Norman Vincent Peale

THE INSPIRATIONAL WRITINGS

Norman Vincent Peale

THE INSPIRATIONAL WRITINGS

Why Some Positive Thinkers Get Powerful Results

◆

Power of the Plus Factor

INSPIRATIONAL PRESS
NEW YORK

First Inspirational Press edition published in 1989.

Inspirational Press
A division of Budget Book Service, Inc.
386 Park Avenue South
New York, NY 10016

Published by arrangement with Thomas Nelson Inc., Publishers and Fleming H. Revell, a division of Baker Book House Company.

Library of Congress Catalog Card Number: 96-77579

ISBN: 0-88486-153-8

Printed in the United States of America.

Contents

Part I
Why Some POSITIVE THINKERS Get POWERFUL RESULTS

To

MYRON L. BOARDMAN,
longtime friend
and associate,
with appreciation
and affection

Contents

To the Reader

Of course you want good results—in doing your job, in reaching your goals, in maintaining good health, and in living your life in general. Here is good news for you: good results can be yours. How? Over years of observing people who attained successful living, I long ago came to the conclusion, based on factual knowledge, that positive thinkers inevitably get positive and powerful results.

So certain am I that there is a definite relationship between positive thinking and positive or good results that I think an invariable scientific formula is involved. Explicitly stated it is this: think positively, act positively, image positively, pray positively, and believe positively, and powerful results will be yours. Helping you learn how to achieve powerful results, according to this formula, is the purpose of this book.

I hope you will stay with me in a reader-author team by reading this book from beginning to end. I have explored practical, workable methods of positive thinking that will greatly enhance your life. By long study and experience I have discovered some simple principles that have worked for me and many others, when they are applied. It is also my pleasure to outline some of the amazing things I have personally found about the power of positive thinking, which I first wrote about many years ago in *The Power of Positive Thinking* and expanded later in other books. So let us proceed to the consideration of an exciting question—the answers to which can improve anyone's life—why some positive thinkers get powerful results.

I wish to express great appreciation to the two dedicated persons who helped immeasurably with this manuscript. One is my secretary, Sybil Light, who meticulously prepared it, and the other, my wife Ruth, who expertly edited it.

Norman Vincent Peale

1.

I've Got It Made

I'm glad that I have never been able to say or even to think that I've got it made. I'm still dreaming, still planning, still trying, still working, and everything is continuously exciting.

We hear people say, "At last I've got it made." About achievers we admiringly exclaim, "He has made it to the top. He's got it made." Or "She has hit the jackpot. That woman sure has everything." So it goes!

But I have sometimes noted something sad about "got-it-maders"; a certain quality seems to have gone out of them. The incentive, the drive, the motivation that took them to the top has declined. The old thrill and excitement of achievement aren't like they once were. Now that these people have got it made, the challenge has dimmed, and maybe the enjoyment of getting there doesn't live up to expectations. As one top achiever complained, "There isn't much fun in life anymore. No challenges or problems like there were."

The president and chief executive officer of one of the most famous corporations in America had a spectacular rise in business. At thirty-five he was top man in a highly competitive industry. He had it made, or so it seemed. At forty he was tiring of it all, and at forty-five he'd "had it," to quote his downbeat evaluation of his career. "From now on," he complained, "I've just got to hold my own, keep some fellow from pushing me off my chair. It was a lot more interesting when I was fighting my way up the hard way. Those were the great days of my life. It isn't the same anymore."

But other men and women are geared differently. Having achieved one goal, they set another and repeat the old tried and true success pattern. They come up with fresh achievements. Having fulfilled old dreams, these people latch onto fresh dreams, bigger challenges, more exciting objectives. Thus it is that they have a perpetual delight in living and working and winning. Their enthusiasm never runs down. Theirs is a constantly renewing and exciting experience. Always they are zestful, eager, creative. They never have it made; they are always striving to make it.

The true flavor, the real fun, the continuous excitement is in the process of making it rather than in having made it. Happiness actually is found in striving for a goal rather than in settling down to enjoy the attained objective. It is found in setting another goal and enthusiastically going for that goal in the same old competitive, innovative spirit.

Happiness at last comes to those who never lose the excitement of going after new goals, who are forever wanting to achieve something better. If you are a winner in a big way or even in a moderate way, you may conclude that since you have it made, you may rest upon your laurels. Be careful, for the result of doing that can be no more laurels.

Perhaps more important, there may be no more of the joy of striving.

One of the most genuinely happy men I ever knew was the late Amos Parrish, perhaps the top sales idea expert in the department store industry. Though he stuttered all his life, store executives would come annually to A. P.'s lectures, packing the grand ballroom of a big New York City hotel to listen to him talk about marketing. This was an outstanding and remarkable achievement, but it was only one of his goal realizations. Even as he grew older, his mind was alert, constantly delivering amazing new ideas. When I would compliment him on some big success, he would brush it aside. "Listen to this idea I'm working on now. This is a h-h-honey," he would excitedly stutter.

When word came that he was dying at ninety-four years of age, I telephoned him. I always loved him and owed him much because he had always inspired me. "Hey there," he said with his usual enthusiasm, "I've got a new idea. This one is a beaut." And he went on to outline an exciting new goal. There was, of course, no talk of dying, only talk about the excitement of living. But two days later he was dead of a progressive disease. A. P. never really had it made, though he was a very successful businessman. He was always involved in the further making of it and having the time of his life in the process.

This unique, unforgettable man brings to mind another equally remarkable friend, the famous baseball executive Branch Rickey. He was successively head of the Saint Louis Cardinals, the former Brooklyn Dodgers, and the Pittsburgh Pirates. His book, *The American Diamond,* is a classic on the game of baseball. At a dinner celebrating Branch Rickey's fifty years in baseball, a reporter asked him, "What was your greatest experience in your half-century in this great American sport?" Pulling down his beetling eyebrows, Rickey snapped, "Don't know. I haven't had it yet." Despite his many distinguished achievements, this man would never assume he had it made. To him it was always still in the making. As a result, his career went from one higher level to another, there being no halting of his achievements.

I was the speaker on a recent Sunday morning in the Crystal Cathedral in Garden Grove, California. This amazing structure was crowded to overflowing by a congregation, according to the newspapers, numbering eleven thousand people in two services and filling every auditorium on the campus. Surrounded by landscaped grounds where sparkling fountains toss their spray, this huge steel and glass church is the spiritual home of millions who receive its message weekly by television.

My presence was occasioned by the observance of the thirtieth anniversary of Dr. Robert Schuller, the minister who, beginning with five hundred dollars and a lot of faith, built this great church. On this special Sunday Dr. Schuller announced plans for another center to serve family needs. One might have thought that he too had it made, but for a unique group of positive people there are always new goals to be built on old goals already achieved.

Regardless of all you may have done to realize your goals, you can do still more; to all your previously achieved goals, you can add other exciting objectives. I want to remind you, if you need reminding, that your future stretches out before you, packed with all kinds of marvelous opportunities. You haven't made it yet, no matter how outstanding your achievements have been. The best, your best, is yet to be. Never look at the great things you have done and say, "Not bad, not bad at all. I've got it made." Instead tell yourself that the splendid things you have accomplished are just indications of what you can do. Believe, always believe, and never doubt that your future lies entrancingly out there ahead of you. Then you will proceed from one level of achievement to another in a life pattern of continuous growth and development.

Basic to our American way of life is the doctrine that any person, under the free opportunities afforded by democracy, can rise to the level of his belief and talent. The quality of one's belief and thinking has been demonstrated to be superior in importance to talent. In fact, thought and faith have often released talent previously unsuspected. Realizing the importance of these features, I have successfully persuaded many people that by positive thinking and by faith in God and in themselves, they can release extraordinary ability from their personalities. By this method many supposedly ordinary persons have become quite extraordinary individuals. But quite beyond anything I or other writers in the field of inspiration and motivation may have done, the climate of America has of itself produced amazing life stories.

In a midwestern city my wife, Ruth, and I were guests in the exquisitely beautiful home of an unusually successful businessman, one who has created an innovative and famous enterprise. Previously I had the privilege of conferring upon him the prestigious Horatio Alger Award given to distinguished Americans who have risen from poverty to positions of honor and influence.

"Where were you born, Dave?" I asked our host.

"I don't know. I think Atlantic City" was his surprising reply. "Nor do I know who my parents were. I was an orphan and grew up with foster parents. I was sent out into the world with only a few dollars in my pocket." After many vicissitudes, this orphan boy got a busboy job with a restaurant owner in Fort Wayne, Indiana.

A hard worker who had the ability to think, Dave did a good job. Eventually his boss sent him to see what could be done with a small restaurant in Columbus, Ohio, which was failing. But Dave had no success with this restaurant until he realized that he had too many items on the menu that required a large inventory, that made it difficult to make a profit. With a limited menu, he turned the restaurant around. He took his profits and opened a hamburger restaurant, because he had loved hamburgers since he was a child. He named his little restaurant after one of his daughters, Wendy, and it gradually took off. Dave Thomas always used the best beef, constantly added new features, and created attractive outlets. He used his good mind and his strong faith to such advantage that currently the Wendy's chain consists of some 3,200 restaurants and is rated at the top of this type of food business.

If you were to ask Dave Thomas if he has it made, meaning that the possibilities for his development have been reached, you would receive a strong negative reply. Men of his stature are the type of persons who constantly improve the American economy. They are perpetual new goal setters who proceed from one level to ever-higher levels of achievement.

It so happens that I am in what may be called the speaking business. That is to say, I accept many engagements to address state and national business conventions, community gatherings, and other functions. Long ago I discovered that this business is one in which you never have it made. No matter how long you have been speaking or how well you may have done it, the engagement tonight is the one that matters. You must do this one to the very best of your ability. Whatever reputation you may have may predispose the audience in your favor before you begin tonight's talk, but that lasts only a few minutes. You will be judged by *this* crowd on what you do *this* night.

At a national business convention meeting at which I was scheduled to speak, I was talking before the session with a young, aspiring speaker. "How long have you been at this speaking business?" he asked.

"About fifty years," I replied.

"Boy, you are fortunate. You have it made. And I'm going to have it made myself pretty soon."

"I am sorry to disabuse you," I said, "but I do not have it made. I must give this speech as if I had never spoken before, and I must give all that I'm capable of to this audience."

Several years later I was on a program with this same speaker, now older and wiser. "I know what you meant back there that night in Chicago. Now just when I think at last I've got it made, I get slapped down in a speech and feel like a beginner all over again."

"You and me both," I replied ruefully as we shared a moment of camaraderie.

On the basis of this philosophy of the "I've got it made" concept, what is the most successful principle of goal setting and goal achieving? As a starter let me set forth some rules that I have known to be effective, and then I will develop them further as I go along.

1. Think about where you want to get in life.
2. Come to a firm decision about your basic objective.
3. Formulate and write your goal in a sharp, clear statement, and eliminate all fuzziness of thought.
4. Study and learn all that you can about your goal and how to get there.
5. Fix a time for achieving your goal.
6. Pray about your decision to be sure that it is right. If it is not right, it is wrong, and nothing wrong turns out right.
7. Give your goal complete and unremitting effort, and never give up trying.
8. Apply positive thinking.
9. Never assume you have it made. One goal attained leads to another and on and on.

* * *

One technique I developed for myself is to write a goal on a card and keep it in my shirt pocket over my heart, the traditional seat of emotional response. My goal, I decided upon in my youth, is to help as many people as possible to live at their highest potential by persuading them to become believers, positive thinkers, people of faith. Many years ago I wrote this goal on a card and have carried it in my shirt pocket ever since. I have had other goals from time to time and have written each of them on cards so that now and then my pocket has been filled with written goals. As I achieved them, I removed the cards. Sometimes I have also copied goals set by other people and carried them in my pocket and prayed about them for friends who also used the shirt pocket technique.

I have often described this method of goal attainment in speeches before sales and business conventions, and many people have used it effectively. For example, a young man attended a national insurance convention where I outlined the shirt-pocket technique in a speech. He was a dedicated agent, but he wasn't doing too well. My speech convinced him that the principal reason for his lack of success was that he really did not expect to set any records. He determined to take a more positive attitude, to visualize himself as achieving better results.

This convention was held early in the new year. Following the speech, he went to his room in the hotel and had a "good ruthless think session," as he described it to me later. Then and there he set a sales goal for the year at a figure that "left him breathless" since it was far beyond anything he had ever done. Here is what he wrote on the card that he carried in his shirt pocket all year long. That it contributed to his success he has no doubt.

> I image this new year as my best year.
> I affirm enthusiasm, energy,
> and pleasure in my work.

As a positive thinker, I believe I will
do 10 percent better than last year.
God will help me reach this goal.

"At the end of that year what result did you have?" I asked.

"Believe it or not," he replied, "I hit that 10 percent increase smack on the nose. Had I not used your shirt-pocket technique I would still be fumbling along near the bottom of our agency. I firmly believe it gave me a new, positive attitude that brought out a talent I didn't know I had. Anyway, I'm moving up now."

"When you went for that 10 percent increase, a figure that is really amazing, how did you feel?"

"Well, you know," he said, "it's funny, but I just knew I could do it. I'm a committed Christian, and every day I said, 'I can do all things through Christ who strengthens me' (Phil. 4:13), or 'If you have faith as a mustard seed, . . . nothing will be impossible for you' (Matt. 17:20)." He added, "Those Bible promises really work. I know that for sure, because they are working for me."

"You've got it made?" I said admiringly with a question mark in my tone.

"Oh, no, I haven't. I'm just starting on my way, and I've got an awful lot to learn. The old failure pattern is still in me and could grab control if I let down. But I'm not going to be lulled into a false sense of security by saying, 'I've got it made.'"

Smart fellow! He was turning his insecurity into a creative motivation.

Turn back to that list of nine rules for reaching a goal, and note the emphasis on knowing definitely where you want to go and the importance of setting a time for reaching your objective. This sort of clear, definite focusing of aim I consider to be very important. If you know exactly where you wish to go and when you expect to get there, you are mentally summoning all the immense force of your personality into action, and you are directing that force to the support of your objectives.

I wish to repeat here an incident I have often used to demonstrate the power inherent in this principle. Playing golf one day, I sliced a ball into the rough at the fairway's edge. A young fellow raking leaves there politely helped me find my ball. "Sometime, Dr. Peale, I would like to talk to you about myself," he said rather hesitatingly.

"When?" I asked.

Startled, he said, "Oh, I don't mean now. Just sometime."

"Sometime seldom comes," I said. "Meet me at the eighteenth hole in about thirty minutes and we will talk." Later, sitting in the shade of a tree, I asked the young fellow's name and said, "Now, what's on your mind?"

"Oh, I don't know. I just want to get somewhere."

"Where?" I asked. "Exactly where do you want to get?"

He looked bewildered. "Oh, I don't know where. I just know I want to get somewhere else from where I am now. I don't know just where."

"And when do you plan to get where you don't know where you want to get?"

Confused by these questions and perhaps even a bit irritated, he grumbled, "How do I know when? Just sometime. I want to get somewhere sometime."

Then I asked him what he could do best, and he replied that he did nothing very well and he didn't know what he could do the best. To my question about what he liked to do, he thought awhile and then answered that he didn't know what he particularly liked to do.

"Well, now, here's your situation as I see it: you want to get somewhere, but you don't know where. And you do not know when you expect to get there. Besides that, you don't know what you can do the best nor what you like to do. Is that about it?"

He glumly nodded his head, "Guess I'm a total flop."

"Not at all. You are just not organized or focused. You've got a nice personality, a good head on your shoulders, and a desire for improvement, and that desire is trying to motivate you. I like you and believe in you."

I suggested that he spend two weeks thinking about his future, that he decide definitely upon a goal, and that he write that goal, using the fewest possible words. Then he was to compute when he might reasonably expect to reach his goal. I asked him to write these decisions on a card and come back to tell me about it.

Promptly two weeks later he showed up quite a different fellow, at least in spirit. He was focused and better organized. He knew what he wanted: to be the plant manager of the company where he was working. He explained that the present incumbent was due to retire in five years, and his goal was to be offered that position at that time. He developed such know-how and leadership ability during that five-year period that when the job finally opened, he had no competition for it.

I might add that now, some years later, he is still in the same position and is indispensable to his employers. He achieved the goal he decided upon following that golf course conference. He is happy and satisfied.

A combination of goal setting, positive thinking, visualizing and believing leads to a successful outcome in most of the problems with which each of us must deal. If you want to have it made, whatever the situation, I suggest putting these four creative factors into active practice.

Take the vital matter of life correction, when seemingly so many things need a turnaround—attitude, health, personality. Sometimes life may break down at many points under differing pressures. Instead of having it made, everything seems to be unmade, sometimes all at once.

A perfect example of this is the man I met on a speaking

engagement in a Canadian city. Seldom have I encountered a more dynamic, positive, and obviously happy man. He presided over the meeting of some two thousand persons, and I was terribly impressed by his spirit and attitude. Finally, out of curiosity, I said, "You are terrific. Tell me, how did you get this way?"

"It's a long story," he said, "but I'll shorten it to spare you. Everything in my life seemed to break up all at once. It all went sour. And later I learned it was because I, as a person, had broken up. I went sour. My concerned wife tried everything to build me up and to improve the distressing circumstances. Finally she remembered your book, *The Power of Positive Thinking*, and asked me to read it. The title sort of struck me, but when I found it had religion in it, I chucked it, for I was off religion, preachers, and the church. But goaded by my wife, to whom I am devoted, I stuck with the book, deciding I would bypass the religious stuff and read only the commonsense parts. But I ended up by taking it all, including the religious part, hook, line, and sinker."

His wife, who was listening to her husband's recital, said, "Just look at that wonderful guy. Everything broke up for him, but through your book God put it all back together again."

"Yes," he said, "but I worked out an idea better than anything in your book. And just to show you how I appreciate what you did for me, I will let you use this terrific idea in your next book."

So here it is: "One day," he said, "the thought came to me that with God's help, I was greater than anything that could happen to me. This resulted in an affirmation I use every day. I pull myself up to full height and say: 'I deny the power of the adverse.' Note I didn't say I deny the adverse but the power of the adverse."

"You have come about as near as anyone I know to

having it made," I said, "because you have obviously become the master of your circumstances."

"Want to know when I became master?" he replied. "Well, I'll tell you. It was in the religious part of your book which, like a dope, I wanted to bypass. I'm certainly no saint, but I am now a believer. To that extent I do believe I am on the way to having it made, though I still have a long way to go."

Let's return to those four basic factors I referred to earlier that are involved in successful outcomes: goal setting, positive thinking, visualizing, and believing. With that combination, almost any adverse situation can be worked out for the best. One big problem relates to health. Judging from the mail we receive in our office, which runs into the thousands, I'd say health is problem number one. Money or job problems rank second, marital problems third. Overcoming a health problem and enjoying physical well-being are the top blessings of this life. Good health is profoundly precious.

Having it made in health is a top achievement, one that is desired by everyone. A combination of overindulgence in alcohol and in food, incessant smoking, and high tension had undermined the once rugged health of a friend I will call Joe (he said I may use his story if I don't use his real name). Joe had become obese and developed high blood pressure. He puffed up stairways, red in the face. His doctor finally let him have it straight—Joe could recover his health if he got on top of the drinking, smoking, eating, and tension. "But," the doctor concluded, "I don't know whether you have what it takes to reconstruct a healthy lifestyle."

This doctor knew that his last remark would anger Joe because he is one of those he-men who think they can do just about anything. So he reacted by bringing the drinking, smoking, and tension under pretty good control, but the eating problem proved his waterloo. He just couldn't push back from the table. He went on diet after diet, but none of them worked. The reason was simple: he didn't really work at any of them. He had to compensate for giving up the liquor and cigarettes, didn't he? So he rationalized his excessive food intake.

The doctor said, "Positive thinking and spiritual treatment are what you need. And, Joe, you've got to take off at least forty pounds. If you do that, added to what you have already done, I'm sure your blood pressure will go right down."

I might explain that the doctor and Joe and I are mutual friends, which is perhaps why the doctor sent Joe to me. When Joe came to see me, he had a negative outlook.

"I just can't change my eating habits. There is no way I can shed forty pounds," Joe complained to me.

"Oh, yes, you can. I know you can. I was told I had to take off thirty-five pounds, and I felt like you, that I couldn't do it. But I changed my mental attitude and took a positive approach. The pounds rolled off, the blood pressure went down, and I have never been healthier, just like you are going to be. So are you ready to start?"

"What choice have I got with Doc and you ganged up against me?" Joe grumbled.

"Not against you, *for* you," I said.

"Now, Joe, here is what I am going to help you do. Set a weight goal, practice positive thinking, visualize the results, and have lots of faith." We subtracted 40 from his weight of 200 to get the goal of a healthy 160.

"Why, I haven't weighed that since college."

"So what?" I said. "We're going back to streamlined youth." He made a face.

Next we added the timing. When was he to achieve the goal? We set a date nine months away. Then we developed a new image of him as a slim 160. He was to think of himself with that midsection bulge gone, clothes hanging beautifully loose on his newly slender six feet one inch frame. And best of all, no guilt feeling for overeating was part of that image.

The last thing we discussed was his need to reread *The Power of Positive Thinking*. He groaned at this one, but I said, "You've got to believe, to know that you can do this. And you will need a big dose of faith to emerge and remain exactly what the insurance table says you should be, namely, 160 pounds. Visualize that blood pressure as normal. Every day affirm, 'With God's help my blood pressure is going down, down, down, as the pounds roll off, off, off.'"

Joe got into the spirit of this slenderizing process. He became enthusiastic about physical renewal. Without his realizing it, he began to have a mental and spiritual renewal as well. He reached his goal in the time set. He felt better than he had in years. He went around telling everyone he had the blood pressure of a twenty-one year old.

"I've got it made weight-wise," he said one day when we were eating a lunch of clear soup, cottage cheese, and gelatin together. "I've got it made . . . thanks to Doc and you and," he added to my surprise, "the blessed Lord Jesus." He flushed a bit self-consciously at this last remark, because he was never one to talk religiously. But a bit belligerently, he said, "I've been praying all the way to 160 pounds."

So name your goal, and apply the positive principles. The day will come when you can thankfully say, "I've got it made." Then go for still another goal. You will be helped toward your goals by reading the next chapter, "Belief Power Gets Powerful Results."

2.

Belief Power Gets Powerful Results

"Born to lose." That ultranegative statement caught my eye as I strolled through a crooked little street in Kowloon, Hong Kong. I stared at those words in the window of a tattoo shop. It appeared that this was one of the slogans a customer could have tattooed on his body. Flags, mermaids, and other of the usual tattoos were also offered.

Astounded, I entered the shop and said to the Chinese man, "Does anyone actually have 'Born to lose' tattooed into his flesh?"

"Yes, some." But then tapping his head, he added in broken English, "Before tattoo on chest, tattoo on mind."

Failure begins in your thoughts when you hold the idea that you are actually incapable, that you are born to lose. So to counteract failure, develop the ability to believe. Tell yourself in no uncertain terms, "I was born to be a winner." To be that, you will just have to be a believer because winners are always believers. Losers are never real believers.

What is a believer? A believer in what? The answer to both questions is a belief in God, in life, in the future, in your spouse, in your kids, in your job, in your country and, last but certainly not least, in yourself. A man objected once when he heard me say this. "I'm a believer in God all right; but as such I am humble and, therefore, not a self-believer."

"Well," I replied, "if you don't believe in yourself, you don't much believe in God. He made you." And I quoted a sign I saw in our drugstore in Pawling, New York, picturing an upstanding little boy: "I believe in me, for God made me and He don't make no junk."

A notable American scholar, one of our wisest men, was William James, a professor of philosophy, anatomy, and psychology. It might be said that he was professor of mind, body, and emotions. (He ranks perhaps with Emerson and Thoreau in his vast knowledge of personality and successful living.) Here is how William James rated belief: "Belief at the beginning of a doubtful undertaking is the one thing that will guarantee the success of any venture."

So what is the *one* thing that guarantees success? Not knowledge, not education, not training, not experience, not money. It is belief. Belief in a project and belief in yourself are vital to success. Naturally other qualifications are extremely important, but the primary factor, the one basic essential, is belief—the belief that *you can* generate the powerful results you want. Another name for belief is positive thinking. It is a fact that some positive thinkers get positive results. William James declared, "Be not afraid of life. Believe that life is worth living and your belief will help create that fact."

Believers are a terrific breed of men and women. Nothing daunts them. They are afraid of nothing. If they have doubts, they rise above them. They become persons of power. These big, rugged souls sweep everything before them. They are doers, achievers, winners. They have the magic word—*belief*.

It is my conviction, based on knowledge of such people over many years and in all kinds of circumstances, that believers can overcome or solve or successfully live with any problem they will ever have to face. Some problems can be extremely difficult, even horrendous. But they don't really appear that way to believers, because believers bring up against any problem the assurance that it can be handled.

The person of belief never goes crawling through life on his hands and knees, whining and whimpering that it's all too much, that he is being treated unfairly. Instead such a person looks adversity straight on and then affirms, "As a child of the good God, I am greater than anything that can happen to me."

I believe that you and I were made to be winners. We were created to be great, not little. To overcome weakness and become a great human being, be a believer. Remember those power-packed words, "If you have faith as a mustard seed, . . . *nothing* will be impossible for you" (Matt. 17:20; emphasis added).

Memory, at the most unexpected times and places, can turn up things, people, and events seemingly long forgotten. This miracle of remembrance happened to me not long ago. I was walking on Fifth Avenue at the corner of Thirty-fifth Street when this flashback happened. In an instant I was transported back to the autumn of 1933 and to Fred.

I had known Fred in Brooklyn a few years previously but had not seen him since then. Now here he was coming along the avenue with the same old squared shoulders and peaceful look on his face. It was an affectionate reunion. "How goes it with you?" I asked. This meeting, I must explain, was at the bottom of the Great Depression of the 1930s, perhaps the lowest period economically in American history. Factories were closed. Empty stores all over the city testified to business failures. People had been let go by the hundreds of thousands, wages and salaries had been cut not once but several times. Soup kitchens and bread lines served long queues of people, some of whom were once affluent. It was widely asserted that no one over thirty years old had the slightest chance of getting a job. Such was the situation when I met Fred on once-prosperous Fifth Avenue that October afternoon.

He was wearing a blue serge suit. When old and long-used, they had the characteristic of becoming very shiny. Fred's was especially evident of long wear. But when he spoke, it was in his same old cheerful tone. "Oh, I'm all right. Just fine. Don't you spend any time worrying about me. It's true that I've been out of work for quite a while, but every morning I come into the city and tramp the streets looking for a job. You see, I just know that somewhere in this big city is a job for me, and I'm going to keep on hunting for it. I'll find it."

"You're keeping that big smile of yours going," I commented admiringly.

"Well, that makes sense, doesn't it? You see, I read somewhere that it requires sixty-four facial muscles to frown and only fourteen to smile. So why overwork your face?" Then he outlined more of his philosophy. He believed that a deep desire for a job would in time be rewarded by a compensatory satisfaction of that desire. "I heard you quote the poet John Burroughs once who said something to the effect that 'mine own will come to me.'"

But the touching thing about Fred was his faith, his belief. "I was raised by believing parents. We had very little, but that never fazed Mother. She would always say, 'The Lord will provide.' And do you know something, He always did. He never failed Mother once," and he added after a pause, his lip twitching a bit, "He won't fail me either." Then standing on the great avenue amidst throngs of unemployed people looking for work, he quoted the old biblical words, "I have been young, and now I am old; yet have I not seen the righteous forsaken, nor his seed begging bread" (Ps. 37:25 KJV). He looked rather defiantly at me. "And no matter how tough it may get, I believe that. Mother and Father—and you [punching me affectionately in the chest] taught me to be a believer. So I just go on hoping and believing and looking."

As he moved along the street, I stood watching him. The sunlight on that shiny old blue serge suit suggested for a moment a knight's armor, its wearer riding in search of the Holy Grail, his sword of the spirit flashing bright.

What happened? He got a job with a man who had some genius for inventing things. In this innovative climate, Fred, who had a fertile mind, had an idea that took off. After a lot of struggle, belt tightening, and belief, Fred and the other man became quite successful. He lived constructively, had a fine family, and was respected by all who knew him.

Some years ago a Sunday was observed in which laymen were invited to speak in the pulpits of New York churches. I asked Dale Carnegie, who was a special friend of mine, to take on this assignment. Dale, author of the American classic *How to Win Friends and Influence People,* probably taught more men and women to speak in public through his courses than any man in America. He gave an unforgettable talk that Sunday morning.

But at one point his voice faltered. He was so deeply moved that he had to stop talking for what seemed a long moment. A hush fell over the big congregation. He was speaking of his youth. He described the poverty in which his family lived; sometimes there was no food in the house. "But not even this daunted Mother's faith," said Dale. "She went about the little house singing the wonderful old hymn 'What a Friend We Have in Jesus.' Calmly she assured Father and all of us children that the Lord will provide. And," he added, "I cannot recall ever going to bed hungry. Necessities came to us in strange and even miraculous ways through Mother's powerful belief."

As I listened to unforgettable Dale Carnegie that day, it occurred to me that poverty was a source of motivation to some of our greatest Americans. It made them determined to lift themselves and their families to a better economic level. A powerful belief, usually derived from their religious training, made them believe that they could do so. I learned from Fred on the street and Dale Carnegie in the pulpit that neither economic depression nor setback such as loss of a job can permanently hold the positive-thinking person down, because in him is the ability to rebound. The lower he falls, the higher he bounces back up. Luck does not do it, nor do fortuitous circumstances, nor does it just happen for some reason. It is the power of belief that makes the difference, a big robust difference.

What causes men and women to get good results even out of harsh situations is this tough, resilient, unshakable belief that pervades their thought patterns. They have what is variously called faith, belief, or conviction that with the help of the Greater Power, they can overcome every difficulty. They have a deep inner feeling that they have what it takes to overcome, and they do not allow self-defeating negative thoughts to overwhelm this positive certainty. So become a believer, no matter how firmly you may have to discipline yourself or how long and hard you may have to work at doing so. Your future depends upon it.

I knew a man who conducted personnel studies for companies. He was also a sales trainer and was particularly successful in developing the unused potential in people. Melvin Evans was responsible for shifting people from jobs in which they were not doing so well to others in which he thought their talents could be better used. He had good to spectacular results. He used to describe his function as the "remaking people business," and he was extraordinarily capable in this capacity. He genuinely liked people, believed in them, and could perceive and bring out their hitherto untapped capabilities.

One case was that of a young man doing a routine clerical job. Evans was impressed by his outgoing, pleasant manner. He worked efficiently and was always thinking up new methods to increase productivity. Besides all this, he motivated others working alongside him to approach their jobs with more enthusiasm. Evans became convinced that this young man, Jack, possessed capabilities not being used.

"How do you feel about this company?" Evans asked.

"Best in the world," responded Jack. "I get a big kick out of working here. I'm going for my CPA."

"Want to know what I think about you, Jack? It may surprise you, but I think you have the makings of a real salesman. You have such enthusiasm for this product that you could sell it effectively and set a top record, benefiting the company tremendously and yourself as well."

At this surprising evaluation, another side of Jack surfaced. It was fear and self-disbelief. "Oh, no, Mr. Evans. I feel comfortable in this job. I know the routine. It's like a second home to me. I'd be like a fish out of water, and I just know I would never make it in selling." This showed his negative self-appraisal and fear of leaving the sheltered nest.

But Evans was firm. "You don't know your own self, son. All you need to do is make a mental shift from a nonbeliever to a believer. You must get acquainted with your real self."

Finally Jack was persuaded to enter the sales training course. To his surprise, he found it interesting, and the instructor told Evans, "I think you've discovered a guy who could be a born salesman. But he still lacks self-confidence."

"That will come," replied Evans.

Finally the time came to go on the road, out among the customers, and Jack was really nervous. But Melvin Evans said, "I'm going with you, Jack. We'll work at least part of the territory together." He introduced the new salesman to some of the people with whom he would do business. They all liked Jack because he was so outgoing. Jack carefully watched Evans demonstrate the selling process. And he picked up something even more important in their time together. Evans let his faith and belief in himself come through, and he transferred this faith to Jack. Soon Jack came to actually believe in Jack. He began to get a new concept of himself and with it the feel of success. As a result, excitement began to take over in him.

Then one day Evans told the young salesman that he had to leave him. He laid out the rest of the sales trip for Jack to do on his own. "Just go on liking people. Be friendly and believe in your product and," he added, "in yourself."

"I'm sure going to feel mighty alone," muttered Jack.

"You're never alone," said Evans.

Jack's subsequent success verified Evans's judgment of the young man's potential. Persuading self-doubting people to believe in themselves, as Melvin Evans did with Jack, is one of the prime objectives of this book.

This belief factor is an amazing force of almost incredible power. It contains all the positives in concentrated form. I have been asked by some people who want to seem nonreligious, "Must you have religious faith to have belief?" My answer is, "It sure does help."

For example, a story that appeared in a Chattanooga, Tennessee, newspaper told of four women in a dress shop, three clerks and one customer. The latter was in a dressing room putting on her clothes after trying on several new dresses. All of a sudden the shop door burst open and in came a big tough-looking man, a knife in one hand and a revolver in the other. "Hand over your money," he ordered.

All the three women clerks could put together was fifty-five dollars. This enraged him. "Lie down on the floor, and if you make a move, I'll kill you." Then he heard the woman in the dressing room. He pushed and manhandled her, taking her money. He threatened her and cut her slightly with his knife. Then the woman reacted. Pulling herself to full height, she said in a strong, authoritative voice to the marauder, "Stop this. In the name of Jesus Christ, I command you to leave us alone. Stop this wickedness!" Bewildered, he turned and ran from the shop, leaped into a car where a woman accomplice was at the wheel, and sped away. Later he was captured by the police, and when interrogated, he said, "That woman had a power like I've never seen before." When this amazing power is turned on, belief gets the most amazing results.

This incident reminds me of a conversation I had with a middle-aged waitress, an outgoing, positive woman, in a motel coffee shop one morning when I was on a speaking trip. Although it was raining hard that morning, she greeted me by informing me it was going to be a great day. Right then and there this charming person made my day. In the course of my meal I discovered that she had put two children through college and had two more coming along. "My faith helped me do it. You see, I'm a believer," she explained.

She stated that, as a young couple, she and her husband lived in poverty. "I came to hate poverty. It destroys the soul. We were on relief and that galled me. It ate at my self-respect. My dear husband was sinking lower into despair. It was then that I read Luke 9:1." She stood by my table in that coffee shop and recited those great words: "Then He called His twelve disciples together and gave them power and authority over all demons and to cure diseases."

She continued, "Now that said something to me. I am a disciple of the Lord, and I am given authority over demons. Poverty is a demon. It is bad, very bad. As a believer, I took that authority. Well, it's a long story and it sure wasn't easy, but with the good Lord's help, my husband and I killed that demon of poverty."

With something like awe I shook hands with this great human being, this great believer, and went away inspired. I considered my own demons; most of us have them. I decided right then and there that I too would take the authority given to us as believers. One thing that came out of that experience is this book in which I want to emphasize that you can be an overcomer through the great power of belief. Whatever the difficulty, you can rise victoriously above what now defeats you. Believe that because it is the truth, the great big wonderful, undeniable truth.

Some of you may very much want this kind of belief going for you, but things have been, perhaps still are, really rough. What do you do when you have had (or are having) an extra tough time or have made some bad mistakes? When this question comes up, I am likely to remember the day a young lawyer came to see me. He was in deep despair and completely hopeless. He had been let go, at least temporarily, by a big law firm for having made a serious mistake. I thought it rather unfair to so penalize a beginner for one mistake, even a big one. I recall reading some years ago that Mrs. Knox of Knox Gelatin had a sign posted in her plant: "He deserves to break his own neck who stumbles twice on the same stone." At least she would give employees a second chance.

At any rate this dejected young lawyer paced up and down, upbraiding himself. "How could I be so dumb, so stupid? Here is my career gone down the drain and at the very start," he moaned, then slumped in a chair, the picture of utter despondency. At the moment I happened to have on my desk a column written by the late Grove Patterson in the *Toledo* [Ohio] *Blade*, a classic article by the great newspaper editor. I read it to the young man, and its effect upon him was miraculous. This column made such a lasting impression on me when I first read it years ago that I incorporated it in my autobiography, *The True Joy of Positive Living*, and I reprint it here.

> A boy, a long time ago, leaned against the railing of a bridge and watched the current of the river below. A log, a bit of driftwood, a chip floated past. Again the surface of the river was smooth. But always, as it had for a hundred, perhaps a thousand, perhaps a million years, the water slipped by, under the bridge. Sometimes the current went more swiftly, and again quite slowly. But always the river flowed on under the bridge.
>
> Watching the river that day the boy made a discovery. It was not the discovery of a material thing, something he might put his hand upon. He could not even see it. He had discovered an idea. Quite suddenly, yet quietly, he knew that everything in his life would someday pass under the bridge and be gone, like water. And the boy came to like those words "under the bridge." All his life thereafter the idea served him well and carried him through, although there were days and ways that were dark and not easy. Always when he had made a mistake that couldn't be helped, or lost something that could never come again, the boy, now a man, said, "It's water under the bridge." And he didn't worry unduly about the mistakes after that and he certainly

didn't let them get him down—because it was "water under the bridge."

The young man listened intently as I read this piece to him. He sat quite still for long moments. Then he rose, gripped my hand, and said feelingly, "Okay, I get the message. I will draw what know-how I can from this experience and let it go like 'water under the bridge.'" He walked out of my office that day a renewed believer in himself, and he also had belief in his future which, incidentally, turned out to be a very good one.

The tendency of people to depreciate themselves is widespread. But seldom have I received a letter quite so depreciatory, such a consummate self put-down, as came to my desk recently. It is from a woman, and I quote it in part.

> I know this letter will probably never reach you personally but I'll write it anyway. Dr. Peale I have this big problem about myself. I have no self-confidence. I feel stupid and so unworthy of God's love. I wonder why He keeps me around, sometimes I wonder why I was born? My husband has a company and he is so smart. The two of us, in my opinion, don't compare.
>
> I'm a quitter! I came from a broken home. I feel insecure and unloved. I guess that's why it's hard for me to believe that God really loves me. I've done so much wrong.
>
> Even as a Christian everything I try to do that's right I do wrong. I hate myself. Dr. Peale, I thought of getting rid of myself but I know that is not right. I sure could use some of your positive thinking right now. I always read how you give someone a card with a Scripture verse on it and it helps them. Do you have anything for me? I have read a lot of your books, but I can't seem to apply things to me. I am a negative thinker.

I've been this way for quite some time. I would appreciate your help.

Thank you very much.

As requested, I did write a card for her. I suggested she carry it with her at all times and read it aloud frequently, especially just before going to sleep at night. I wanted to get belief thoughts working powerfully in her mind. Even if her disbelief in herself was deepseated, I have found that such affirmations, as the ones the following card contains, often have a powerful effect. Here is the card I gave her.

> I like me. I believe in me.
> I was created by God who never made
> anything badly.
> His creation is wonderful
> so I am wonderful.
> Divine perfection is within me.
> I love life. I love people.
> I have ability. I can do things well.
> I am happy. I am grateful.
> I treat myself with respect.
> As a child of God, I believe in me.

The woman used this affirmation as directed and is definitely emerging from her appalling self-depreciation.

When such personal disbelief exists, when there is a lack of personality control, or when failure is persistent, then the need for basic self-change is indicated. It is utterly foolish to continue in such a sorry state because it is a fact that self-change is taking place in people every passing day. Such a change of attitudes and conditions can occur in anyone. We can all change. I can change, and you too can change.

My cousin, Lew Delaney, was a successful salesman who became the national sales manager for a large company. Once we were talking about the remarkable change that can take place in a person and Lew said, "When a person is forthright about himself or herself, honestly admits the need for change, and then firmly sets about changing and has belief, that change will come. If he or she takes God into the process, that person can for sure change, and I mean change. Let me tell you about one of our salesmen named Tim. Did he change? Why, you wouldn't know him for the same man."

As Lew told me about him, I got the impression that Tim was a genial, likable man but lacking in force. He was, as Lew put it, the "lowest man on the totem pole," bottom salesman in production. As much as management hated to do it, Tim was about to be let go. Then to the surprise of everyone, Tim suddenly began to deliver. His sales mounted, and in one year's time he went from the bottom to the top one-third of the company's salesmen in productivity. At the end of the second year he was top man in sales nationally in the company. It seemed a miracle.

At the annual sales meeting when salesmen came together from all over the country, the president called Tim to the stage to receive the award for best salesman of the year. He ambled up, sort of embarrassed, and the president said, "I don't know when it has given me so much pleasure to make this award. Tim, you have become a truly great salesman, but even more you have become a truly great man. Actually you've got us all mystified. What a change in your record and in you! You just aren't the same Tim. Do you mind telling all the boys here how you did it?"

Lew said Tim was no public speaker, and he shifted from one foot to the other, became red in the face, and stammered in getting started. "Well," he said, "boss and fellows, I like you all and I think you'll understand. I was a failure, a flop, and I knew it. Nobody had to tell me. One night I said to myself, 'I don't want to be this way anymore,' and I got to thinking. I was sitting in our living room, and on the lower shelf in a bookcase I saw a Bible. I've got to admit I hadn't cracked it in years. Well, I got it out and at the front inside was written, 'To Tim. With love, Mama.' I just sat there leafing through it, and then a statement sort of leaped out at me that said I could change, that I could become a different man. And suddenly I just believed that.

"Well," continued Tim, "next morning I went downtown and bought myself a completely new outfit—a new suit, underwear, socks, shirt, shoes, tie—the works. Now I know the old saying that clothes don't make the man. But anyway I went back home and took a bath. I scrubbed my skin until it was red like a newborn baby's. I shampooed my head to get all those old negative thoughts out of my thick skull. Then I got dressed, and a new Tim went out selling. With God's help I started making sales, and I just kept on selling. Boss, I guess that's all there is to it."

Lew said, "It was unforgettable, fabulous! Those seven hundred men sat still a minute; then as one man they leaped to their feet, shouting and clapping and pounding each other on the back. It was pandemonium and," added Lew, "I've got to admit I was choked up and had tears in my eyes and so did just about everyone else."

And why not? A man had changed, become a new man. So much so that you wouldn't have known him for the same person.

"Everyone wanted to know what the statement was that leaped out of the Bible to effect such a complete change in Tim," Lew said, "but nobody felt like asking since it was pretty private to Tim. But one day later when we were together, I asked him. He took his card and wrote 2 Corinthians 5:17 on the back. 'Look it up' was all he said. I was curious and did look it up. 'If anyone is in Christ, he is a new creation; old things have passed away; behold, all things have become new.'

"You know, Norman," said Lew, "you and I first heard that in Sunday school as kids back in Lynchburg [Ohio] and I never thought much about it. But do you know something? It really works. Tim's experience proves it."

How right he was—belief power gets powerful results.

In Chapter 3 we will discuss how to succeed in dealing with problems, and I hope this will be of real help to you.

3.

Success in Dealing with Problems

The positive thinker is an achiever who gets powerful results for several reasons. He is not afraid of nor abashed by that phenomenon known as a problem. As a practical, positive-thinking philosopher, he knows that every problem contains the seeds of its own solution. If there are no problems, there will be no solutions and progress will stop. The positive thinker knows that good outcomes are rooted in the fertile soil of tough problems.

When the good Lord wants to give you some great value, how does He go about doing it? Does He wrap it up in an exotic package and hand it to you on a silver platter? Hardly. He is too subtle, too sophisticated for that. His method is much more adroit. He often buries that great value at the heart of a big, difficult problem. And how He must watch with delight to see if you have what it takes to break that problem apart and find at its heart, if you please, that pearl of great price.

But even so, wherever I go, either by direct statement or by implication, people seem to say, "Wouldn't life be simply wonderful if we had fewer problems, easier problems or, better still, no problems at all?" Would it?

I would like to answer this question by telling of an incident. Walking on Fifth Avenue in New York City, I saw a friend named George approaching. Judging from George's disconsolate and melancholy demeanor, I could see that he was not filled to overflowing with the ecstasy and exuberance of human existence. To put it more simply, George's spirit was dragging bottom.

This excited my sympathy so I asked him, "How are you, George?" For some minutes he meticulously enlightened me on how bad he felt. The more George talked, the worse I felt. "What has you so upset and discouraged?" I asked. This question really set him off.

"Oh, it's these problems," he fumed. "Problems and more problems, nothing but problems. I am fed up with problems." He became so exercised about the matter that he quite forgot to whom he was talking and lambasted these problems virulently, using in the process, I am sorry to report, a great many theological terms. But he certainly did not put them together in a theological manner. However, I understood what he meant all right, because he had "the ability to communicate."

"George," I said, breaking into his diatribe about his problems, "I would like to help you if possible. Tell me what I can do for you."

"Do for me?" he shouted. "Rid me of these problems. If you can do that, you will be my friend for life."

Since I always welcome an opportunity to become anyone's friend for life, I meditated upon George's situation until I finally came up with a solution. Although it may not have been the most pleasant suggestion, at least it was realistic. "George," I said, "let me get this straight. You want to be rid of your most difficult problems or perhaps most of your problems. But you are certainly not going to stand here on the street today and seriously tell me that you want to be rid of all your problems."

"The latter is what I want. I have had it," he insisted glumly.

"Okay. That being the case, I believe I can assist you. The other day, George, I was in a certain place on professional business, if I may thus characterize it. An official told me that approximately one hundred thousand people were there and not one of them had a problem."

The first glint of enthusiasm flashed in George's eyes and suffused his countenance as he eagerly exclaimed, "Boy, that's for me! Lead me to that place."

"You asked for it," I replied. "It's Woodlawn Cemetery."

That is a fact. No one in that or any cemetery has a problem. They couldn't care less what is reported in the newspapers, on television, or over the radio. They have no problems at all. But they are dead. Therefore, it is logical to assume that problems constitute a sign of life. I would go so far as to say that the more problems you have, the more alive you are. But if you have no problems at all, you are in great jeopardy. You are on the way out. I recommend that you pray to the Lord, saying, "Lord, what is the matter? Don't You trust me anymore? Give me some problems!"

The positive thinker is alive, alive mentally and spiritually, and knows that with the good Lord's help, he has what it takes to handle any problem that may arise in his lifetime.

Good results are not obstructed by the fear that he is not capable of problem management. He attacks problems by intelligent thinking and, accordingly, gets positive results.

The concept of problems as suggested here would seem to indicate a mentally healthy attitude. Indeed one way of determining your state of mental health is to examine your reaction when a tough problem suddenly appears. Do you whine and complain that you are being unfairly put upon, petulantly asking, "Why me?" If that is the case, you might very well seek counseling in the hope of developing a more logical, philosophical understanding of difficulty. On the contrary, if you have a sturdy, clear-eyed mental attitude when a problem suddenly comes at you, then you will stand up to it fearlessly and confidently knowing that you have the capacity to handle it successfully. This attitude would seem to indicate the possession of good mental health. By this test the positive thinker has the quality of healthy-mindedness that enables him or her to bring positive results out of even the most difficult problems.

Some years ago the eminent psychiatrist, Dr. Smiley Blanton, and I founded the American Foundation of Religion and Psychiatry, the name of which was later changed to the Institutes of Religion and Health. As a result, I have been closely associated with psychiatrists and psychologists for many years. I respect them highly from a professional standpoint and hold them in affectionate regard as colleagues. We have had fun together as well as cooperated in exciting ventures.

A national convention of psychiatrists was held in a New York City hotel, and the lobby was constantly crowded with these doctors. Around the corner from the hotel is a big railroad station around which there are always huge flocks of pigeons. As far as anyone can determine, these are well-oriented, normal pigeons going about the daily functions of pigeons. But apparently the mental disorganization of the multitudes thronging in and out of the station finally transmitted itself to one of these pigeons. By a process that has never been accounted for, this pigeon presently found itself in the lobby of the nearby hotel, flying around among the psychiatrists. In fact, it is reliably reported that this pigeon flew around for two whole days before any psychiatrist would admit to another that he saw a pigeon!

But, however that may be, our clinic has had considerable success in giving many people the great blessing of a healthy-minded attitude toward problems and the constructive know-how to handle them successfully. In this clinic we have dealt with just about every known human problem. You name it, we have seen it.

One problem is worry that besets multitudes of persons. Worry is not to be minimized as a personality problem. The English word *worry*, I am told, is derived from an Anglo-Saxon word, *wyrgan*, which literally meant "to choke or strangle." If someone seized you about the throat, pressing with maximum strength, he would be dramatically doing to you what you do to yourself if you are a victim of worry for a long period. You are, in effect, literally strangling or choking your own creative powers.

Among the hieroglyphics revealed during excavations on a cliff in Britain was a rough drawing chiseled out of the rock depicting a huge wolf sinking its teeth into the throat of a man. This drawing was deciphered as the ancients' effort to illustrate worry. It seems that way back in the misty past people were plagued by that devastating, self-destroying emotional problem we call worry.

Another personal problem we often see is that of fear. It may be described as worry in-depth. In addition, there is that of anxiety. What is anxiety? A dark, irrational, conflicting, and terrifying feeling that something awful may happen. The late Dr. Smiley Blanton used to say that "anxiety is America's greatest plague."

The Institutes of Religion and Health also deal with marital, alcohol, drug, and youth problems and many other situations that frustrate the free, creative flow of human potential. But perhaps the most common difficulty besetting modern, educated, and highly organized persons generally is the inability to cope with the ordinary problems of human existence.

A most viable procedure for developing a person well able to cope is turning him into a person of faith. Faith is the greatest of all therapies, barring none. Faith in what? In God, in people, in your job, and in yourself. When an individual develops strong faith and when doubt and attitudes of inadequacy are minimized or even eliminated, that person no longer has any serious problem with coping. That person becomes thoroughly changed in his mental and spiritual nature. A former weakness becomes a strength. The result is that a previously inadequate person can now undertake and handle problems with verve and power. Problems that formerly overwhelmed, frustrated, and defeated him no longer do so. Now he surmounts them. He solves them or becomes philosophically able to live with them. And he does so with the positive attitude that instead of being obstacles, problems are actually career builders, super know-how producers.

I had to go through this change in mental attitude myself. As a young man I was anything but a positive thinker. In fact, I had a dominating inferiority complex. Learning how to shake it off and live normally was one of the greatest problems I ever had to face in life. I had some ambitious dreams and set big goals. I had boundless enthusiasm and energy. But I was plagued by self-doubt and feelings of inadequacy. I endured the sneering message from my subconscious: "You can't do it, you haven't got what it takes."

For example, one of my goals, my chief goal really, was to be a public speaker. But the mere thought of appearing before an audience frightened me. When I did attempt it, my knees shook, my mouth was dry, and I hesitated ineffectively. Still I wanted to speak in public; I miserably desired to do so. I felt strongly motivated to do things, to accomplish objectives, and to realize ambitions. If you ever wanted to do something and believed that you could not, longed to be somebody and yet had a self-doubting attitude, then you had a problem. And that problem, of course, hatched a lot of other problems. How could you possibly handle situations in your life and make good decisions if you were a defeated disbeliever in yourself?

I was fortunate in encountering four men in my youth who helped me with myself. The first was Ben Arneson, a professor at Ohio Wesleyan University. He saw and understood my pathetic dilemma. One day he said, "Peale, please remain after class." He sat studying me. "What's the matter with you, Norman? I know you work hard and have mastered the material in this course, but you never speak up unless I call upon you. And then your face gets red, you flounder and stammer. You are embarrassed and self-conscious. Why? Tell me why?"

He did not give me time to try to come up with an excuse. "I know why. You have an inferiority complex that you've been nursing until it dominates you. Actually you are egotistical in thinking that everyone is watching you, that you are the center of attention." He sat bouncing an eraser up and down on his desk. Suddenly he said, "See that eraser? A wonderful thing, an eraser. It can rub out mistakes, make the paper clean." And hurling it against the desk, "Look at the bounce it's got built into it.

"Same thing with you, son. Wipe out that inferiority attitude, get the bounce going that almighty God built into you." He continued along this line, "You've been reared in a godly home to have faith, and faith can always cancel out fear. And you've got fear—the fear to live, to be your own good self. Take it up with the Lord, Norman. Let the good Lord remake you. He will if you ask Him."

I stumbled down the hall with a mixture of feelings. Anger was one. Frustration was another, but a strange emerging hope was there also. Walking down the long flight of stairs, I stopped on the fourth step from the bottom. I remember it precisely because on that step one of the major events of my life occurred. I knew the professor was right about what I was and what I could be, if —! Fortunately I knew what to do. I prayed, "Dear Lord, I have seen You change bad people into good people. I have seen You change drunks into sober men and women, and thieves into honest persons. Can't You also change a poor defeated boy like me into a normal person? Please do, dear Lord." I really meant those words I prayed.

James Russell Lowell in his poem "the Cathedral" wrote:

> I, that still pray at morning and at eve . . .
> Thrice in my life perhaps have truly prayed,
> Thrice, stirred below my conscious self, have felt
> That perfect disenthralment which is God.

Those lines perfectly describe what happened to me in that unforgettable moment. But there was no apparent miracle except that I felt strangely peaceful and happy.

One day another professor, named William E. Smyser, kept me after class. "Norman," he said, "here are two books I want you to read." One was the *Meditations of Marcus Aurelius*, the other *The Sayings of Ralph Waldo Emerson* edited by Bruce Perry. "They will help you to understand the greatness inherent in the human mind when faith is dominantly present in the thoughts." Many times since then I have stood by that magnificent statue of Marcus Aurelius on the Capitoline Hill in Rome and tried to thank him for all he did for me in helping me develop that normal self-confidence I call positive thinking.

The struggle to solve my personal problem of inferiority was certainly not an easy or a short one. A deep-seated problem may require lots of time and patience and stick-to-it-iveness to get positive results. The perseverance to hang in there in the tussle with a tough problem is of the utmost importance. The tendency to accept defeat will strongly resist this ousting process, but the problem must be attacked repeatedly with positive thoughts and faith until it gives way, as it assuredly will, if one has the will and fortitude never to give up.

Perhaps six years after that experience on the college steps, I was the young pastor of a church in the Blackstone Valley of Rhode Island. The going was tough because of a long strike at the New England textile mills and a divided congregation. All this I was trying to heal and deal with. My old self-doubt began once again to emerge, but I had the rare good fortune to have a wise and discerning friend, a man of strong and rugged faith, a real positive thinker. His name was Rob Rowbottom. Listening to my negative remarks, he came up with a statement that has lived powerfully in my mind ever since. It was one of the wisest utterances I have ever heard in my lifetime. Rob simply said, "Never build a case against yourself."

Write those six words on a card, and carry it with you every day. Better still, write those words indelibly upon your mind. With that positive thought going for you, no problem you will ever face can be too much for you.

Still I struggled with the problem of myself. It is a fact that of all the problems we ever have to deal with, the problem of the self is often the most complex, difficult, and tenacious. But if we solve that one, all other problems become immeasurably less difficult.

Approximately ten years after the experience on the college steps, I was the young, inexperienced pastor of an outstanding church near a university campus, the University Methodist Church of Syracuse, New York. It had a beautiful edifice, but the congregation had declined and the financial debt had increased. I might add that it seems I have always been favored in difficult jobs. I say favored because the bottom is a most advantageous place. The only direction one can go from the bottom is up. And at the beginning of my incumbency this church was at the bottom. Once again that old die-hard feeling of inadequacy began to reemerge. The whole enterprise became, in my thinking, a horrendous problem. My entire view was dominated by what I viewed as a mountainous difficulty.

Again fortune favored me. In my congregation was one of the greatest businessmen Syracuse ever had. His name was Harlow B. Andrews. He was said to have been one of the early inventors of the dishwasher. He operated one of the first supermarkets in the United States, bringing in fresh fruit and vegetables from Florida and California by express train and selling them off season in prime condition four days later on Salina Street. He was a very religious man, head of the Syracuse Rescue Mission, but he had the fastest team of trotting horses in Syracuse and would race them down James Street in summer and on frozen Onondaga Lake in winter. A local banker once commented that Andrews had the most acute financial sense of anyone in town, that all he had to do was extend his fingers and money sprang to them. I was so fascinated that I cultivated his company assiduously in the hope of acquiring his gift but, alas, I had no success.

So I took my problem or problems to this pious, wise, and astute man. He listened as I outlined all the difficulties in the situation. Finally when I had run down a bit, he asked, "Is that all of your problem?" I nodded, whereupon he waved his hands in a sweeping motion as though he were piling up a lot of stuff. "Quite a pile," he grinned. "Sure is a big problem, isn't it?" Then he said, "Come here, son, let's walk around this problem," and he made as though to poke at the pile. Fascinated, I noticed his rough big forefinger. He had arthritis in that finger, causing it to be crooked, but he could point mighty straight with that crooked finger.

"Every problem," he said, "has a soft spot. I've learned that fact over the years and don't you give me an argument about it. Every problem has a soft spot. When you find it, the problem can be broken apart, and you can put a right solution together." So he proceeded to walk around the problem, muttering to himself. Then, "Ah, we've got it. Here is that soft spot," meanwhile wiggling that forefinger into it. "Let's handle it at this point. This is the essence of your difficulties. Let's take it from here and go forward." Then he added, "Apply some positive faith. Believe, believe, believe. Pray big prayers, have a big faith, get some big ideas. See yourself getting big results. Go to it, son, with God's help. You've got what it takes." As I started to leave, he pointed that big old finger at me. "And in the name of God, believe in yourself." What this unforgettable character was whimsically saying is that positive thinkers get powerful results.

Some years ago the head of one of the largest industrial corporations in this country made an appointment to see me. I had often heard of this man and read of his activities, but I had never met him. When he came into my office, I at once sensed the force of his personality. I realized that no one could have attained his eminence in the business world without great mental capacity and lots of talent.

But Mr. X, as I shall call him, was very shaken and showed symptoms of a nervous breakdown. He explained that his doctor ascribed his deteriorating emotional and physical condition to pressure and overstress. He told me that he had read one of my books and lately had been attending Sunday services at the church. Both the book and the talks had been helpful to him, he indicated. Then he came up with a unique suggestion. "When I do not feel up to par physically, I consult my doctor, and he gives me a prescription. So now that I am in a bad way emotionally and maybe also spiritually, why can't I come to you as a mental and spiritual doctor? Please study my case and write me a prescription. I have faith in you, and I promise I will follow it."

In our conversation I learned that he had become terrified of making decisions concerning the important problems facing him almost daily as president and chief executive officer of his corporation. This reaction astonished him by its unaccountability. Previously he had been keen-minded and quick and accurately decisive. In some way the pressure under which he had broken had resulted in a mind-gripping fear that he would decide problems erroneously. As a result, he had become timorous and indecisive. Aides, forced to cover for him, had protected his position thus far, but sadly he said, "I know I can't get away much longer with my inability to deal with problems."

One must handle people with sensitivity and with whatever know-how one may have picked up by study and experience. I had several meetings with this man and became convinced that by restoring his once-positive thought processes, he could be healed. Since the reason he came to me, a minister, was due to his religious inclinations, I would treat him on that basis.

"Well, Mr. X," I said, "I believe that if you add deep mental peace to your mind, your drive will be enhanced and confidence in your judgments will be restored." I quoted those great lines from the poet Edwin Markham: "At the heart of the cyclone tearing the sky is a place of central calm." That is to say, the cyclone or elemental power draws its force from a calm center. A human being, in the mind, derives power from central calmness. "Now I prescribe for you the following daily affirmations":

1. The peace of God that passes all understanding is in my mind and my body now.
2. I am not alone. The Lord is by my side and all day long He will be near me.
3. God will help me with every decision; and since there is no error in the Lord, wrong things will be removed from my mind.
4. I believe that God is guiding me. I receive that guidance. I will act upon it without hesitation.

"When you retire at night, thank the Lord for being with you. Know that you have decided rightly. Then go to sleep in peace."

"That makes sense," he said thoughtfully. He folded the paper on which I had written this prescription under an Rx to make it more authoritative. "I'll follow it." And he did regularly and completely. It was not too long before he was his old competent self again.

A long time later the head of a big soft drink company said, "Thanks for pulling me out of a mental funk." When I expressed surprise, he pulled a paper from his wallet. I was astonished to see the prescription I'd given Mr. X. "He passed copies of that around among his friends," he explained. "You see, he is a real positive thinker. And he says to be a positive thinker, you've got to have the peace of God in your mind because then you are afraid of nothing. Isn't that something?" He added, "But it does work, it really does."

As I said early in this chapter, a positive thinker is never afraid of nor abashed by a problem. He knows that problems contain solutions, and the tougher the problem, the tougher he must be. Better results will be attained by tackling the problem resolutely and intelligently.

My longtime friend, George Cullum, Sr., whose firm laid much of the underground piping at the Dallas-Fort Worth Airport, said, "When we strike tough hard rock, we simply get tougher and harder than the rock." Naturally George was always a thoroughgoing positive thinker. It has often been demonstrated that a tough problem, when met head-on with courage and with positive anticipation of success, will yield greater results than a soft or easy problem.

Branch Rickey, one-time head successively of the Saint Louis Cardinals, the old Brooklyn Dodgers, and the Pittsburgh Pirates baseball clubs, told me admiringly about the famous player Stan Musial. Branch said that he asked the outstanding hitter how he had attained his high batting average. Musial replied, "I always wait for the tough pitch. I like the tough pitch best because when you connect with it squarely, it goes, really goes."* So too when you and I are not afraid of a tough one but stand up to it and resolutely swing at it, we are very likely to connect with it squarely. Then we go, really go.

I often think of my old friend R. P. Ettinger. He was my publisher until his death. Some rated him as one of the most capable businessmen in New York. He lost his voice due to cancer and could no longer speak. One day his wife called me. "Dick wants you to talk to him. Remember he published your book, *The Power of Positive Thinking*. Just say something to encourage him."

"Hello, R. P.," I said, "do you know something? I think you're just about positive thinker number one. And even more important, God loves you. He knows you can handle a problem, for you have a tough, strong faith. You've always gotten big results out of big problems, and you will do the same out of this one."

*From *The American Diamond*. Copyright © 1965 by Branch Rickey and Roger Riger. Reprinted by permission of Simon & Schuster.

He told me years later that those words from a friend who loved him and believed in him "brought him out of it." And when one day I heard him make a thrilling talk to a large group in a rather husky but clear voice, it was another powerful demonstration of the fact that some positive thinkers get powerful results.

As head of the Chicago Bears, George Halas won more football games in his career than the legendary Alonzo Stagg. He was the only man the famous Vince Lombardi would embrace, the only one he would call Coach. George Halas had a large framed sign in his office and a similar one in his bedroom—"Never go to bed a loser." That's great. And here is one that is perhaps just as good—"Always get up a winner." As we follow these two mottoes, we too may be positive thinkers who get powerful results. We will turn problems into good outcomes.

The negative thinker does a very dangerous thing. Constantly, this person pumps out negative thoughts about everything. Accordingly, the world around him is activated negatively. There is a law, that law of attraction, that like attracts like. The old saying, "Birds of a feather flock together," sums this up. Thoughts of a kind have mutual affinity. Send out negative thoughts, and negative results will return. It is an immutable law of mind, of cause and effect.

The positive thinker, on the other hand, sets very different forces in motion. He sends out robust thoughts of faith, hope, and optimism. Positive thoughts flow vigorously from his mind, and the world around him is activated positively. On the basis of the same law of attraction, positive results come surging back to the positive thinker. This process also is a law of mind. It is the way life works.

How fortunate one is to learn and use this creative process of positive thinking early in life! But it can be learned and applied to good effect at any age. I received a letter from a ninety-three-year-old man, a lifelong attorney-at-law. He said:

> I have had an inferiority complex all my life for 93 years. [It's the longest one I ever heard of.] But I read your book and I believed it. I put it into practice and want to report that I have finally made an end to my inferiority complex. Thank you very much.

But the P.S. was the payoff. "P.S. The future looks great."

Turn now to the next chapter. We are going to talk about the positive thinker as an achiever.

4.

The Positive Thinker as an Achiever

"I'*m* just a country boy working at positive thinking," he said with a shy smile. "Mind if I walk along with you a ways?" He explained that he had been reading motivational books for several years and seemed proud of his collection. "The first one I read was your *Power of Positive Thinking*. Mom gave it to me for Christmas when I was a kid, and I was sort of brought up on it. I'm trying to believe that I can reach my ambition."

"And what may that be?" I asked.

"I want to be a lawyer and maybe get into politics, but that all seems like a dream that can't ever come true."

"Why can't it come true?"

"Because we're poor. And you have to go to college and

law school to be a lawyer. Nobody in my family ever went to college. We're just farm folks up country."

This conversation took place as I was walking back to my hotel. I had just given a speech at a motivational rally which was packed mostly by ambitious young men and women working in sales.

My companion said, "I'm nineteen years old, and when I saw in the paper about this meeting, I came down by bus. Cost nearly my last buck. I watched you leave the hall after your talk and followed you. Tell me that you think I can make it. Just tell me that and give me some pointers on how I can reach my goal."

It was all rather pathetic, yet inspiring too. He really touched me. He was so traditionally American. A poor boy wanting to be a lawyer and to get involved in his country's life.

"You have all the makings," I said. "You have intensity of desire, a definite goal, a worthy purpose. You have shown perseverance by coming to this meeting by bus, using up your few dollars. You have a good mind, for there is intelligence shining out of your eyes. You say you are working at faith. So believe you can. With God's help, there is no doubt that you can be what you want to be."

I took a pad from my pocket and wrote these words: "I can do all things through Christ who strengthens me. Philippians 4:13." Then I asked, "Are you a believer in God?"

"Oh, yes, I believe."

"Well, belief and a positive thought pattern are the secrets along with hard work, determination, and imaging your goal." I pointed to the words I'd written. "Saturate your mind with those words. That will help a lot."

He went off with a swinging gait. I watched until he rounded the corner on his way to the bus station for the long trip up country. He waved to me. It may reveal sentiment on my part when I confess that I had a catch in my throat. Our country is still the same wonderful America where youths can follow their dreams. That my young friend will make it I haven't the slightest doubt.

It seems that everywhere I go I encounter men and women, young and old, who are working on goals and on self-improvement. And I must admit that they help build up my own motivation.

In the Atlanta airport I ran into an old friend, a business executive, and we had a stimulating conversation about positive thinking and how it changes people into goal achievers. On the back of his business card, he had written that the *positive principle* is the mental and spiritual process by which a person moves from self-limitation, deterioration, and failure to self-improvement, growth, and accomplishment.

When a person is not succeeding as well as desired, it only makes sense that some change is indicated. And often, perhaps usually, such a failing person assumes that the solution to the problem is to change jobs. But actually the better way may be not to change the job but to change the person. A changed individual may make the job altogether different. The job may become a remarkable opportunity instead of continuing to be the dead end it seems. A changed person often results in a changed everything. Mental and spiritual alteration may be just the process that will carry a changed person to a success he wouldn't have dreamed possible before the personal change took place.

At a sales motivational meeting, a young man said, "I go for this positive-thinking stuff, but I have a stupid, lousy job. What do I do about that?"

"You know something," I said, "you might have the opportunity of a lifetime in that job you put down. You might be able to become one of the top executives of your organization if instead of depreciating what you are doing and instead of wanting to change jobs, you really changed yourself. Do that and maybe you will change what you call a 'stupid, lousy job' into an exciting one. Why not visualize yourself as exactly the kind of man your employer thinks you are? He wouldn't have you in that job unless he thought you could handle it. He is pretty smart in his insights into personality qualities. Maybe he actually knows you better than you know yourself. Practice liking everyone, and deliberately start liking your job. I'm guessing you will soon have a better time at work. Do this, and you will start moving up."

Basically, he was a disbeliever in himself. That seemed obvious. But I sold him on what he really was underneath and on what he could do. Fortunately he was goal oriented, but he seemed mentally disorganized and pretty negative. "I'm not really a positive person," he explained. "How the boss ever got the impression that I am mystifies me."

"He probably sizes you up as a potentially outgoing and motivated individual," I suggested. "Anyway, did you ever hear of the 'as of' principle? I explain it to everyone."

He shook his head, "No, that's a new one on me."

"Well, it's a sound psychological principle, one that can really change people, provided they want change to take place. It was, I believe, first stated by William James, who is often labeled the father of American psychology. It means that if a person is dissatisfied with himself as he is or with his job, he may image himself as he wishes to be and the job as a terrific opportunity. Then he acts as if he and the job were that. If he persists in this alteration effort, the strong psychological and spiritual forces inherent in his personality structure or in his nature will conspire to make him and his job just that."

I explained that I had seen the "as if" principle put into effective action so often by people who want to change that I had strong faith in its efficacy. He listened with growing interest as I told him of dull, unenthusiastic men and women whom I had persuaded to act as if they were enthusiastic. In due course, they actually took on enthusiastic attributes. And I told him of others who were shy and introverted, who deliberately acted as if they were extraverted and outgoing, and who ultimately became genuinely that kind of individual.

Well, he seemed to get the message, and fortunately he didn't overdo it. Next morning he did not go bounding into the office breathing out joy and enthusiasm. He continued to be low-key, but he began to take a real interest in his assignment and in his associates, especially in the shy ones who are in every group. He went out of his way to talk with them. He encouraged those who seemed to be feeling down and depressed. But the main thing is that he gradually got beyond his old gripy self, and in acting as if he were a positive, caring, and outgoing person, he gradually became one in fact. I saw him only once after that when I spoke at a national convention of his industry. He introduced himself and told me of the minor executive position he was then holding. Here was a man who had experienced alteration and, as a result, was now gaining on goals that formerly had seemed far beyond him.

It is pathetic that so many people who could do a terrific job in life just don't do it. Instead they settle apathetically for something less. The famous writer James M. Barrie stated the matter very well: "The most gladsome thing in the world is that few of us fall very low; the saddest that, with such capabilities, we seldom rise high." Perhaps another way of saying it is that we are self-made victims of mediocrity. We make ourselves content to be what amounts to mediocre when the actual fact is that we do not need to be that at all.

Why does a person fail to become what he or she could be? There are probably many answers to that question, but a simple one is that the person doesn't give the job or the effort the whole mind and doesn't let the entire self become involved. It has always been true that the world gives itself to the all-outs and denies itself to the half-outs.

When I think of the goal achievers I have known, they all had certain characteristics in common. Always, without exception, they had a goal, not an indefinite, indistinct, fuzzy object, but a sharp, clearly defined goal. They knew precisely what they wanted, and they went for that goal with focused determination and unremitting effort. They all had enthusiasm, a burning, glowing enthusiasm, and it was sustained through all manner of difficulty. These high achievers never gave up, no matter how tough the going. Add up all the positive qualities, and these achievers had them all. Then the big plus was that they were all believers. Every day all the way they never doubted; they were never negative thinkers. All the goal achievers I have ever known have been positive thinkers who got powerful results.

In Chicago you will see the name Rubloff on building after building all over town. Arthur Rubloff is one of the greatest real estate men in this or any country. He made North Michigan Avenue one of the notable thoroughfares of the world, known everywhere as "The Magnificent Mile." He was the innovator of the shopping center—his Evergreen Plaza is a spectacular example of a free enterprise restoration of the inner city.

Arthur is an art collector, a philanthropist sharing his wealth for the benefit of all people. He had no rich father and no help along the road to the top. He got there on his own; he sold newspapers, shined shoes, and worked as a galley boy on a Great Lakes freighter. He was a poor boy with a dream and a goal plus the willingness to work. Add to that formula the will never to give up, enthusiasm for life, intelligence, positive thinking, always positive thinking, and he had the makings of successful achievement.

Also from Chicago is another famous goal achiever, W. Clement Stone, who began in the classic Horatio Alger pattern as a poverty-stricken kid selling newspapers on the South Side. He is now worth, so they say, a third of a billion dollars. Also a generous philanthropist, Stone has given his life to motivating others to become what they have within themselves to be.

In an article in his magazine *Success*, Clem Stone says to ignore those who dolefully say you can't. He offers some wise advice on how to give the lie to the "it can't be done" excuse. Here is what he says:

> Millions of people in every walk of life have never tried to achieve high goals that were achievable or solve problems that were solvable. Why? They were told or believed "It can't be done." And they never learned or applied that essence of the art of motivation with a positive mental attitude (PMA) that could have helped them achieve any goal that didn't violate universal laws, the laws of God, and the rights of their fellowmen.
>
> They could have achieved the highest goals and solved the most difficult problems:
>
> . . . If they had motivated themselves to Recognize, Relate, Assimilate, and Apply from what they read, heard, saw, thought and experienced. . . .
>
> . . . If they had set high desirable goals, written them down, engaged in concentrated study, thinking, and planning time for a half hour or more daily on their goals. The subconscious will come up with the answers through repetition, repetition, repetition.*

I frequently stay overnight with my longtime friend John W. Galbreath at his 4,400-acre farm, Darby Dan, near

*Reprinted with permission. © 1983 Success Unlimited.

Columbus, Ohio. John has led in the remaking of the downtown and river front areas of the city and has built huge installations in all parts of the world, notably the great Mei Foo section of Hong Kong. He was the owner of the Pittsburgh Pirates baseball club.

Galbreath was born on a poor twenty-acre farm on the outskirts of Mount Sterling, Ohio, and as did all American kids prior to the school-bus era, he trudged to school on foot. A lovable, outgoing person, he preserves, in older years after achieving great success, the same down-to-earth humility that has always characterized him. But along with this self-effacement is a sharp, keen mind that led him from poverty to a high-level position in the world. The country boy who came out of poverty is now the friend of presidents and Queen Elizabeth II.

When he takes off from his private airport on Darby Dan Farm, the flight path often takes him over the stony twenty acres where he grew up as a boy and where his father struggled to wrest a few dollars from the soil to support his family. How was this miracle of achievement attained? John Galbreath will tell you that it was done first by desire, intense desire. That is his basic formula for goal achieving—intensity of desire. To that he has added a humble faith in God, an upright character, and an outgoing interest in people who today strive to do him honor, not because of his riches, but because of what he is—an honorable, lovable, humble, and very able human being. His story, like the others I've mentioned and scores of others I would like to mention, is that of a positive thinker—a positive thinker who set goals and reached them. I'm sure he would unhesitatingly tell you that you can be a goal achiever too if you follow the basic principles laid out in this book.

To reach a goal an individual has to have a strong motivating force as well as an intense desire and the belief that it can be done. While I was writing this chapter, Abraham

Spector, a longtime friend and associate, came into my office. He is an outstanding CPA, a leader in his profession. I have worked with Abe as a personal adviser for a good many years. He is a real achiever. So I put the question to him, "Abe, what made you a successful man? Did you have a goal?"

He replied, "I was born in the Bronx and grew up there in a poor family. I don't use the word *poverty*. That's a later term. But back then we were poor people, a poor Jewish family. And," Abe hesitated, then continued, "I just didn't want to be poor anymore."

How many Americans have been motivated by being poor as Abe Spector was? Legions of them. Another Abe, Abe Lincoln was poor, very poor. Americans hate poverty. Lincoln's mother said to her son, "Abe, be somebody." I was of a poor family myself. Being poor causes hardships, but it has been one of the great American motivators. It has stimulated many to rise higher, to become achievers in life. They didn't want to be poor anymore, so they developed goals and became positive thinkers. They worked and worked and thought and thought and believed and believed. They built their lives on the "of course you can" principle, and they attained their goals. They were activated by strong motivational force.

One of the greatest demonstrations of how a motivated positive thinker reaches goals is the story of the unforgettable Olympic champion Jesse Owens. I had the privilege of personally knowing this superb athlete, this great American. Some sports writers judged him to be one of the greatest athletes in the history of this country. Jesse Owens himself vigorously disclaimed such high evaluation, but there is no doubt about his athletic prowess or about his greatness as a sincere Christian and as a notable human being.

One evening during a dinner program of the Ohio Newspaper Publishers' Association in Columbus, Ohio, I sat by Jesse Owens at the head table. I got him to talk about his life and career, and he related the following story. He was born into a black family of extremely limited means. "We were poor materially but rich spiritually." He also said that as a young boy, he was slight of build, even skinny, with a below-average physique. But his believing, positive mother told him that he was destined to do great things in life, that he was going to be somebody. He didn't see how that was possible. His family was poor and had no influence. Everything seemed against him, but his mother kept reminding him of the Lord by saying, "You just be a believer and keep faithful. You will be led."

One day at a school assembly the speaker was Charlie Paddock, one of the most famous athletes of the time. On many a sports page he was hailed as "the fastest human being alive." I saw him run once in the Boston Arena, and he was like greased lightning. Having long since retired from his athletic career, Paddock gave his time to motivating kids everywhere, and he had a tremendous influence on youths.

Over a thousand kids packed the school auditorium that day to hear the renowned runner speak, and little Jesse Owens was on the front row. Owens said that Charlie Paddock walked to the front of the stage, put both hands in his hip pockets, let a deep silence fall, and in a full strong voice shot out the question, "Do you know who you are? You don't, eh? Well, I'm here to tell you. You are Americans, and you are the children of God. You can be somebody. You can be anything you want to be if you have a goal and will work and believe and have good moral character. You really can be what you want to be with the help of the good God."

Jesse Owens told me that in that moment, in a flash, he knew just what he wanted to be; his goal was instantly formed. He wanted to be the next Charlie Paddock, the fastest human being alive. He could scarcely wait for the speech to end, and immediately he rushed up and clasped Paddock's hand. With a touch of awe in his voice, he told me, "When I grabbed Charlie's hand, an electric impulse passed up my arm and through my body."

Then he rushed to the coach, shouting, "Coach, I have a dream, I have a dream. I'm going to be the next Charlie Paddock. I'm going to be the fastest man on earth!" The coach was a wise man, a motivator and guide. He put his arm around the shoulders of the frail little boy. "That's right, Jesse. Have a dream, a big dream. You will never go any higher than you can dream. But you can go as high as you dream if you work at it, believe in it, and stick to it. To reach your dream, you must climb a ladder on which there are four rungs. Mark them well. They are (1) determination, (2) dedication, (3) discipline, and (4) attitude."

The coach went on to say that attitude is of primary importance, even more than the other three qualities taken together, because attitude deals with how a person thinks and believes. And before anyone can be determined, dedicated, and disciplined, he must make a mental and spiritual commitment to the goal. He must continue to think positively about it all the way to its attainment.

I was fascinated as Jesse Owens told me this story of his awakening to his possibilities, his goal, his dream and how it could come true. What followed? He thrilled the world in the 1936 Olympic Games by winning four gold medals. He tied the record for the one-hundred-meter race and ran the two-hundred-meter race faster than it had ever been run before. His broad jump record set in the games lasted for twenty-two years, and his performance on the relay team was spectacular. And finally, when the American Hall of Athletic Fame was established, the name that led all the rest was that of the frail little boy from Cleveland who followed a dream, a goal to athletic immortality. Reflect on the story of Jesse Owens and know, really know in your heart, that you too as a positive thinker can reach your goal.

To help you do just that, here are ten "of course you can" principles. Engrave them on your mind. Believe they will work when used. By applying them, the positive thinker gets powerful results.

1. Stamp your goal indelibly on your mind.
2. Always image yourself as succeeding with God's help.
3. When a negative thought enters your mind, immediately cancel it out with a positive thought.
4. Mentally minimize difficulties; maximize your strengths.
5. Deny the power of difficulty over you. Affirm the power of faith to overcome.
6. Believe in yourself.
7. Always be genuinely friendly.
8. Keep on learning, growing, improving yourself.
9. Build a ladder to your dreams—Determination
Dedication
Discipline
Attitude
10. Every day practice the greatest of all positive affirmations, "I can do all things through Christ who strengthens me."

But let's face it, the problems of life can gang up on us. Difficult situations develop out of various causes. A temporary letdown of positive attitudes could be one. So, in the next chapter we will explore an important issue—how to make things go better for you.

5.

You Can Make Things Go Better

"Shoot for the moon. Even if you miss it, you'll land among the stars." So said Les Brown, a former member of a state legislature but now a popular youth motivational speaker. "A big shot is a little shot who keeps on shooting," declared Stanley Kresge, a prominent Detroit philanthropist.

One man says aim high, the other keep it going. Both principles are basic in knowing how to make things go better for you.

When things are not going well for you, ask yourself whether you are thinking good things or bad. It is a well-established fact that there is a strong tendency for outward manifestations to match inner thought patterns. Thoughts are alive and produce vibratory influence. They have acute drawing power. It is summertime as I write this, and last evening a friend complained that he just cannot be out-of-doors on a summer evening because he "draws all the mosquitoes in the county." I do not claim that thinking draws mosquitoes (though it could just be), but it is a fact that nonpositive thinking draws nonpositive results which can cause more trouble than mosquitoes ever did.

I knew a man once who had attained some success, but a recession adversely affected the industry in which he was an employee. Many workers had to be laid off, and he was among them, temporarily he was told. Something happened to his spirit as the layoff continued and he was reduced to dire financial straits. Finally he had to take a low-status job, and he was lucky to get it. It was all he could find to bring in some money to care for his wife and children. His negative attitude deepened, triggered perhaps by the fact that his brother was a distinguished and successful, even famous, man. But he plugged away and did a good job.

I was in his city on a speaking engagement, and he found me in the coffee shop of the motel where I was staying. It seems that he had read one of my books and felt that perhaps I could help him. His immediate problem, he said, was that one of his children was ready for college and the others were just a few years behind. The question was, how was he ever going to be able to put them through college? After all he was the "no-account failure in his family" while his brother was "a big shot success."

"Just what does your brother's success have to do with this problem?" I asked. "It's you and your children we are talking about."

"Oh, I'm a flop, always was. My brother has all the brains. He gets all the breaks in life."

"You need a larger income, don't you?" He nodded. I continued, "You have just stated several reasons why you do not gain the required increased resources. One is that you are not competing with yourself but with your brother. Another is self-depreciation, always putting yourself down.

Don't you know that there is a tendency for all of us to be taken at our own self-appraisal? I suggest that you start holding yourself in higher respect and you might also start being proud of your brother. Generosity toward him will actually activate a flow of generosity and prosperity toward you."

Obviously this man possessed more ability than he realized, but he had been putting himself down for so long that he had come to believe he was second-rate. He was a confirmed self-depreciator. Daily he was violating one of the basic principles of success—never build a case against yourself. This man's self-image had been so constantly self-tarnished that he had mentally come to assume a picture of himself as a complete failure. This mass of negativism had been compounded by his resentment of his brother's success. Mentally he was in competition with his brother and had developed a built-in failure attitude that took refuge in a no-ability, no-account concept of himself. Yet there was enough lingering hope still flickering in his mind to bring him to consult someone who he thought might provide some help.

I suggested a plan for him, and he followed it. It helped to get him started on the road to a successful life. The first step had to do with his attitudes toward his brother, himself, and his job. He was to stop being jealous of his brother and to quit competing with him in his mind. Instead he was to get into real competition with himself. He was to image himself as daily doing a better job. This meant challenging himself, believing in himself, and definitely visualizing successful achievement.

I encouraged him to list on paper all his assets of personality, intelligence, experience, and native ability, to compel him to recognize himself as a somebody instead of as a nobody, his current self-appraisal. Such self-image psychology, when developed, has the power to create a rational self-knowledge and lead to normal self-confidence. This man's basic quality was indicated by his ability to discard the crutch of self put-down and venture into a healthy-minded self-esteem. He learned to believe in himself in a normal manner.

Gradually he developed a good feeling about his brother. They grew closer together, and ultimately a mutually caring relationship resulted. As healthy-mindedness increased and with it self-esteem, people regarded him more highly, and the final outcome was a higher position. Naturally this sequence of self-improvement did not work out overnight. It seldom does that quickly. The emergence from sickly negativism and self-depreciation does not come speedily or easily. But once a person wants self-improvement, devises a plan, and follows it sincerely, the desired result will come. Things will go better because the person is becoming better.

Just one sequel to this fascinating story of a once-defeated man who must remain nameless because of my promise to him. It concerns his original problem about getting his children through college during the tough time of his personal reconstruction. I suggested the principle of imaging or visualization. He was to picture each child in turn entering college as a well-prepared student, to "see" each of them working to help pay the costs, and to hold the picture of each going forward in cap and gown on commencement day to receive her diploma.

"I don't know, indeed will never know, how we did it," he told me a long time later. "But all of us held the 'image,' and things just worked out. It was a miracle," he concluded wonderingly.

"You practiced scientific positive principles of thought and attitude," I said. "And because of your strong religious faith, you had the power of spirit going for you." This man and his entire family found the priceless secret of making things go better, much better.

When things are not going well for you and you are looking for ways to make them go better, here is another procedure I urge you to consider. Start and continue practicing the amazing law of supply. It will work miracles in your life. I personally know this to be a fact because this law has done just that for me. The law of supply is one of the greatest secrets of successful living that I have ever discovered. Considerable numbers of people to whom I have suggested this marvelous way of thinking and doing will enthusiastically endorse the positive assurance I give you here.

What is the law of supply? It is the operation of the principle of abundance spoken of by Jesus Christ when He said, "I have come that they may have life, and that they may have it more abundantly" (John 10:10). It is stated again in Luke 17:21, "The kingdom of God is within you," which is a reference to all the great values and blessings of life—hope, health, love, joy, and every good thing built into you by the Creator. According to the law of supply, your own good seeks to come to you and will continue to flow abundantly toward you if you do not block the flow by negative thought and action. When you become a true believer and are positive and outgoing in your faith, thinking your best, doing your best, and being your best, the law of generous supply starts working. Then God can activate your good, which He provides, and send it flowing unhindered to you.

My wife, Ruth, and I have practiced this principle since we were first married. We began married life with a minimum of financial support, but Ruth, a natural-born positive thinker and a woman of undiluted faith, always stoutly affirmed even in our times of dire circumstances that the Lord would provide. If we did our part and tried to help people as much as we were capable and trusted and had faith, we would, she declared, be taken care of and always would be given strength to carry on. In developing this philosophy, she had stumbled on one of the subtlest of all laws, the law of supply.

We had been practicing this principle for twenty years before we heard a name put to it. Our son John had been entered as a student in Deerfield Academy in Massachusetts, and there we came to know Dr. Frank Boyden, one of the greatest headmasters America has ever had and certainly one of its outstanding schoolmen. Frank was spiritually and intellectually wise, and he was a true positive thinker. As he showed us over the magnificent campus with its splendid buildings and superb equipment, I marveled, since I knew he had built this school from a minuscule beginning.

"How did you ever do it?" I asked.

He smiled and said, "I'm sure the bank wrote me off a good many times, but I felt that I was doing God's work in helping boys to become good and successful men. And since the heavenly Father had, I felt, called me to do this job, I knew He would never let me fail. So the funds always came and they keep on coming. I was on the receiving end of God's law of supply. When you give all you can, God will give abundantly in return," he concluded.

As Frank spoke, I found myself thinking of that significant reference to this law of supply in Malachi 3:10:

> "Bring all the tithes into the storehouse,
> That there may be food in My house,
> And prove Me now in this,"
> Says the LORD of hosts,
> "If I will not open for you the windows
> of heaven
> And pour out for you such blessing
> That there will not be room enough to
> receive it."

Ruth and I had been tithers, even when we had practically no material things. And we had been recipients of God's boundless blessings. So in this conversation with Frank Boyden, I knew that we had been working with a basic law of prosperity. As we drove away from Deerfield that day, Ruth said, almost with awe, "The law of supply—why, that is what we have been practicing all our lives. That's our big secret of living."

"It's yours, honey," I said. "I learned it from you, and you learned it from the Lord."

Now, years later, we are still tithers, giving not 10 percent but often 20 and even 30 percent. I would never even consider modifying this practice, for I believe it to be the activation of the continuous law of supply. And when to financial giving one adds the giving of love and help to people, then good returns in even more abundance. The original meaning of the word *abundant* meant "to rise up in waves"; your good rises up in the full flow of divine generosity.

When things are not going well and you are striving for the answer to your problem of how to make them go better, I suggest that you give thought to this basic way of turning adversity around, the practice of the law of supply. The truth is that God the Father wants you to prosper. The first psalm says so:

> Blessed is the man
> Who walks not in the counsel of the
> ungodly. . . .
> He shall be like a tree
> Planted by the rivers of water,
> That brings forth its fruit in its season,
> Whose leaf also shall not wither;
> And whatever he does shall prosper (vv. 1,3).

The Bible, in which we have the most perfect use of language to describe the greatest things, finds it difficult to describe the riches almighty God desires to give us. In 1 Corinthians 2:9 is stated, "Eye has not seen, nor ear heard, / Nor have entered into the heart of man / The things which God has prepared for those who love Him." The Creator of all scientific law also created the law of supply to deliver marvelous values to us out of His boundless supply. So it would seem that when things are not going well, we are out of creative contact. Therefore to make things go better, we have only to establish a more perfect connection with the abundant flow of good.

The wise Dr. Samuel Johnson once declared, "It's worth at least a thousand pounds a year to have a bright point of view." I think it is worth much more than that since gloomy-thinking negativism is so contrary to prosperity as to actually chase it away. Prosperity turns away from the doubt-filled mind. Remember, doubts tend to produce doubtful results. "All things work together for good to those who love God," the Bible tells us in Romans 8:28. Every morning remind yourself that since all things are working together for good for you, doors will open, new opportunities will come, and things will go better for you. By lifting anxiety from your mind, this powerful, sound belief will stimulate creative thinking and shift circumstances in your favor. But you must believe this, really believe it, to activate your mental process accordingly. Continue to believe and you will experience perhaps the best of all descriptions of spiritually induced prosperity, the words of the old hymn, "There shall be showers of blessing sent from the Saviour above."

Never say that blessings are scarce or even that money is scarce; the very assertion can scare both away from you. The only difference between the words *scare* and *scarce* is the one little letter *c*. Do not say that times are hard, for as

Charles Fillmore wisely asserted, "The very words will tighten your purse strings until omnipotence itself cannot slip a dime into it. Fill every nook and corner of your mind with the word *plenty, plenty, plenty.*" Every day at morning, noon, and night affirm aloud "plenty, plenty, plenty" and then, again aloud, say "opportunity, opportunity, opportunity." Meanwhile, image, visualize, picture plenty and opportunity. Empty out your negative, gloomy thoughts that scare away prosperity, and fill your mind with these bright, optimistic, positive thoughts that attract and draw the good that a generous God wants to send your way through your creative thinking.

Never think or talk lack because the grave danger is to actualize lack. When you send out such negative thoughts, the result is to activate the world around you negatively. Remember that like attracts like. When you constantly send out negative thoughts, you strongly tend to draw back negative results. You should never entertain or express an idea unless you wish it to take form in your life. In the Old Testament is the promise, "You will also declare a thing, / And it will be established for you" (Job 22:28).

When you say, "I am poor," you are in effect declaring poverty. Your word is the expression of your mental image. It is vital when things are not going well to avoid holding a failure image. The mind, which always works to serve you, will grasp at it to establish failure as a fact. Instead you must compel better things to develop by thought discipline. Thoughts and words can speak life or death to your future. Remember, lack thoughts and lack words tend to produce lack as fact. Remember also the truth that prosperity thoughts and prosperity words move you in the direction of prosperity and increased success, because you tend to become what you think and affirm, pray and visualize.

The principles outlined in this book are demonstrable truths, evidenced in the experiences of many persons. People who believed in these principles and put them to work in real situations have found that they definitely cause things to go better, much better. They discovered the proof of the pudding, so to speak.

If you *can* only believe! If you *will* only believe! Then nothing, *nothing,* will be impossible for you! That is the truth and the gospel, and it is wonderful. It's the good news.

I visited an industrial organization that had signs all over the factory and the offices adjoining the plant. On each sign was the one word *Think.* That was all the sign said. Curious, I asked the head of the firm about the signs. He explained that they were his idea. The purpose was to stimulate employees to come up with new ideas to add to the company's total efficiency. But beyond that purpose, the company president was enthusiastic about developing people who worked for him, "and," he said, "if you can get a person into the habit of really doing some hard, constructive thinking about his or her job, that individual is destined to advance in responsibility and income."

He told me about a number of people who had thought up innovative procedures. Some were just small things, but others were revolutionary. The result was a company spirit of participation that benefited the total organization. But in a few cases, getting people to think revolutionized the life and career of employees who, while they would have done satisfactory routine jobs, would otherwise never have gone up the ladder.

Any job will respond to sound thinking; out of thinking come ideas that make things go better. And when the thinking you do is positive, you have a double-pronged tool for achieving improvement.

If you are convinced of the truth and practical workability of what you are reading here, the smart thing to do is to act now on your conviction. You may get an immediate result or it may be delayed. But in either case, go with your faith, hang in there with it. Keep on believing, believing, believing. And keep thinking. Keep action going and you will enjoy improved circumstances.

In the home of Commander and Mrs. Geoffrey Kitson in Bermuda, I noticed a framed quotation on a wall. It read, "Everyone has inside himself—what shall I call it—a piece of good news." What is that good news? Well, it could be that you and I are greater than anything that can ever happen to us. Or it could be that we have it in us to overcome anything that would ever get us down. Certainly those words can mean that we have what it takes to improve a present situation and make things go better. There is an achiever, a winner, in every one of us, and that is good news.

Thomas A. Edison also had a framed sign on his studio wall: "There is a better way of doing it. Find it." You can do that better job and get things going better all the while. As I think along this line and reflect upon the remarkable men and women I have known who improved their situation by improving themselves, I always recall an unforgettable verse from the book of Job: "If you return to the Almighty, you will be built up" (22:23). Being built up, you will be bigger than any discouragement, any setback, any failure.

That is a valid piece of good news within you, one for which you can be grateful. You and I can be built up so as to tower above our failures and, despite all difficulties, make things better than ever before. We can get into the habit of expecting and experiencing self-improvement and the habit of turning a current condition into a better state.

After I finished a speech in a city auditorium, a man came backstage who really was in a miserable state of mind. He was young, perhaps thirty years of age, and he told me he faced a hopeless situation. He added glumly that I was "his last hope." How could he improve his situation, rebuild his shattered career? I stated quickly that I was not his last hope—he and God were—but I told him that I would be glad to help in any way possible.

I let him talk for a while, ventilating his depressed thoughts. I noticed that he was about six two or three, but he was slumped down, bent over, his head on his chest while he told me all the reasons why he could not meet his situation, to say nothing of improving it. Suddenly with seeming irrelevance, I asked, "Will you do me a favor, my friend?"

Surprised he said hesitantly, "What do you want me to do?"

"Stand up, stand up as tall as you can." He complied, but he stood with his shoulders slumped. I asked, "How tall are you anyway?"

"Six feet two when I stand up straight."

"Well, please stand up straight now. Make your height your total six two. I'd like to see it. Nature has been good to you to give you height like that." Thus prodded he struggled to achieve his full height. "Look at that," I exclaimed in admiration, "six two! What a man!"

He still looked at me in some surprise, but it was interesting to see him straighten up, trying to reach even higher. "Doesn't that feel much better than when you were lopped over to about five five a few minutes ago?" I asked.

"Yes, I do feel better, funny but I really do."

So I gave him a formula. "Here is how you can meet your situation and turn it around. Do the following three things. First, several times each day stand tall, reaching for the sky with the crown of your head. Lift your head up as far as it will go, and try to reach for infinity. When God created you, He made you on your two feet to stand tall. And He gave you a head, and the head is supposed to be carried high. When a person maintains this erect stature, whatever his height, he has a commanding power over life and circumstances. So stand tall.

"Second, think tall. Think big thoughts, victorious thoughts. Think winning thoughts. Stand tall mentally. You have been giving me a desultory, gloomy mass of negative, unhappy, frustrated, defeated thoughts. Now that you are standing tall physically, also stand tall mentally. Positively practice positive affirmation." And the first such affirmation I gave him was "It can be done and I can do it!" I said, "Please say that."

"You mean out loud?"

"Certainly! Let's say it together. It can be done and I can do it." So I had him there standing tall, thinking tall, and affirming that he had a stature physically and mentally that towered over his so-called failure situation.

"Third," I suggested, "stand tall spiritually. Think of the greatness of God. Think of yourself as an undefeatable child of God. Ten times every day repeat aloud one of the greatest affirmative statements of faith: 'I can do all things through Christ who strengthens me.' And make a start by doing that now." By this time he was getting the message and actually getting into the spirit of overcoming.

Almost word for word, this is the conversation we had in about ten minutes. I could already see him changing into a victorious, winning person as a new positive attitude began taking hold. "Okay, Dr. Peale, okay. Thanks a lot. I know I can improve my situation, and with the Lord's help I will do it." So saying, he walked out into the night.

This man actually returned to the Almighty and became built up. Of course he had his moments of uncertainty, even slumping down occasionally, but he made the grade because he was changed in his thoughts. His attitude was revamped. He found the good news that was built into him. In the last analysis, nobody ever changes a situation unless he gets changed himself. Every outside situation is a reflection of the internal condition. Get changed on the inside, become a changed person, become a new man or woman, and you can handle and improve any situation. And that is a fact, a big, certain fact.

So I end this chapter as it began: shoot for the moon. Even if you miss it, you will land among the stars.

We are now ready to talk about today, this wonderful, opportunity-packed today. In the next chapter I have a winning slogan for you: "Today is yours, seize it!"

6.

Today Is Yours, Seize It

Positive thinkers get positive results because they appreciate the inestimable value of a day, this day, not the next day, but *this* day, and every day. Today offers at least sixteen waking hours that may be crammed full of opportunity, joy, excitement, achievement. The positive thinker knows that today was made for him and for everyone who will go for it positively. Today is his, so he makes it a marvelous creative experience. The positive thinker's optimistic attitude toward today and every succeeding day strongly tends to make every day a great day. It becomes what he visualizes it to be.

Every morning for many years, the first thing upon rising, I have quoted a dynamic, upbeat statement that I found in the most creative of all books. It has done wonders for me. Sometimes I repeat it aloud, sometimes I think it quietly, but always it vitalizes my attitude and activates my faith. It really gets me going at full power for the day. Moreover, through speeches and books and by one-on-one contact, I probably have persuaded thousands to adopt the same get-up-in-the-morning habit. There is no doubt whatsoever that it effectively conditions the day. Here are those life-packed, inspiration-filled, get-going words that help me every morning, rain or shine, to take my day and do something with it: "This is the day which the LORD has made; / We will rejoice and be glad in it" (Ps. 118:24).

And every now and then my wife will say at breakfast, "Let's have a good day today," and we proceed to do just that. A positive attitude toward every day works out so well that I am motivated to write this chapter, "Today Is Yours." You must seize it because it is fleeting, only twenty-four hours that are soon gone by. If you live to be eighty years of age, you will have only 29,200 days. Each of them, therefore, is a precious fragment of a gift called time, your time. It only makes sense to use every day well. Today is yours. Use it well.

The place was Korea. The hour 1:00 A.M. The temperature was below zero. It was so cold that bare fingers stuck to metal. A big burly marine was leaning against a tank and eating cold beans out of a can with a penknife. A newspaper correspondent watching him, aware that a big battle was building up, asked a philosophical question. "Look, if I were God and could give you anything, what would you ask for?"

The marine dug out another mouthful of beans with his knife, thought the question over, and then said, "I would ask for today."

I believe we all should. Fortunately, we have today. What are we going to do with it? The answer is easy. We are going to carry on working toward our goals. And despite any reverses, setbacks, or difficulties that may come, we are going to be achievers because we are positive thinkers. We are going to reach those goals and have a rare good time in the process. We are going to have the immense satisfaction of being winners.

Positive thinkers get positive results because they love life, see good days, get in there, and give themselves to their days, every one of them, with enthusiasm. In turn, their days will come back to them. It is a fact that if people love life, life will love them back. And it will joyously give back to them in proportion as they give to it.

My wife, Ruth, and I were out in that great country of Alberta, Canada, where the vast prairies surge up against the mighty Rocky Mountains. I had given a speech in Calgary. Early the next morning, Ruth and I went to the airport. The temperature registered twenty-five degrees, the air was crisp and pollution free. The sky was a clear blue, not a cloud in sight. It was a beautiful, cold but sunny November day.

We had over an hour before departure, and feeling alive to our fingertips, we decided to take a brisk walk. Soon we were out of the airport grounds onto the prairie itself. Then we turned about, and there in clear view were the Rockies in breathtaking panorama. They were covered with snow, sparkling like thousands of diamonds in the sunlight. We counted sixty-two snowclad peaks. "Isn't this terrific!" I exclaimed. Ruth's eyes were bright with the delight of the morning and the beauty about us.

Later when our plane took off over a low hill, there, spread out before us from north to south against an azure sky, were many more white peaks. I was so moved by it all that I said, "You know, honey, I love this. I really love it all. I don't want to leave this incredible, wonderful world. I want to live a long time. This is so fascinating, so very great."

Always of a practical turn of mind, Ruth responded, "Well, if you practice that positive thinking you talk about, you will live a long time. You'll have lots of days yet to come. Tell you what. Let's take today and every succeeding day and fill each one full of the beauty and romance and joy of the life God gives us."

So today is yours, dear friend. Seize it! Grab it! Love it! Live it!

Someone might glumly object that all this sounds like a lot of moonlight-and-roses stuff. Such a person might ask, "But what about the tough breaks that come along? How are you going to equate all the dark, even tragic days, with this beautiful talk about good days every day?"

Well, no one has actually raised this question with me, but I have raised it with myself. Having had quite a lot of so-called tough breaks of my own, I long ago faced up to the necessity of working out a positive philosophy about tough breaks in life's total experience. Actually the problem is not so much what happens to you as what you think and do about what happens to you, because a lot of harsh things can come to you.

This one day, whatever it may bring, belongs to you and to me to handle so that the best results can be obtained from what may seem the worst. The secret, of course, is to inject hope into despair and faith into defeat.

The late Casey Stengel, famed manager of the New York Yankees, had the idea in simple form. It was said that defeat did not awe Casey because in every defeat he was always looking for victory. It seems that defeat only motivated him to win more victories. The tough breaks that made some days difficult impelled him to turn the breaks his way the next day.

Personally I have found a lot of help in the truth that to every disadvantage there is a corresponding advantage. And it has always helped me when the going was hard to recall an old proverb, "The hammer shatters glass but forges steel." If you are made of good stuff, then the tough breaks will not break you but will make you hard like steel. And you will think of bad days as good days because of your attitude.

Captain Max Cleland was a vigorous young man on that morning back in 1968 in Vietnam. But before night came, his strong body was wrecked—an exploding grenade took off both his legs and his left arm. Then followed months of physical suffering and mental agony and adjustment. It seemed unlikely that any days ahead could be his to seize and do with creatively. But Cleland had strong, tough faith. He had been noted for a ringing laugh and an infectious smile, and he kept that laugh. Of course he had times of despair and days when it seemed he could never make it.

But Max Cleland went home to Georgia to serve two terms as a state senator. Then he ran for lieutenant governor. When he lost, he was crushed, and depression seized him once again. It was then that something happened to restore good days to Max. Driving in the rain to Washington, D.C., to take a Senate staff position, he suddenly realized, as he described it, "I could go no further by myself. On that rain-swept highway I threw myself at the Lord's feet and cried out, 'God forgive me and help me.' When I reached out, He came to me.

"Since then I really have become stronger at the broken places. And today I find more meaning, more purpose, and more joy in life than I ever thought possible." Despite being able to move only by wheelchair, Max Cleland is in the midst of an illustrious career. President Carter appointed him administrator of the Veterans Administration, the largest department of the federal government, in which capacity he served with distinction. Later he was elected Georgia secretary of state by a large majority. I have watched admiringly as he fascinated large audiences by his matchless speaking ability, persuasive sincerity, and upbeat positive faith. If I were to name the ten happiest persons of my acquaintance, "handicapped" Max Cleland would be on that list.

How did he become a good-day expert, a genius in victorious living? He cites three principles: (1) Strive for acceptance of the problem. He prayed the famous prayer, "God grant me the serenity to accept the things I cannot change." (2) Find another door that opens, because when one door closes, another swings wide open. Don't look so closely at the closed door that you miss the one that is opening. "I still had my mind and one strong arm to propel a wheelchair." (3) Let God help you.

That God is helping him over the rough spots, keeping him happy all the way, is obvious to all who know him. Despite the horrendous things that happened to him, Max Cleland did not fold up in defeat. He had the tremendous positive spirit to know that today was still his; he grabbed it and made something extraordinary of it.

Ann Person was flat on her back in the hospital. Her husband, Herb, was ill. The family was practically destitute. The future looked grim indeed. But Ann wasn't defeated because she could do two basic things, think and pray. As long as one can do that, there is always hope. And an idea focused in Ann's mind that led to a spectacular success. But let her tell her story in her own words as she related it in part to *Guideposts* magazine.

> In October 1965, I lay flat on my back in the tuberculosis ward of Oregon's state hospital. Bleakly, I stared up at the ceiling. With my illness had come depression. I realized that I didn't have much to show for the past 40 years. I had frittered my adulthood away; dabbling in everything, but committing myself to nothing.
>
> As a child as I stitched my first doll's dress I was sure

I would grow up to be a world-famous fashion designer. And for many years I pursued my goal.

But somewhere along the way my enthusiasm waned and my dream of a glamorous career faded. My life, once full of vitality and purpose, became lackluster and drab. Even my health began to decline.

Never had I felt so alone and empty—and scared—as in that hospital bed. "Lord," I whispered, "I'm scared. If You'll just get me out of this, I promise I'll do something worthwhile with my life. I know I can't do it without Your help. You've got to show me the way. But give me a chance."

In the silence that followed there was an indescribable feeling of comfort. I slept peacefully, secure in knowing that by turning the situation over to God, I had done everything I could.

I felt rejuvenated—excited, somehow, about what the future held in store. Remembering my prayer, I felt confident that I would find my niche soon.

It was in my sewing classes that I felt most strongly my old enthusiasm bubbling up inside me. Students would often tell me they'd never felt so motivated.

One day, an appreciative student sent me a huge carton of knit fabric remnants from a mill-end factory outlet. Knits, at that time, were new on the market and virtually unknown to most home seamstresses. Those who were familiar with the fabric considered it difficult, if not impossible, to work with. Countless times, I'd heard friends complain how knits bagged, sagged and raveled hopelessly.

Still, the riot of colors and textures peeking out from that box were irresistible. "Try me," they seemed to say. I pulled out a large kelly green remnant, sat down at my machine and began experimenting. Once I started, it became difficult to stop. I felt a tingle of excitement as one discovery followed another.

The best results, I learned, came from using big stitches, *stretching* the fabric as I sewed. Word spread, and before I knew it, my classes were devoted entirely to my new "stretch and sew" method with knits. Came a phone call from a woman in a small town. Would I be willing to drive down and demonstrate my techniques to a few of her friends? *Do it*, a small voice urged, and I accepted. When I arrived 70 ladies were waiting. And that one session initiated a chain of classes that kept me on a 500-mile, statewide weekly circuit for the remainder of the year.

I was on fire with an enthusiasm for my work and life that I hadn't known since childhood, and I knew without a doubt that the source of this vitality was God. For the first time in my life, I was finally doing what I *should* be doing. I had found my niche.

We copyrighted the name "Stretch and Sew," and I began training and licensing others to conduct the "Basic Eight" series of lessons. Six months later we opened the first Stretch and Sew Center, where classes were held and exclusive Stretch and Sew knit fabrics, notions, and patterns were sold. I put together one of the first books every published about sewing with knits, featuring easy-to-understand language. Incredibly, the book *Stretch & Sew* sold more than a million copies, and its success led to a five-year national television series called *Sewing with Ann Person*.

Herb came up with the idea of a franchised Stretch and Sew Sewing Center system. Today there are 239 such centers throughout the U.S. and Canada, where millions of women are learning the Stretch and Sew way. Recently, at the close of a workshop in a midwestern city, a small woman came up to me.

"Ann," she said quietly, "I'm a widow. For years after my husband died, I was alone and desperate. I didn't know who I was; I didn't want to live. I signed up for

> your classes just to pass the time—but through them I gained a sense of self-worth I never had. I learned how to set goals and make decisions. I made friends. It was just the boost I needed, and I just want to thank you . . . and thank God."*

The more we read such success stories, the more we should realize that we can do things ourselves. Amazing creative power may be lying unused within you. Never allow potential in your personality to languish. Do not let it wither and die. All you need to do is stop thinking negatively and start taking a positive attitude about yourself. Cultivate belief. Make yourself believe in yourself and in your hidden talents and ability. Think and think and think some more and, to thinking, add prayer; these two procedures are miracle workers. And to both of them, add courage and fortitude. Such action can find and release talents you never realized you possessed. Then will come a day, a big wonderful day, when you will clearly picture who you are and what you can be. Then you will exclaim, "Today is mine!" You will seize it and that will be the day. Ann Person did not know that she had a creative enterprise locked within her, but by the process I've outlined here she found that she did.

I was riding one night with a man taking me to a speaking engagement. As we passed a farmhouse, he said, "Funny thing happened there. A man lived in that house who let it run down until it was almost in ruins. And he seemed rundown also. He dressed in such a shabby manner that he appeared extremely poverty-stricken. He lived from hand to mouth. Then he died, and shortly afterward the county

*Excerpted with permission from Guideposts Magazine. Copyright © 1981 by Guideposts Associates, Inc., Carmel, New York 10512.

put a feeder road through his farm. In excavating for the road, workers unearthed several milk cans. They were crammed with money, about $200,000 in bills—fives, tens, twenties."

It was discovered that this "poor" man had at one time owned stock, but he had sold it and buried the cash in the milk cans. "Foolish, pathetic fellow," we say, but he was certainly no more foolish or pathetic than those of us who bury our talent under a mass of negative thinking and, as a result, live in a personality poverty. The positive person will see clearly the resources and opportunities available to him. He will make the most of every day and every situation. He will even see opportunity where none appears to exist and do something outstanding.

I was lucky enough never to be offered a job that was already succeeding. I think I was lucky because a job already at a high level has to be maintained there or upped still further. If the job is at low ebb, an individual can become successful by developing it and improving it. I was offered and I accepted four churches in my life as a minister, and each one was at the point of failure, even disintegration. In each case I had the opportunity to turn the situation around and bring the four churches to a successful condition.

I did not know it at the time, but this was the big good fortune of my professional life. In fact, I recommend taking on a position that is down in preference to one that is going well. In making the low one successful, you make yourself a success. Anyway, such was my opportunity, and each time I took a poor job, it proved to be the greatest chance to come my way.

How do some positive thinkers get powerful results when faced with difficult situations? I think of Dr. Raj Chopra, a successful educator who received an offer from a midwestern city board of education to become superintendent of their school district. A CBS "60 Minutes" television report on this particular school system had declared that students' test scores in that city were the worst in the state, that it was a failing school system, consisting of twenty-two elementary, five junior high, and two high schools. But, even knowing all this, Dr. Chopra went to see for himself whether this job might be a challenge for him. He is a positive thinker who likes to tackle difficult jobs.

What he encountered was a pretty negative situation. The hotel clerk recognized his name when he checked in and sardonically said, "Good luck. You'll need it." The clerk told him that demoralized teachers were fleeing to other jobs. As Dr. Chopra went about town talking to people, he sensed a generally depressed attitude toward the town, a poor self-image caused perhaps in part by the television report. Hardly anyone had anything good to say about the local schools, and some advised him not to take the job. "You'll only hurt yourself," they warned.

But Dr. Chopra met the one person who finally convinced him that he ought not to accept the job. The man was sitting on his front doorstep and drinking a can of beer. There was an elementary school next door. Dr. Chopra asked him what he thought about his community's schools. "The man stared at me for a moment," said Dr. Chopra, "lowered his can of beer, turned toward the school, and snapped, 'If that place was on fire, I wouldn't throw a bucket of water on it.'" That was the last straw, and Dr. Chopra couldn't get home fast enough.

At dinner in his home he described this depressing situation to his family, saying that there was no hope for the school system. The family was quiet for a moment; then his young son Dick spoke up, "But Dad, what about your faith? You're always telling us how problems should be opportunities." The father knew that his son was right. So he reversed his decision and took the job.

He said of his experience:

My first priority was getting out into the school and visiting with students and teachers. One morning as I walked through a school hall, a teacher came toward me. I greeted her, "Good morning, Mrs. Jones."

"What's good about it?" she grumped.

"It's good because I have this opportunity to look at your beautiful face."

She looked a bit startled, but I continued. "Mrs. Jones, the morning is good because both of us are looking forward to working with young people today. It's exciting to know that we are going to make this day better for them."

She stared at me dubiously.

"Well, isn't it a good morning?"

"Absolutely!" she laughed.

Enthusiasm is contagious; it's transmitted from one to another. But you can't generate it in others unless you have it yourself.

One way to become enthusiastic is to look for the plus sign. To make progress in any difficult situation, you have to start with what's right about it and build on that. When a hue and cry is raised that 20 percent of the students cannot read, I've found that first I have to tell parents that 80 percent of the students *can* read. After that we start talking about what to do with the other 20 percent. With any tough situation, the best hope is to start working on it from the positive side.

When I visited my first classroom in the run-down school system I was impressed by the inquisitive young faces I saw there. Were these the same children who had ranked so low on test scores? They didn't look any different from students I'd seen in other cities. In fact, they looked very intelligent to me. And I decided to tell them so.

"I want you all to know that I think you are among the brightest children I have met," I said, "I'm proud to be associated with you." As I told them how certain I felt that they would do exceedingly well in the coming year, I saw a look of expectancy brighten their faces.

In telling our teachers that we appreciated their skills, we also let them know we *expected* the best.

We always tried to impress upon our principals, supervisors, and teachers the power that lies within each and every one of us to make a difference in other people's lives.

How did it all work out? Were the gloom-and-doom prophets right?

Student test scores soared to a new high, teacher morale was up, and parents were proud—so proud that they'd begun sponsoring an annual "Pride Week" with a big parade down Main Street honoring their school and community.

What made the difference? Simple principles of positive thinking, or "power principles" as I like to call them. No matter where you are, you can use positive attitudes. Here they are:

1. Be enthusiastic.
2. See the good.
3. Expect the best.
4. Learn that "I can make the difference."
5. Believe!

Dr. Chopra was subsequently called to be superintendent of one of the great school districts in the nation, the Shawnee school system in the Kansas City area.

There is an old saying, "One never knows what a day will bring forth." You have only one day at a time. No day is just another day, another routine twenty-four hours. This day, any day, may contain your golden opportunity, perhaps even the big opportunity of a lifetime. You may make a decision today that may affect the rest of your life. Be alert today because opportunity may come.

If you have missed opportunities, turn your thoughts to today. Acquire know-how from past experience but never bog down in postmortems. Appreciate the precious value inherent in this one new day. Visualize other and greater opportunities in store for you. Above all, never minimize the opportunity that may involve a tough situation. Gold comes laced in rocks. So does the chance of a lifetime. As a positive thinker, you will get powerful results if you believe that this day is yours and seize it.

It has been my privilege to speak at many positive thinking rallies or, as such meetings are sometimes called, success motivation conventions. These usually attract large crowds numbering from five to ten thousand, mostly young men and women who come to listen to several speakers for the avowed purpose of doing more with their lives. Sometimes employers, wanting to encourage their employees, buy blocks of tickets for these meetings.

All speakers can no doubt tell of people whose lives were turned around in such meetings. There is something about a big meeting, a kind of creative atmosphere, that seems made for miracles of personality change. At any rate, time and again men and women have told me that "something happened" to them and they were never the same again. They became focused; they found themselves discovering powers they never knew they had. Thus it was that on one particular day they became new persons, surprising even themselves, by the hitherto unknown potential they demonstrated. They found that this was their day, and they seized it and went on to outstanding success.

One night I was speaking with two men in Chattanooga at a motivational rally. Being the last speaker of the evening, I went from backstage to almost the last row of the balcony to watch the effect of my fellow speakers on the huge crowd. An obliging young man moved over to give me the aisle seat, and before the rally began we had a pleasant conversation. But he did not know who I was.

Shortly after the first speaker began, I noted that my fellow seatmate was nodding and presently was sound asleep. He roused a bit when some humorous remark caused general laughter, but then he quietly sank back into sleep. The applause at the conclusion of the talk awakened him. "Pretty good, wasn't he?" observed my friend.

How would you know? I thought of saying but didn't. But I did say, "This next speaker is one of the best. He found the success secret for himself and tells about it. I know of many fellows who were not getting anywhere but who listened to this speaker and were literally blasted out of sleepy indifference. They became balls of fire and terrific successes."

"I'll sure listen," he said. To my surprise, he did listen. The speaker seemed to get this sleepy fellow with his first remark. "Listen, whoever you are, wherever you are. This can be your great day. You can be changed in the next few minutes. Your great unreleased potential can become activated. So listen, listen, listen," he thundered. "Destiny is calling you now, this day."

The young fellow didn't slump into sleep. He sat up straight, leaned forward, and drank in every word. He was fascinated, sitting spellbound for the next forty minutes. At the conclusion of the speech he muttered, "I've got to touch him, shake his hand. He got to me, he got to me." With a word of apology he brushed past me and rushed down the balcony steps toward the stage.

I never saw him again, but later I asked the speaker whether a young man six feet plus with blond hair might have grabbed his hand with more than the usual zeal. "He did indeed, and he said something had happened to him. He declared that he would never forget this day."

Several years later I asked this same speaker if he remembered this incident. "Oh, yes," he replied, "and that fellow is one of my greatest examples of how, under the influence of one minute of motivation that really connects, a person can find his day, seize it, and never be the same old failure anymore."

We can never know in advance when our big moment will come. However, if we believe that our purpose in this world is not yet fulfilled, our day will come. And then we must surely seize it and go on from there to achieve our destiny.

That fulfillment of your life can begin any day. It can get into motion now, today, as you read this book. If the impulse is sufficiently strong, the motivation definite, a person drawing deeply upon the basic potential locked within can produce astounding results.

Recently I dedicated a chapel in a large industrial plant in Philadelphia. On the day of dedication the exquisite chapel was filled by a large gathering of the leaders of the city to honor the company's founder, Michael Cardone. He and his wife overcame poverty to create the huge factory now employing many hundreds of persons.

These capable people had their day when the idea came to them to redo or reclaim old automobile parts and accessories, from windshield wipers to motors. Many persons would not have seen the astonishing extent to which this idea could be developed, and few would have undertaken it. But the Cardones had faith, they believed that the Lord was guiding them. They seized the day and went with the idea of making new windshield wipers and new motors out of old ones. Today Cardone Industries, a complex of buildings with a chapel for the worship of God at the center, is one of the outstanding examples of the American system of free enterprise. And it is an example of two believing people who lived by the truth that today is yours, seize it.

Of course the positive approach to life has an enemy, a sly, devious enemy called discouragement. Discouragement lurks nearby to get in its depressing work whenever possible, but there is a weapon that can effectively destroy discouragement. I will tell about it in Chapter 7, "The Positive Thinker Wins Over Discouragement."

7.

The Positive Thinker Wins Over Discouragement

Does the positive thinker ever get discouraged? Of course. He is a human being, subject to the rise and fall of moods. But the positive thinker does not remain discouraged because he learns how to deal with this feeling.

Spirit is variable, a mixture of light and dark, up and down, joy and gloom, a rhythmic variation of levels. It is easier to let the down cycle take over than to maintain the up cycle of spirit. The latter requires desire, will, and effort with a pattern of uplifting thoughts.

Hence as a positive thinker, you must take authority over the rhythmic mood cycle. When it goes down, ride with it, but mentally make your thought control bring it upward quickly. As a result, while discouragement comes at intervals, you must not give in to it or settle down in it. Turn on your mental lifting power and rise up over the discouraging mood. The positive thinker wins over discouragement.

It is not necessarily an easy process to become proficient in mastering discouragement. It requires know-how. You have to understand the causes of discouraged attitudes. Once you become knowledgeable about the variableness of spirit, the next step is to develop insight into the law of spirit and understand mood cycles.

Then you must study workable and effective techniques of spirit acceleration. You must investigate and experiment with various mood lifters until you find procedures that work for you and are adaptable to your particular personality characteristics.

In this chapter I will suggest some practical techniques for overcoming discouragement that have been helpful to me and to many others. You might try them separately or in combination. By experimentation you can arrive at an antidiscouragement methodology that will give you a perpetual mastery over the dark moods that attack your positive, enthusiastic spirit.

Here is antidiscouragement suggestion number one: *you must really want to overcome discouragement*. It is as simple as that. You must truly want to be healed of the discouragement tendency. But you may ask, "How can anyone not want to be rid of the habit of being discouraged? How can anyone in his right mind not go all out to banish discouragement from his life?" The answer is that perhaps few of us are always in our so-called right mind. That is to say, we have a certain amount of the illogical within us. All of us are a mixture of reason and unreason. We do not always think straight.

We can use discouragement to cover up failure and to rationalize our inability to make it successfully. So we can tell ourselves defensively, "You see, I always knew I didn't have it in me." And then we can retire to the dark shadows in the mind and console ourselves. In a sense, discouragement is a kind of retreat where we can escape reality and soothe ourselves in self-pity. Accordingly, the semidefeated person, the halfway negative thinker, does not quite want to let go of the crutch of discouragement, because without it he has lost his mechanism for escape from a competitive world.

Moreover, there is in all persons, though in some more than in others, what may be called a masochistic or self-punishment streak. Such people seem to have a need for self-flagellation, not in any dramatic form, but in the milder form of holding dark, gloomy thoughts. They get a certain satisfaction from retiring into gloom and depression. Granted, this reaction verges on the abnormal, but not everyone is completely normal in all reactions. Yet it is possible to be normal, which is one of the objectives of positive thinking.

Take charge of your thoughts. You can do what you will with them. When you want to get through with discouragement, when with all—completely all—of your mind and all of your heart and all of your soul you definitely, absolutely want to cast it out of your life forever, then you are on the victory trail. When you want to badly enough, you can stand up to your thoughts and direct them instead of letting them push you around.

A good example is Merton DeForrest, who passed over the river not so long ago with all his flags flying and bugles blowing. He had a long fight with discouragement and often retreated glumly into dark, gloomy thoughts to nurse his mental wounds. But finally he became fed up with his pathetic life-style. He had a powerful spiritual experience, which completely changed him deep in his nature. He read *The Power of Positive Thinking*, and what is more important, he practiced it. One day he faced his discouragement tendency. Mentally he took it in hand and authoritatively declared,

"Listen, you, get this straight. I'm in charge of my life. Not you. So you get out and stay out."

Seems strange to talk thus to an attitude, but it is not strange. It is realistic. When you become assertive and mean it, a destructive attitude will inevitably back down, and if you continue to assume control, the attitude will eventually give up, as DeForrest discovered.

Sounds like bravado? Whistling in the dark? Not at all. It is the magnificent assertiveness and authority of a sovereign individual, a child of God. It is the power of great personality in action. Remember what the Bible says about dominion? "Then God said, 'Let Us make man in Our image, according to Our likeness; let them have dominion. . . . So God created man in His own image; in the image of God He created him; male and female He created them. Then God blessed them, and God said to them, . . . 'have dominion'" (Gen. 1:26–28). That is what you are to do—take dominion. Take charge of your thoughts. Master the dark ones. Put your positive thoughts in charge. Take control of your life as God said you could. That is antidiscouragement suggestion number one.

A second technique is to *use silence* as I described in a plan I put in a thirty-four-page pocket-sized booklet *10 Minutes a Day to a Better Way*. It has been read and practiced by over one million people. (If you would like a copy of the booklet, write to the Foundation for Christian Living, P.O. Box FCL, Pawling, New York, 12564, and say you read about it in this book. They will be glad to send you a free copy.) The following is the outline of this plan and its application to the problem of discouragement.

The plan is to spend ten minutes every day in carefully selected thought procedures. A successful outcome will depend upon the regularity with which this routine is followed. Doing it for one day, two days, three days and then skipping a day or more will nullify the values that constant regularity of the ten-minute period brings.

Some have their ten-minute period in the early morning; others after breakfast; and still others at varying times during the day or evening. Being rigid about this practice is not recommended, but at some time within every twenty-four hours, the ten-minute period should be observed. If the plan is followed regularly, beneficial results will soon become apparent.

All of us, because of circumstances, think we have to let some things pass. But the person who seriously wants a better way must establish the rule of never letting a day go by without observing the ten-minute period.

Go into a room, close the door, and sit quietly. If the telephone rings, do not answer it. The same with the door-bell. Let nothing interfere with the spiritual, profoundly creative silence you will experience in the next ten minutes. Remember the wise words of Thomas Carlyle, "Silence is the element in which great things fashion themselves together." Scrupulously observe the silence.

Turn your mind to thoughts of God. Think only about Him for five minutes. Picture Him as a wise, kindly, loving Father. Say these words:

> "Silence. Silence.
> Heavenly Father.
> Kindly Father.
> My Father."

See Him as just that.
Then say:

> "The great God,
> the loving God,
> the protecting God."

Then add:

"Jesus Christ,
my Lord and Savior,
is helping me now."

If you do this as directed, you will be enveloped by a sense of peace.

For the second five minutes, image yourself as dropping discouragement into the eternal quietness, the everlasting silence, the great hands of God. Let go of it. See God taking it into His big hands. Let God handle it. As you do this, your mind is swept clean of dark shadows. Light fills every crevice in your mind. You are now able to think more clearly. Ideas by which you can successfully handle discouragement will emerge into consciousness.

As a young man, I was in a period of discouragement. I was crossing the Atlantic at the end of a vacation. Being unable to sleep, I dressed and went up to the top deck. It was totally dark. I stood watching as the darkness turned into gray and there were shadows everywhere. Then a faint glow of pink appeared on the eastern horizon. A sliver of the rising sun projected upward. Long shafts of light cut across the waters.

At this point a miracle happened. The great round sun seemed to leap out of the sea and burst forth in all its glory. Then I saw something I have never forgotten. The shadows, lurking in every nook and corner, started to run. Like mice, they scampered across the deck, seeming to jump into the sea, leaving the white ship without a shadow as it sailed serenely across the blue waters of the Atlantic. Suddenly my discouragement was gone.

When discouragement really begins to dominate, the positive thinker employs a third method for getting out from under its effects. *Have someone listen.* That helps get you back into a normal attitude.

I recall one day when my secretary came into my office to tell me that a woman demanded to see me.

"Has she an appointment and who is she?" I asked.

"No appointment and I do not know who she is beyond her name. She states that she was walking on the avenue and noticed your name on the sign board. She says she is a positive thinker in a bit of trouble, and she believes you can help her."

"Well, okay. Show her in. I'll talk to her."

The woman was businesslike. "Thank you for seeing me without an appointment. I'll state my business briefly. Then you can advise me, and I will get out of your hair and be on my way." Trouble came through despite her assumed jauntiness.

She then proceeded to talk without interruption. She had been studying to make a positive thinker of herself, but she said, "A lot of troubles and difficulties ganged up on me. Try as I can, discouragement has all but knocked out my positive attitude." She expressed her belief that if she could get on top of the discouraged feeling she "could get back on track and handle things."

"Empty it all out," I said. "I'm here to help you, so go ahead and talk. Ventilate the discouragement. I'll listen; and when you finish, I will come up with whatever I think might be helpful." So she went on steadily pouring out her troubles, not repeating them as some disorganized thinkers do, but in an orderly sequence of thought. Obviously she was a thinker, and I judged she had a rather important job.

After talking steadily for thirty minutes, she suddenly looked at her watch. "Oh, I have taken far too much of your time. Please forgive me. You have helped me a lot. I'll not forget your kindness to a total stranger." Then she departed my office as quickly as she had entered it. She left me wondering exactly what I had done for her. Then I realized I had helped by listening, and she had helped herself by emptying her mind.

When discouragement piles up, threatening to crush your spirit and frustrate your positive attitude, go to some understanding person who will listen creatively. Completely empty out the mass of accumulated dark and dismal thoughts. The mind, if it is to function well, must never be overburdened by negative thoughts, discouragement included.

Years later, when I was speaking at a motivational rally, a woman came along in a line of people waiting to speak to me following the talk, and she referred to this incident. "You helped me through a crisis that day," she said, "and thank God I've been on top ever since." That is what we are "in business" to do, to help people get on top and stay there.

Of course, it is not to be expected that the simple act of listening can always drain off discouragement as effectively as in this instance. But, that it did happen in this circumstance shows the validity of the mind-emptying process.

Let me give you a practical three-point formula for getting rid of depression and discouragement: (1) pray it out, (2) talk it out, and (3) think it out. Ventilate it by praying to the great God who listens and understands. Talk to some person who will, in His name, listen and understand. Finally, use your own reason, your own rationality, and think it out. The secret is to talk out the problem to God, to another person, and to yourself. Such a mental and spiritual process of eliminating discouraging thoughts, if continued rationally and not emotionally, has a powerful, curative effect.

A friend, whom I shall call Harold, had a series of adversities, one after another, enough to take the life out of just about anyone. But this man had a strong faith and stood up admirably under the onslaughts of trouble. He was a level-headed thinker who did not emotionally blame God when things went badly. He figured that much of the difficulty was his own fault. "The rest was just the way things bounced," he said. "You have to expect some setbacks."

He applied strict reason to his situation, carefully thinking out better procedures, analyzing his mistakes, trying to eliminate the error factor. In fact, he did everything that an intelligent man might think of. But, even so, discouragement had, as he explained, "grabbed him and just wouldn't let go." Slowly but certainly he was yielding to depression. It was infiltrating his thought and control center, and his strong faith was beginning to erode.

But suddenly Harold "took corrective action." That phrase is not his or mine. I heard it from my friend Jim Knapp, and I have quoted it often. When I heard Jim use it, the wisdom of it struck me. Really, the way out of any defeatist situation is to stand up to it with strength, common sense, and spiritual guidance and take corrective action. *Action* is the key word. Right action corrects rightly.

And *that* is an important fact. It is not what happens to you that matters. It is what you think about what has happened to you. When you begin to think right, objectively rather than emotionally, positively rather than negatively, you can resolutely take corrective action.

Since a thought is something that goes on in your mind and something that you can control if you have the will to do so, and discouragement is an accumulation of gloomy thoughts, you can choose to either entertain these thoughts or throw them out. That was the down-to-earth conclusion my friend reached. It made sense to him because when he directed discouraging thoughts to get out, they actually obeyed. Of course, they tried to fight back, but he faced them with power. In time he was on top of them. "Action was what I took. Just plain, old action. I was fed up with moaning and grumbling and the self-pity that goes with that type of nonthinking. Action, action, and more action, corrective action, that is the idea," he declared exultantly.

"What form did your action take? Just what was your corrective action?" I asked. It seems that it first took the form of physical action. He stopped slumping and sitting around dismally going over and over in his mind, "Why me?" He went out and walked and walked; he swam and swam; he began hitting golf balls again. This action took the strain off the cerebral center that governs thought and shifted it to physical activity. His mind began to clear, he felt better, the blood surged through his veins, and his heart rate accelerated. As he walked and stepped up physical activity, he was taking action, and he began to think eagerly not glumly. Ideas began popping up in his mind. Then one day the moment came when he exclaimed jubilantly, "Why I can work out of this!" He recovered his normal verve, not immediately to be sure, but it did not take as long as one might assume. When a person takes strong corrective, vigorous action, things soon begin to improve.

Following the physical action came an upgraded mental attitude and thought process. Harold looked in succession at each trouble or setback and asked what each one had to tell him. He fell back on a phrase I had quoted in one of my books, that great statement by W. Clement Stone, "To every disadvantage there is a corresponding advantage." So my friend scrupulously and diligently looked for advantages in what seemed hopeless disadvantages. He was surprised to find quite a few that subsequently turned into successes. With his new positive spirit everything looked better, and things began to go better for him. Action had driven off the dull inertness created by his negative mental attitude of discouragement.

An old friend of Harold's said, "Haven't seen you lately. Where have you been hibernating?"

"I've been licking my wounds," Harold replied, "but, thank God, I'm coming out of a rough down period."

To which his friend said, "You're thanking the right person. I've found that you can pray and praise your way out of any setback and discouraging condition." Harold said he followed the praying bit, but he wasn't sure he understood the praise part. The friend stated his belief that rough going is one of God's ways of teaching us something, of helping us to grow big. He had found that praising the Lord opens up new meanings of adversity. Harold took up this new idea and added the prayer and praise action to his physical and positive mental action. He discovered that in doing so, a balanced corrective action plan lifted the dark curtain of discouragement even further. Ultimately he became his normal self again. The alternative to the corrective action treatment Harold employed might have been failure and breakdown. But it didn't happen that way. This man did not break when adversity came; he responded by breaking new records.

His story reminds me of another friend of longstanding. I refer to the late great merchant J. C. Penney. He achieved notable success out of poverty but was dogged by adversity over much of his successful career. I knew him quite well. One day it occurred to me to ask him, "J. C., please give in one sentence the secret of your success in life."

"I can do that in four words—adversity and Jesus Christ." He explained that adversity made a man of him and that Jesus Christ was his Savior and guide.

My total memory of J. C. Penney, who lived well up into his nineties, is that of a happy man. He drew his happiness from his strong Christian faith. Only once did I know him to become discouraged or depressed. It was following one of the greatest adversities in his business life. He was in the depths of despair, utterly disconsolate.

Then off in the distance he heard singing. It was an old favorite hymn, "Be not dismayed whate'er betide, God will take care of you." Suddenly his discouragement lifted, and as if by a miracle, he was set free from its devastating effect.

Years later when I spoke at his funeral service, that same hymn was sung at his request. He believed that God would take care of him, that Jesus Christ was at his side. In that faith he conquered discouragement. J. C. Penney was a convinced, practicing positive thinker made so through hardship and the belief that God will help anyone who thinks and has faith.

Positive thinking is vital to the processes that are guaranteed to keep your spirit always high, so high indeed that discouragement cannot break it. The positive thinker is a creative thinker, a cool, objective thinker in whatever situation he finds himself. He is never emotionally overwhelmed by problems. He knows that every problem contains the seeds of its own solution, that in all difficulty there is buried some great possibility. Therefore, to him a problem is not inherently bad, something to flee or avoid. It is a challenge or an opportunity containing some inherent good. When an apparently tough problem presents itself, he is not frightened by it, certainly not discouraged by any lack of ability to handle it. Instead, he stands up to it, believes it may contain amazingly great values, and humbly knows that he has what it takes to extract those values from it. Problems are men makers, women makers, life makers.

If the problem or difficulty may temporarily prove baffling, defying his best efforts to effect a solution, the true positive thinker does not get discouraged and walk away from it in defeat. It is not in his nature to give way to discouragement or to take a licking. He just sticks with it, believing that there is an answer for every problem. This characteristic is sometimes called persistence or perseverance or stick-to-itiveness. Call it what you will, in addition to faith, it is the chief enemy of discouragement and always wins over it, if maintained.

I have indicated earlier that in my working life, it has been my good fortune never to have an easy job. I have been the pastor of four churches, and when I started with each of them, they were heavily in debt and low in membership and had an unpromising, even doubtful, future. Each was at the bottom, but the bottom is a propitious place to be because the only direction from there is up. I cannot overemphasize that fact. If you take a job that is already up, you must keep it up or lift it higher. To me, that hardly affords the satisfaction found in taking on a job that is down, perhaps way down, and bringing it up, way up. That is good fortune indeed.

Now I must admit that in the case of each of these four jobs I got plenty discouraged, but in each church I met persons from whom I learned much. Out of the situation I formed the technique of positive thinking. Trouble, difficulty, and hardship are three great teachers. Fortunate is the person who in keeping company with them keeps his eyes, his ears and, better still, his mind open; they can teach him valuable things.

Four significant ideas were given to me along the way, ideas that helped me to gain a lasting victory over discouragement.

1. Never build a case against yourself.
2. Love the Lord and love people. Forget yourself.
3. Think big, pray big, believe big, act big, love big, be big—big all the way.
4. Be a believer—a believer in God. Be a believer in people, in the future. Be a believer in yourself.

Positive thinkers become discouraged at times simply because they are human beings. As I pointed out earlier, all men and women are affected by the rise and fall of moods, by the variableness of emotional reactions. But positive thinkers develop the mental and spiritual capacity to keep their thinking operative, whatever the situation. They are mentally controlled rather than emotionally conditioned. As a result, even though positive thinkers may at times experience discouragement, by their sound, mentally controlled, and objective attitude, they are able to rise above the discouragement and handle it. Nor do positive thinkers accept an attitude of discouragement as the final answer to a failure situation of any kind. They forget it and try again.

On a plane en route to a speaking engagement at a business convention, I sat by a pleasant fellow who said that he was the principal speaker at the same meeting where I was scheduled to speak. "I thought that I was the principal speaker," I replied, laughingly. He then announced that he was a humorist, a comic, and produced one of his folders that billed him as the "funniest speaker in the world, the funniest man alive." One of the captions was "Hang onto your seats, folks, or he will rock you into the aisles." Another was "Hold your sides. You're going to die laughing."

"Believe me," I said, "I hope I come on first. I certainly don't want to follow you." But as it turned out, the humorist was the first speaker, and I was to follow him.

The emcee of the evening went all out in describing my fellow speaker. He used extravagant phrases, assuring the audience that they were in for the time of their lives. But apparently he built the speaker up too highly. The humorist got good laughs, but they began to taper off to titters, finally to grins. Perspiring but undaunted, he said to me out of the corner of his mouth, "Tough crowd." Finally he gave it up and sat down to rather perfunctory applause. "Whew," he said as he mopped his face, "hard going for sure."

I had no better luck when my turn came to speak. Again the effusive emcee went all out in the introduction. To hear him talk, you would have thought I was the greatest speaker who ever orated. Such is human nature that the more he eulogized me, the more the audience wanted to know "who is this guy?" Sensing the cooling-off mood of the crowd, I decided to try no jokes at all, though I do have a few that always seem to get a good response. I used nothing but serious material. The trouble was that the audience laughed when they were not supposed to. "Tough crowd," I said to my friend out of the side of my mouth. They gave me a fair hand, but I knew it was out of generosity.

On the way back to the hotel, the humorist said, "I'm discouraged, are you?"

"Well, I'm not exactly elated."

"Tell you what," he continued. "Let's forget it, wipe it out, relegate it to the past. Have you a speaking engagement tomorrow night?" When I said that I did, he nodded. "That's good. So have I. Let's take the positive attitude that we will do better next time." Then he added a wise remark that has stayed with me: go after a success after every failure. That is the way a positive thinker handles a failure situation. It is also the way a positive thinker wins over discouragement. This leads us directly into Chapter 8 in which one important characteristic of a positive thinker is discussed: how the positive thinker drops the negative word habit.

8.

Drop the Negative Word Habit

Positive thinkers are word droppers. They drop every negative word that gets in the way of personal growth and development—words such as *if, can't,* and *impossible.* They simply and forthrightly chuck them out of their vocabulary and thinking.

A negative word is a symbol of a negative concept that can be harmful. Dropping it is of superimportance. In fact, it is good to go so far as to bury such failure-generating words.

One man I heard of did just that. A group of people purchased land on which to build a big human service institution. But, as always, some among them doubted that it could be done. They said, "If we had more support, if we had more money, if . . . if . . . if." More enterprises and more people have probably gone down to failure on the little word *if* than any other, unless it is the word *can't.*

Others in the group discouragingly opined, "It can't be done. There is just no way. It can't be done, can't . . . can't . . . can't."

Still others were even more explicit. "It's impossible," they declared. "No way can we accomplish it. It is impossible . . . impossible . . . impossible." So the deadening, negative words droned on hopelessly.

But one positive, innovative man came up with a unique idea. He was a generous donor to the undertaking, and when he asked for a little piece of land that had been acquired, his request could not very well be denied. But everyone was curious and surprised when he explained that he wanted it for a "cemetery." He fenced off the little enclosure and set three small gravestones.

At the announced time for the burial service, people were assembled, and he unveiled the stones. In one was carved the word *If*, in another *Can't*, and in the third *Impossible*. "Here lie buried words that could cause the failure of our enterprise. Leave them buried," he said. The people got the message.

This creative outcome was due to a positive thinker, a word dropper. He dropped and buried those negative and defeating words.

The famous psychiatrist, Dr. Smiley Blanton, noted how often patients would think back glumly "if only I had not done that," "if only I had done that," one futile "if only" after another. His imaginative treatment was successful. He instructed each patient to imagine an opening in the head from which a recording of the words *if only* could be removed and the words *next time* inserted. The patient was to "listen" intently until he heard the click of the new recording in place. This imaging process proved remarkably successful in eliminating the negative "if only" concept and in substituting the positive "next time" affirmation.

The thoughts, ideas, and concepts that lodge in our minds result in attitudes and beliefs, and these in turn determine whether we experience failure or success. The "if only" attitude is a despairing, totally ineffective look back at something that has gone by: if only I had bought that stock; if only I had not sold when I did; if only I had taken that job; if only I had not nagged my husband so much that he left me; if only I had not mistreated my wife. I'm sure you could come up with some examples too.

The positive thinker is free from all such futile recriminations. His idea is not "if only." It is a much stronger, forward-looking idea, one full of hope and expectation. It is the dynamic thought, "next time." With this concept he gets unlimited positive results. If he makes a mistake, doesn't do what he should have done, or does what he should not have done he turns his back on all of it and simply affirms, "Next time I will do better, act more wisely. Next time I will have improved judgment." "Next time" thinking is geared to going forward, to doing better! Do not be an "if only" thinker because that is related to the past—to mistakes, errors, losses, bad judgments, situations that you can no longer do anything about.

My wife, Ruth, once met a Dakota farmer at a church dinner on the western plains late one summer. As national president of her denominational board of domestic missions, she was a speaker at a church conference. Seated across the table from the farmer at dinner, she tried to engage him in conversation, but he was not very articulate, obviously unaccustomed to small talk. Seeking to identify with his interests, she asked, "How are the crops this year?"

"Not good, ma'am. In fact, there aren't any crops. I saved maybe 10 percent of my crop, but my brother lost everything."

Appalled, my wife asked, "But what happened?"

"We had a tornado. In ten minutes everything was gone." Then he was silent.

"But what do you do when everything goes bad like that, sir?"

"Do?" He paused as if looking deeply into his mind. "Do? Why we just aim to forget it."

This man had lived with nature for years. He had lived with the element of wind, cold, heat, and tornadoes. He had experienced good years and bad. He worked in partnership with God, the Creator, who gave us the good earth and who watches over us in the good and the bad times. This man of stature had calmly accepted the fortuitous and the devastating as facts of life. He did not pathetically cry "if only," but sturdily determined that next time he would go forward. He always regrouped, he always went forward, building, ever building.

He fitted the definition of a positive thinker: one who is tough and rugged mentally and spiritually, who sees every difficulty but sees it straight. He knows that ultimately the good in this world overbalances the evil. He knows that with the help of the good God, he has what it takes to take it. He finds the answer and always overcomes.

When the ifs and the can'ts and the impossibles gang up on you, what then? Why, just counter with the next times and the cans and the possibles. It is that simple, though it isn't all that easy. Sometimes it can be hard, very hard indeed, but if you persevere, think positively, and have faith, you will come through a winner, perhaps even a big winner.

Furthermore, you learn to be a philosopher. Often what seem to be destructive adversities turn out to be creative assets, and those assets would not have become yours if something hadn't happened that at first seemed to ruin everything for you. When things go wrong, ultimately they may turn out right. So when your hopes and dreams and goals get dashed, poke around among the wreckage. You may find your golden opportunity in what seems to be ruin.

Remember the story of Mordecai Brown, one of the greatest big league baseball pitchers of his time? His parents were very poor, but like real Americans, they never really knew they were. Their son had his heart set on being a big league pitcher, and he showed extraordinary talent at a young age. Mordecai worked on a farm to help support his family as did other kids in those days. One day he got his hand caught in some machinery and lost most of the forefinger on his right hand and badly crushed his second finger.

"There goes all my hope of being a pitcher," so the negative thinker would moan. "If only I hadn't had that accident. Now I can't pitch with that ruined hand. Out the window go my dreams. It's just impossible." But that was not the way this boy thought and talked. He accepted it and got along with that poor hand as best he could. He learned to throw the ball with the fingers he had left. Eventually he made a local team as third baseman.

One day the team manager happened to be directly behind the first baseman when Mordecai threw from third. He was astounded to watch the twists and turns, the amazing gyrations of that ball as it sped true into the first baseman's mitt. "Mordecai," he said enthusiastically, "you are a born pitcher. You have speed and control and, boy, with that gyrating ball you'll have every batter swinging but only hitting the air."

Mordecai would throw the ball in such a way that it would come fast, dancing, twisting, turning, gyrating up and down, sliding directly over the plate. The batters were totally baffled. Mordecai mowed down the batting order. His strikeout record was impressive as were his games won. He became one of the great pitchers of American baseball.

How did this boy accomplish this feat of turning disaster into an asset? Those injured fingers, the abbreviated forefinger and gnarled second finger, gave the ball those extraordinary twists and turns. This boy, a believer raised in a faith-filled home, simply believed that he could take what he had and make something of it. He was a positive thinker who, with incredible skill, handled his life's impossibles. His word dropping—tossing out the ifs, the can'ts, and the impossibles—made him a baseball immortal.

Now I know you might say, "I'm no superperson like Mordecai Brown. I can't come back from hard luck like he did." But when Mordecai had the accident to his hand, he was no superperson either. The plain fact is that all of us have far more qualifications than we realize. Just affirm those creative words—*next time, can,* and *possible.* And be like every good positive thinker, be a word dropper and throw out *if, can't,* and *impossible.*

In addition, fasten your mind onto another word, a victory word, an overcoming, wonder-working word—*miracle.* The positive thinker is a believer. He believes that nothing is too good to be true, so he believes in miracles.

A negative-thinking man was married to a positive-thinking woman. This was back in the depression time, and like most families, they had problems, mostly financial. He griped steadily, "If we could only work out of this situation, I could see our way through this. It's all impossible."

But the positive-thinking wife sang a different tune. "How do we go about solving this problem? I know we can handle this one. It is no real problem. It's perfectly possible." The two loved each other, and she pulled him along, supplying faith and optimism for both. He managed to hold onto his job while a lot of others were losing theirs. Her faith in him had a lot to do with this.

He worked in a shop where merchandise from Great Britain was sold, mostly woolens. This man, Henry, was undoing a package of goods one day, and on top of the contents he found a folded piece of paper. He picked it up and read, "Expect a miracle—it can happen." *Wonder who wrote that and why?* he said to himself. He started to toss it in the wastebasket, but something stopped him. *Guess I'll show it to Helen. She falls for fool stuff like this.* He put the paper in his pocket.

That night he shoved it across the table. "Honey, funny thing. Some oddball in Britain put this message in a box I was opening today. Kind of a nut, I guess."

She read it, then sat thoughtfully looking down at it. "No, Henry, I don't think the person who put this in that box was an oddball and certainly not a nut. He or she must have had some sort of trouble, maybe like the ones we have, and was guided to pass it along in this curious manner to help someone else, us, for example.

"We haven't been able to see our way through some things. Tell you what. Let's take one of our small problems and really expect a miracle, test it out, so to speak."

"Oh, come off it, honey. A miracle is some dreamy-eyed, goofy thing that only happens in fairy tales. Miracles don't happen in this scientific age." And they were off on one of their friendly arguments. Helen went to the bookcase. "Let's see what our friend Mr. Webster says about miracles." She read from the dictionary, "Miracle—'a wonderful happening.' And," she declared triumphantly, "it doesn't say anything about its being contrary to science. I wonder if we call something a miracle simply because we do not understand it. And when we do understand, then it is part of the whole scientific body of knowledge. Airplanes were once in the category of miracles. They were wonderful happenings. The electric lights were too, and the telephone. Someday what we now call miracles, like healing outside the known laws of medicine and psychic phenomena, will all be part of scientific law. And finally," she concluded, "perhaps we will come to realize that even faith itself is part of the laws of God, the Creator who made them all."

"Smart girl" was all Henry could manage to respond. "You could be right." So the two agreed they would expect a miracle, a wonderful happening in connection with one of their smaller problems. They brought positive thought to bear, her strong positive attitude, his weaker one. But even a weak positive thought pattern is not without power, as is taught in Matthew 17:20, "If you have faith as a mustard seed, . . . nothing will be impossible for you."

Sometime later Henry and Helen had occasion to be thankful for a rather strange series of coincidences and circumstances. The matter to which they applied the "expect a miracle—it can happen" principle began to work out. The outcome was not exactly what they wanted or thought they needed, but it proved to be a right answer. Even Henry came to believe in miracles. But Helen, a positive-thinking word dropper, was responsible for starting miracles working in their lives by dropping the idea of the impossible and concentrating on the possible. There came a time when Henry also became a full-fledged positive thinker. He came to it the hard way, but when he became convinced that we become what we think and that what we think comes to us, he joined his wife in positive thinking. They became a really effective team of positive thinkers who got positive results.

Positive thinking brings the best values to those who are dedicated to achieving the best. And we all, I believe, want the best for ourselves and for our families. Would you like to have the best, or are you actually waiting to settle for something less than the best? Of course, you would choose the best. How can you have the best? Think the best, not the worst, because in the long run you tend to get what you think.

If you really want to know what you are likely to be five or ten years from now, all you need to do is read the thoughts that are now dominant in your mind. In time the continuity of your dominant thought pattern will activate the forces about you to produce the outward conditions that correspond to your basic thinking. Your thoughts form your future. Thoughts externalize into actualization. You cannot see a thought, but you can trace its effect. And all your thoughts add up to a result. In due course you become precisely what you habitually think.

The positive thinker succeeds in life. As a word dropper, he has cast out of his life-style a pernicious mental sickness called negative expectation, always expecting things to be bad.

Common expressions that indicate negative expectation are "things always go wrong for me," "I know I can't make it," "it's going to be a lousy day." Some people actually think they were born to lose. Negative-thinking parents render a profound disservice to their children by conditioning their minds to failure, though they do so unwittingly.

A young woman stopped me on the way out of an auditorium where I had just finished a talk on positive thinking. She was very concerned about what she called a "longtime mind-set" from which she was trying to extricate herself. "Ever since childhood I've had a failure pattern. I would do well in school when it began in the fall, but some weeks later I would start doing badly. From then on I would go down until I was failing in my work. Often I just plain flunked," she said hopelessly.

After finishing school a year behind her class, she got a job. She was a pretty girl and had a nice way about her that enabled her to make a good first impression but eventually the old failure pattern "would grab her" again.

I asked, "What do you think is the cause of this deeply rooted failure pattern that holds you back?"

She hesitated. "I hate to blame anyone and hope I'm not being unfair, but to tell the truth, I think it's my mother's fault. Oh, I don't want to say this because Mother is really wonderful and I love her. But ever since I was little, she was always talking about her worries. She was negative thinker number one. For her, nothing was ever going to turn out right. Everything was bound to turn out badly. She used to say, 'Honey, you might as well expect the worst so you won't be disappointed.' So I guess I have always been subconsciously expecting the worst and I haven't been disappointed. But I sure am an unhappy person. What can I do?"

As I listened to this unhappy and mixed-up but obviously bright young woman trying desperately to find herself, I admired her perceptiveness. She recognized that she was caught in a self-defeating complex of thought, one that was deeply rooted in her consciousness. I suggested that the mental roots of negative expectation had to be cut. Then they would wither, and she could pull them out of her mind like persistent weeds in the lawn.

My impression of her sharpness was verified by the alacrity with which she picked up the figure of speech I had used, "roots of negative expectation." "But give me a prescription right now for getting release," she declared. "I just know you can."

"With all your negativism, you're pretty positive about this," I said with a smile. "So let's try.

"Any ingrained, long-held habit can be eliminated and a healthy thought pattern substituted if you will do the following: (1) Want such change to take place. An all-out intensity of desire is the first requirement. It must be more than a half-hearted wish. (2) Know specifically how you want to be different. In your case you want to substitute a success thought pattern for your hitherto dominant failure pattern. (3) Fix an exact time when you will start the process of eliminating the failure pattern and also when you expect the success pattern to be established."

"Oh," she exclaimed, "I already know about that. I will start now, and the date for the change is today, right now."

"Hold your horses," I replied, "we are not talking about an easy process. Mental habits are formed slowly and have been intricately wound around in your subconsciousness. The unwinding process takes time."

"But," she said, "I remember reading about you, Dr. Peale, having an awful inferiority complex. You prayed to the Lord and reminded Him that He could change thieves into honest people and drunks into sober people and that He could also do that right off."

"Yes," I agreed, "and I believe that, but the Lord didn't do that right off in my case. He took a while with me. I was a tough case, but He did change me and He will change you too."

Then I continued: "(4) Start right now visualizing or imaging yourself as you want to be. See yourself as having dropped that old failure pattern and as now taking on a vital, dynamic success pattern. (5) Begin at once practicing the 'as if' principle. If you want to be something that you are not, act as if you possess the desired quality. If this is done with persistence, you will ultimately attain this quality. In your case, begin now to act as if you are success oriented. Acting as if it is so can make it so. (6) You are now ready for the dynamic process of life changing through faith. Acknowledge to the Lord that you cannot effect such profound personal change on your own. The Bible says, 'If you can believe, all things are possible' (Mark 9:23). If you can believe, and if you want to and will to, ask the Lord who created you to re-create you. If you have faith that such a result will happen, it will happen."

This is not fanciful, dreamy-eyed, nor some sort of religious stuff. This process has worked over centuries for millions of people and works today in this modern world.

Had it been only a theory or a vague unsubstantiated claim, it would have been discredited long ago. But the validity of spiritual and mental change of personality is recognized widely as scientific (it works) reality. The young woman whose experience is related here is just one example of a person who, by a process of idea dropping and substitution, became a new person. She put this process into operation. She did not find change to be quick or easy, but it did come gradually and the goal she set was eventually attained. She did eliminate the long-held failure pattern. She became successful in her occupation, but more important, she became successful as a person.

If we take on wrong ideas, we can also drop wrong ideas. If we grow into wrong thought patterns, we can, if we want to and will to, drop the erroneous thought patterns. And if we are motivated by real desire, we can take on a new, more positive life-style. There is extraordinary power in creative positive expectation.

Life can be a wonderful, satisfying experience. Despite all of its adversities, life itself is good. Believe in the value of life and its infinite worth. Built in it, for those who believe and endure, are ultimate joy, peace, and achievement. Fulfillment is offered to all by almighty God, the Creator and the Re-Creator of all who want the good for their lives.

Unfortunately some people fail to see the great values of life because of sadly twisted thought processes. A chief reason I write about having faith and practicing positive thinking and finally winning over every form of defeat and adversity is that I believe in life and love it. I want to encourage others to believe in it and love it too.

USA Today carried a full-page story about teenage suicides. The writer said, "Nearly everybody seems to have a theory about the cause: drugs, alcohol, sex, unemployment, child abuse, divorce, the decline of churchgoing, pressure to achieve, conflict with parents, the threat of nuclear war, excessive television watching, the availability of handguns, biochemical imbalances. But nobody has a satisfactory answer."

But one writer in the same issue, Don Wildmon, has come up with sound reasoning, I believe. He asks:

> Why are we suffering from this tragedy? Because for the past two decades our society has been on a hedonistic binge, placing materialism and self-indulgence high on our scale of values. We have tended to play down man's spiritual nature. . . . Mass media, especially television, no longer allow the child to be a child, or the adolescent to be adolescent. By exposing them continually to an adult world, which is basically materialistic, we have robbed children of the privilege of childhood. They have been told over and over again that things bring happiness and that happiness is the chief goal in life. We have sold our youth a big lie. . . . What can we do? Restore time-proven, traditional Christian values. . . . Expose hedonism for what it is—a big lie, a mirage that always fades.*

Hedonism—the concept that the primary aim of life is sensory pleasure—is, of course, a crude falsehood, a bold lie. The truth about life is found not in the cynical mutterings of the unwashed but in the clean facts of the Bible: "Whoever finds me [the Lord] finds life" (Prov. 8:35) and "I [Jesus] have come that they may have life, and that they may have it more abundantly" (John 10:10). So positive thinkers who are smart enough to spot a lie are again ruthless, sophisticated word droppers. They drop hedonism

*Copyright, 1983 USA TODAY. Reprinted with permission.

into the garbage can where it belongs and go on being happy, actually reveling in life. Positive thinkers love life and do something wonderful with it every day.

As I write this chapter, I am at a convention to give two talks. The meeting is composed of hundreds of people, each of whom achieved over a million dollars of sales last year and won a trip to this convention.

Mingling with these people who became outstanding achievers, I heard story after story of men and women who dropped negative thoughts, negative attitudes, negative ideas. They cast them out and turned their backs on defeatist concepts. They embraced the positive. They went to work. They believed. They visualized. They worked and worked, believed and believed. They became winners and achievers, and they and their families found great happiness in the process. And that is exactly what you can do.

One man who attended this convention unhesitatingly told me, "I don't deserve any credit for my performance. My wife made me a successful man. She pulled me out of a failure psychology and got me going."

The wife standing by said, "Don't you believe it. He has always been a great man. All I did was to remind him of what and who he is."

It seems that this man was a self-doubter. He felt inadequate. He didn't believe that he could. He had a low and erroneous opinion of his abilities and potential. Gradually his daily conversation was filled with downbeat ideas and negative expressions: "It won't work," "Yeah, maybe he can do it, but I can't," "Guess I'm no good at this job." When awards for top performance were given, he would come up with a classic negativism, "I can't see myself ever winning an award." Classic because it indicated he had never imaged or visualized himself succeeding.

Well, at breakfast one morning when he was glumly getting off his usual negatives, his wife really reacted.

"Listen," she said, "I'm going to tell you something. You make me tired with all that put-down stuff. I know you, and you are a very able, indeed a superior and effective person, and you are constantly lying to yourself about yourself. I am sick of it. I'm fed up with your negative conversation. If it were true, I'd go along with it, but since it's all untrue, I'm insisting that you stop it."

Her husband started to interrupt this flow of wifely indignation, but she said, "I'm not through with you yet. I love you, I know you in and out, and I believe in you. I am not going to stand by and watch you destroy yourself by a stupid inferiority complex. For heaven's sake, start thinking positively. Be a man and stand up to yourself." She concluded blazingly, "I won't listen to this negative talk any more."

She really got to her husband. Basically he knew she was right. Now, afraid to speak any more negatives, he found he had to talk positively. In time he began to try thinking positively. Then he tried positive action. He tried and tried and finally succeeded. His sales topped a million dollars that year. He became a prize winner. That is how I happened to meet him at the convention. He put his arm around his wife's shoulders and looked down at her proudly. "Isn't it great to have a wife who makes you be what she knows you can be?"

In the next chapter I will show you how positive thinking relates to vital aspects of your life, health, and energy.

9.

Positive Secrets of Health and Energy

God wants you to have the best of life all your life. He wants you to feel a glorious aliveness—physically, mentally, and spiritually. Jesus said, "I have come that they may have life, and that they may have it more abundantly" (John 10:10). Or, as another translation, the Good News Bible, puts it, "I have come in order that you might have life—life in all its fullness" (TEV).

Do you have a vibrant quality in your life? Or are you only fractionally alive, only partially healthy? Does your energy run out, leaving you tired, even exhausted?

If this describes you, this chapter is for you. It offers no advice about diet or physical exercise. Nor is it medical advice, since I am not a doctor of medicine. It outlines ways that can produce vibrant health and abundant energy every day. It is not theoretical because I have personally tested every suggestion offered. I make no claim to have been a great athlete or superstrong man, but I have had good, sound health and great reserves of energy all my life, energy that has never run down. I think my good health and great energy are the result of my sincerely attempting to base my life on spiritual laws and principles found in the Bible—principles that never change. They have always helped me, and now I hope they will help you.

I have always taught faith as an important way to a good, healthy life. Now leading medical men are speaking of the health-producing "faith factor." Herbert Benson, M.D., says:

> I'm not at all interested in promoting one religious or philosophical system over another . . . I'm most concerned with the scientifically observable phenomena and forces that accompany faith. . . . My research and that of others has disclosed that those who develop and use the Faith Factor effectively can:
>
> - Relieve headaches
> - Reduce angina pectoris pains and perhaps even eliminate the need for bypass surgery (an estimated 80 percent of angina pain can be relieved by positive belief!)
> - Enhance creativity, especially when experiencing some sort of "mental block"
> - Overcome insomnia
> - Prevent hyperventilation attacks
> - Reduce blood pressure and help control hypertension problems
> - Enhance the therapy of cancer
> - Control panic attacks
> - Lower cholesterol levels

> - Alleviate the symptoms of anxiety that include nausea, vomiting, diarrhea, constipation, short temper, and inability to get along with others
> - Reduce overall stress and achieve great inner peace and emotional balance
>
> The Faith Factor should be used in conjunction with modern medicine. It should be an addition to the awesome cures that the medical profession can now perform. The two approaches—the Faith Factor *and* modern medicine—can enhance each other's impact and, together, bring about optimal results (*Beyond the Relaxation Response* [New York: Times Books, 1975], p. 88).

We live in a material world, and, of course, the material world is important. We couldn't survive without it. But we also live in a mental and spiritual world, and that is even more important. A psychiatrist once said, "Attitudes are more important than facts." That is another way of saying that the world of ideas is just as real and significant as the world of material things.

It is also true that an underlying force, or power, links the material, mental, and spiritual worlds. Your awareness and acknowledgment of this force have much to do with your degree of health and the amount of energy you have in life.

Let me tell you about a woman whose life was turned around. She was only thirty-four years old, supposedly in the prime of life. But, because of frail health, she could do no housework, and she was considered too delicate to have a child. She often took to her bed for lengthy intervals, her energy at low level.

The negative and apprehensive thought pattern thus created siphoned off her joy in living and contributed to her decline in health and energy. She developed into a perennial patient and was a familiar figure in doctors' offices. Her husband sadly accepted the conclusion that he had a semi-invalid wife whose life expectancy was limited.

She was a nominal Christian and a regular church-goer. Her religious training and upbringing had given her a sincere faith in prayer. She accepted the teaching that guidance in solving problems could come through prayer. Gradually, as she prayed for help in her physical problem, she began to believe that an answer would come.

One day, while reading the Bible, she had a thought that amazed her. It is one now commonly accepted, but then it was revolutionary in concept. And her thought was this: physical health can actually be strengthened or weakened, even gained or lost, depending upon one's basic, continuous mental attitude.

In a flash, the insight came to her that as one thinks or images in deep consciousness, so will one tend to become. This independently conceived idea burst with life-changing force into her mind. It was a revelation. Without any involved or complex process of reasoning, she perceived the truth of this idea with such clarity that she accepted it totally.

On a spring day immediately following this mental and spiritual experience, she was walking along a quiet tree-lined street with her husband. The trees were in bud, and the reemerging life of nature was dramatically in evidence everywhere. Suddenly she stopped. "I see it. I see it. That's it!" she exclaimed. "It is the life-force, the wonderful life-force!"

Her startled husband asked, "What do you mean, the life-force?"

She pointed to the leaves bursting from buds, to the brown grass turning green, to the jonquils, hyacinths, and daffodils pushing up from the soil. "That," she declared, "is the life-force. And that same marvelous, re-creative power of new life is in people too. It has to be. Aren't human beings the highest form of creation? They can be re-created by the same miracle of new life." As she spoke, she seemed to be transformed. Her heightened color and dancing eyes attested to a new aliveness within her.

Suddenly she declared aloud, "I affirm that the life-force of almighty God, my Creator, is now re-recreating me. This powerful life-force is surging into my mind, my heart, my bloodstream, all through my being. Health, energy, vitality, and new life are now being renewed in me just as in the trees, the grass, the flowers."

By an act of intense thought, belief, affirmation, and developing faith, this woman began the process of rejecting semi-invalidism and frailty. She acquired, in time, rugged health and energy that enabled her to live an outstanding, very busy life for ninety-six years. She became strong and healthy of body, clear and sharp of mind, enthusiastic and dynamic of spirit. And her faith-filled life inspired thousands until her triumphant departure to the higher life just four years short of a century.

It is amazing how sturdy health may be developed through a combination of insight, belief, in-depth faith, and affirmation of the re-creative power of the Creator. To reach and tap this endless source of energy, repeat or affirm aloud the following words at least once every day. As you do so, stand tall, take a deep breath, and say:

I am vigorous.
I am vitally alive.
I am filled with boundless energy.
I am radiant with good health.
I am joyful.
I am enthusiastic.
I am filled with the life-force.

I know that in Him is life and His
life-force is at work in me,
giving me health and energy and power.
Praise His holy name!

As you do this faithfully, believing sincerely, you will be taking creative spiritual action, and the power of the spiritual universe will flow toward you.

God wants you to be well, to be vital and vigorous all of your life. Believe that. Give thanks for it every day, saying aloud: "God wants me to be well." The Bible confirms this: "Beloved, I pray that you may prosper in all things and be in health, just as your soul prospers" (3 John 2).

In creating the human body, God made the most intricate, amazing instrument ever devised, packing into it complex organs designed to last for long years and work perfectly in a harmonious, balanced whole. To that He added a brain, consisting of about three pounds of tissue, able to think, reason, remember, conceive ideas, and produce noble works. To top it all off, God placed at the center of each human being a spirit or soul by which he or she can know the Creator and live with Him through time and eternity. Amazing!

The verse from 3 John relates the health of the body to the health of the soul. If the soul and the mind are kept free of evil, negative thoughts and attitudes, the body will be healthy. On the other hand, sickness of the soul can result in death: "The soul who sins shall die" (Ezek. 18:4).

Today we know that sickness of soul can result in bodily illness, but people were not really aware of this fact a generation or so ago. I remember well the first time the connection was made plain to me. As the young pastor of a church in Brooklyn, New York, I was called to a hospital to see a patient who was very ill. This man was a well-known politician, prominent in the community. His doctor told me that he was a devoted family man and a pillar of the church. The doctor also admitted that he was puzzled by the man's failure to respond to treatment. "Something seems to be blocking my attempts to cure him," the doctor said.

When I saw the man and looked into his lackluster eyes, I had the feeling that something was wrong with him spiritually, that the illness was spiritually based. I was very young and somewhat hesitant, but I said to him, "I know you are a man of good reputation, but tell me: is there something on your mind that is troubling you?"

He looked at me for what seemed a long time. Finally, in a tremulous voice, he said, "Yes, there is. I know I'm considered a good family man. I'm a deacon in my church, and I have a position of trust in government. And yet I have done things of which I am ashamed. To put it bluntly, I'm a sinner and a hypocrite. If people really knew me, nobody would respect me."

I offered him a threefold solution to his problem: penitence, confession, and restitution, after which would come forgiveness, peace, and healing. I listened to a recital of the sins he had committed, the wrongs he had done. Then he humbly asked for forgiveness. When he finished and I told him that God loved him and had forgiven him, he gave a deep sigh. "I feel so much better," he murmured. "I think I can sleep now."

That was the turning point in his illness. He recovered and went on to a useful, honorable life. The balance between body, mind, and soul was restored. He was made whole again.

This wholeness is what all of us should strive for at all times. Jesus taught us to ask God to deliver us from evil. When we sincerely ask for forgiveness, we are reborn and renewed—actually re-created in mind and soul. This process is described in Psalm 103:2–5:

Bless the LORD, O my soul,
And forget not all His benefits:
Who forgives all your iniquities,
Who heals all your diseases,
Who redeems your life from destruction,
Who crowns you with lovingkindness and
  tender mercies,
Who satisfies your mouth with good things,
So that your youth is renewed like the eagle's.

Attaining health and energy is basically a spiritual process. The spiritual life stimulates vitality not only in the mind and the soul but also in the body. We become healthy to the degree to which the mind thinks healthy thoughts and the soul is morally clean. A clean soul actually sends continuing newness of health throughout the entire system.

In a clinical study of some 500 cases, it was found that 383 of the persons studied were sick, not because they had suffered accidents or organic diseases, but because, according to a doctor's vivid description, "Those patients were draining back into their bodies the diseased thoughts of their minds."

Generations ago Plato wrote: "Neither should we ever attempt to cure the body without curing the soul." Modern thinkers are just now realizing the sound thinking of this wise philosopher of ancient times.

Strive always for wholeness. Keep the three basic elements of your being—body, mind, and soul—in harmony and balance. Remember that good health is possible only when these three elements work with, not against, each other.

Health, wholeness, holiness—these three words have a common origin. At the deepest level, they have a common meaning. Say this simple prayer:

Lord, give me health.
Lord, give me wholeness.
Lord, give me holiness.

Those words will bring a deep peace and restfulness to your mind and body.

There is a powerful phrase in the book of Joshua: "Choose for yourselves this day whom you will serve" (24:15). The choice in those far-off times was between worshiping false gods or remaining faithful to the true God. But the challenge may also refer to many aspects of modern life. We make continual choices between the negative and the positive. We can choose a way of life that will bring us health and happiness, or we can choose the opposite. We can choose between faith and indifference. The choices really are endless.

Happiness, prosperity, and success in life really depend on making right choices, winning choices. There are forces in life working for you and others working against you. To have health and energy, you must be able to recognize beneficial and malevolent forces and choose correctly between them.

Every day when you arise, choices are waiting for you. On the one hand are positive attitudes: creativity, enthusiasm, love, faith, hope. On the other hand are negative attitudes: hate, fear, worry, anger, anxiety. These negative attitudes will seize you if you permit them to do so. Once they fasten onto you, they will work steadily to produce negative results: loss of energy, loss of creativity, loss of enthusiasm and, ultimately, loss of health.

Fortunately, as an intelligent person, as a student of human nature, you can use the positive forces to maintain a healthy body and repel all negative forces. That is a crucial choice, a winning choice. Making this choice requires clear thinking and a strong, resolute faith. When faith declines, doubt takes over, and it can ultimately poison any personality. Dr. Charles Mayo said, "I never knew a man to die of overwork, but I have known many men to die of doubt."

I knew a woman whose eighty-seven-year-old father was killed in an accident crossing a highway. An autopsy revealed that this man had within him conditions that should have developed into serious illnesses. But they hadn't. The doctors told this woman, "Your father had all sorts of potential illnesses that might have progressed. Actually, he should have died twenty years ago. But you say that he was active and energetic as he approached ninety years of age. That's remarkable."

The woman said, "My father was in the habit of saying every morning, 'This is going to be a fine day!' If someone pointed out some ominous or threatening situation, his reply always was: 'I have hopes.'"

Obviously this man had the life-force working in him. In spite of the seeds of illness in him, his body was totally alive. His faith, vitality, enthusiasm, and love of life were more powerful than the negative forces of illness working against him.

The late Wilbur Cross, governor of Connecticut, had a similar outlook on life. Each day he would exclaim enthusiastically, "It's a great day for it!" Every day always had something great to offer—and when you stop to think about it, that is true. Each day is a great day for *something*.

Tomorrow, go to an open window, take a deep breath, look out at your particular corner of the world, and say aloud:

Thank You, God, for being alive.
Thank You for family and friends.
Today is going to be a great day.
I have high hopes for all that this day will bring.

I intend to live every minute of it fully.
The Lord made this day; I will rejoice and be
glad in it!

Use this affirmation as a morning action-motivator. It will help make each day a great day.

Sometimes I am complimented on my energy. Actually that energy isn't mine at all. It comes because I try always to keep my mind open and receptive to the energy that comes to me from God the Re-Creator.

Once, after I had made an energetic speech of some forty-five minutes, a reporter asked, "Where do you get all that vitality? What is the secret of your amazing energy?"

He probably expected some remarks about exercise, diet, sleep habits, or inherited characteristics. But I looked at him in silence for some moments. Finally I said, "Do you want to know the real secret of health and energy?"

"I sure do," he replied fervently.

"It is in the book of Isaiah, chapter forty, verse thirty-one":

But those who wait on the LORD
Shall renew their strength:
They shall mount up with wings like eagles,
They shall run and not be weary,
They shall walk and not faint.

That one statement has had so much to do with my personal continuing health and energy that I suggest the use of it to anyone who really wants to be healthy and energetic. Strength is promised to "those who wait on the Lord." That means, of course, an attitude of belief that you will truly be healthy and strengthened by God Himself, as you center your life and concentrate your thoughts on Him.

The passage from Isaiah describes strength as a powerful upthrust akin to the takeoff of an eagle. Have you ever seen an eagle "mount up"? I did once, years ago in the Rocky Mountains. The gigantic bird was perched on a huge needle of stone, high up on a mountain, clutching the apex with rugged claws. It remained poised on that lofty perch for long minutes. Finally, spreading its wings to the fullest extent and sending out a reverberating scream, the eagle took off, heading up and up into the blue until, as a diminishing speck, it disappeared over a mountain peak. I found myself deeply moved, repeating, the lines, "They shall mount up with wings like eagles."

But the Scripture passage reaches its climax not in the mounting up but in the steady continuance: "They shall run and not be weary, / They shall walk and not faint." The outcome of the mounting up is being able to walk in the tough, hard ways and keep going, always keep going.

As you rise up in thought and spirit like an eagle, you are given insight, stamina, and patience to maintain strength, energy, and determination to persevere no matter what difficulties may come upon you. And those energies derived from spiritual upthrust will not ever run down.

This truth is simple and basic, like all great truths. Those who wait on the Lord are putting themselves into the life-force that God has built into the universe. It is possible to exist on the edges of this great power, or even outside it; but that is mere existence, not real living. Every truly successful, happy person I have ever known recognizes this and opts for the life-force.

For those who are unsure of what is meant by that phrase, "wait on the Lord," the Lord Himself has provided rules and guidelines spelled out so clearly that anyone can understand them. That is why reading the Bible regularly is important. It offers a blueprint for spiritual and physical health.

Here are three simple pledges of intent. Follow them and they can change your life.

1. I resolve to read one chapter of the Bible each day.
2. I resolve to commit to memory one passage of Scripture each week.
3. I resolve to give thanks for the energy and health that are mine.

The Bible is available to all of us. All we have to do is open it, read it, believe it, practice it.

Every careful observer knows that life ranges from mere existence at the lowest level to spiritual joy at the highest level. Some persons I have known have attained this state to a high degree of perfection. One was Dr. John Reilly. He was a member of my church, a great doctor, and a wise, understanding Christian. At one time, he professionally attended a president of the United States.

Every morning it was Dr. Reilly's habit to thank God for every organ of his body and to ask Him to bless each one that it might function perfectly. This action formula for sustained good health is a procedure well worth imitating. Here is what Dr. Reilly affirmed aloud:

Thank You, God, for my clear mind.
Thank You for my sturdy heart.
Thank You for my sound lungs, my marvelous
network of veins and arteries, my reliable
digestive system.
Thank You for my eyesight and my hearing.
Thank You for the perfection of Your creative
workmanship as it appears throughout my body.

All his life Dr. Reilly remained healthy, alert, and very much alive. Then one afternoon, when he was ninety-five years of age, he lay down for a nap. While he slept, the heavenly Father called him home.

His nurse later told me that before he slept that day, Dr. Reilly said, "Tell Dr. Peale that I will be working for him from the other side." Believe me, I am glad to have him do so, because he was a spiritual giant and medical expert on this side, and God might indeed choose him as one of His angels of mercy over there.

Dr. Reilly often told me that he was convinced that our bodily health is largely determined by what we habitually think. And he added that a primary rule of good health is to avoid any kind of behavior that can set up feelings of remorse or guilt. Guilt can actually plant the seeds of sickness in the soul, a sickness that proceeds to damage the mind and, in time, the body. If a person has fallen into a pattern of conduct that causes guilt feelings, such a behavior pattern should be discarded, and discarded quickly, if the individual wishes to remain in good health.

A woman once wrote to me, saying, "When you come to our city, please see my husband." Formerly this man had been successful in business, active in civic groups, popular and outgoing. But then suddenly he seemed to lose vitality. He would sit and stare into space. His condition was finally diagnosed as a nervous breakdown. No one was sure of the cause, but one perceptive doctor remarked that the patient could have something weighing on his mind, which might perhaps mend if he could be persuaded to empty it out.

Eventually I saw him. His manner was dull and apathetic, and at first, he would reiterate that he "felt ill." Finally, I asked, "Is there something on your conscience that you have not told anyone? I am a pastor, and nothing you can say will shock me. So I suggest that you come clean and empty it out." I explained the effect on the body of an unhealthy mental condition. Gradually, bit by bit, out came things he had done, which he knew were wrong and sinful. When at last he had emptied out everything of this nature, he sat back, spent.

I made a heaping motion with my hands. "What are you doing?" he asked curiously.

"Heaping up all that part of your past that has weighed so heavily on your mind. Quite a mass of evil and sick stuff, isn't it? How could you expect to feel well with all that on your mind, on your soul?" I then suggested that he ask the Lord to forgive him, asserting my belief that if he did, he would get well again. He did so, then and there, praying aloud rather simply. It was a moving experience to listen to him.

Then we sat in silence for a few moments. Suddenly he stood up, raised himself on tiptoe, brought his arms over his head, took a deep breath, and exclaimed, "My, but I feel good! Oh, thank You, God, thank You, thank You!" Such was the beginning of his return to health.

It is important to remember that God not only created you, He is constantly re-creating you. The life-force in you is always working in a rebuilding process, causing every organ to function perfectly in harmony with God's laws. One way you can aid this process is by the use of positive affirmation. At least once every day affirm:

> God's life-force is now flooding my being.
> My entire body is being filled with health.
> The healing grace of the Great Physician is
> sustaining me.
> In Him is life; His life is in me.
> I am well and strong. Praise the Lord!

Strength of body, mind, and soul is what God wants for us. He wants us to be "strengthened with all might" (Col. 1:11).

The Bible speaks of the Lord as the One who heals *all* your diseases. This is an encompassing promise. God's healing power is available for anything that may be amiss in your physical, mental, and spiritual structure. This, of course, is not to minimize in any sense the great value of medicine and surgery. On the contrary, God heals in various ways, not the least of which is through physicians, surgeons, medicines, and the instruments created by science.

Always thinking health, practicing health, affirming health will go far toward giving you good health. Dr. Paul Tournier said,

> Most illnesses do not, as is generally thought, come like a bolt out of the blue. The ground is prepared for years, through faulty diet, intemperance, overwork, and moral conflicts slowly eroding the subject's vitality. Every act of physical, psychological or moral disobedience of God is an act of wrong living, and has its inevitable consequences.

Fortunately the Lord has given antidotes against deterioration. One important method of His healing is that of joy. The Bible declares that "a merry heart does good, like a medicine" (Prov. 17:22).

Dr. John A. Schindler, a famous physician who practiced for many years in Wisconsin, wrote an important book, *How to Live 365 Days a Year*. He regularly asked his patients: "Look, are you happy and peaceful enough to live a long time?" He claimed that if he could get patients to lift their thoughts into an area of pure joy for only ten minutes each day, he could get them well, keep them well, and help them live a long life.

Robert Louis Stevenson said, "To miss the joy is to miss all." Paul Tillich, a famous scholar, said in his book *The*

Meaning of Joy, "Where there is joy, there is fulfillment, and where there is fulfillment, there is joy."

A middle-aged man, whom I shall call Steve, had suffered two heart attacks. The doctors had taken good care of him in both cases, but he lived in terror of a third heart attack. He had the notion that he could survive two heart attacks, but that a third was bound to be fatal.

"Steve," I said, "you could bring a third heart attack on yourself by your fear. I get the impression that you are not happy. You exude gloom, despair, and negativism. I want to share with you what a doctor friend of mine says: 'If you are happy, you will be peaceful. And when you are peaceful, you will be happy.' Furthermore, Steve, you will be healthier as well."

Dr. Herbert Benson, quoted earlier in this chapter, says: "A positive attitude opens the vast positive possibilities of healing." Also, Dr. Benson indicates the wisdom of the Tibetan sages: "The state of your mind is the most important single factor in your physical health" (*Beyond the Relaxation Response,* pp. 88, 63).

The Bible is actually a book on health and well-being, and whoever practices its teachings fully and faithfully is very likely to be a healthy individual. To Steve I quoted Jesus' words found in John 14:27: "Peace I leave with you, My peace I give to you; not as the world gives do I give to you. Let not your heart be troubled, neither let it be afraid."

"Now, Steve," I continued. "When you go to bed at night and are trying to go to sleep, place your hand over your heart and imagine that it is the healing hand of Jesus. Then say, 'Let not *my* heart be troubled, neither let me be afraid.'"

Steve was deeply moved. Tears came to his eyes. So I continued, "As a pastor and a practitioner of the truths in the Bible, I suggest that every day you do as suggested. You will become joyful and peaceful. You will move into the area of pure joy. This is a powerful procedure." Steve, a sincere believer, did as I suggested. He did not have that third heart attack.

One trouble with Steve was that he had fallen into the habit of thinking too much about himself. When you put yourself in the center of all your thoughts, to the exclusion of everyone else, you are close to committing personality suicide. Self-love, self-pity, and self-interest are destructive maladies causing the personality to wither and die. A person at any age, under any circumstance, can feel better by reaching out to others. Helpful people are joyous people, and joy "does good, like medicine."

Still another mental and spiritual medicine is that of hope: "And now abide faith, hope, love" (1 Cor. 13:13). Every day send down into your mind three great words—*faith, hope,* and *love*—and your health will be stimulated.

Shakespeare said, "The miserable have no other medicine, but only hope." And he also pointed out that hope is a healing potion. Hope is indeed medicinal in its effect. When you have hope, you stand straighter, you throw back your shoulders, you breathe deeply of God's good air, and your mind is filled with healthy thoughts.

My mechanic told me my car needed overhauling. He said, "A clean engine delivers power." That is true of a human being too. Lubricate the mind with hope, and it will operate with power because with hope come aliveness, enthusiasm, vibrancy, and vitality.

Elbert Hubbard gave some priceless advice full of hope and health:

> Draw the chin in, carry the crown of the head high, and fill the lungs to the utmost; drink in the sunshine; greet your friends with a smile, and put soul into every handclasp.
>
> Do not fear being misunderstood, and do not waste a minute thinking about your enemies. Try to fix firmly

in your mind what you would like to do, and then, without veering off direction, you will move straight to the goal.

Keep your mind on the great and splendid things you would like to do, and then, as the days go gliding by, you will find yourself unconsciously seizing upon the opportunities that are required for the fulfillment of your desire.

Picture in your mind the able, earnest, useful person you desire to be, and the thought you hold is hourly transforming you into that particular individual.

Thought is supreme. Preserve a right mental attitude—the attitude of courage, frankness, and good cheer. To think rightly is to create. All things come through desire and every sincere prayer is answered. We become like that on which our thoughts are fixed.

Never think of yourself as old, weary, sick, or discouraged. Never think of yourself as defeated. Hope is a form of imaging. Get hope into your mind, and change all negative thoughts into positive thoughts. Remember, there is a tendency to become what you image or visualize.

Pull yourself up, physically, mentally, spiritually, by filling your mind with hope. "Hope thou in God: for I shall yet praise him, who is the health of my countenance" (Ps. 42:11 KJV). As you hope in God, you will have health in your countenance, because you will have health of body, mind, and spirit.

A doctor had a seventeen-year-old patient who was in a coma. The boy's parents were divorced, and he had been deeply troubled before his illness. The doctor gathered the members of the broken family together, and a neighbor farmer who loved the boy was there also. The doctor sat studying his patient, then said, "All the medical signs indicate that this boy may die by morning. But actually, from a medical viewpoint, he should not die. He simply does not have the will to live. What we must do is give him a transfusion at once."

Immediately, all volunteered to give blood, but the doctor said he did not want blood. He wanted the transfusion of healthy ideas. "If we can penetrate this boy's unconsciousness, and drive faith thoughts into him, perhaps we can counteract the disease."

The farmer was a man of simple faith. He held a Bible in his big hands. He knew that Bible almost by heart, and he turned its pages lovingly. He knelt by the boy's bed, and for a long time, he read aloud passages that dealt with life, faith, love, hope, the goodness of God, and the mercy of Jesus Christ.

The family stood around the bed, each one mustering faith and transmitting it to the sick boy. Finally, as dawn was beginning to break, the boy opened his eyes, looked around, and smiled, then sank into a peaceful sleep. The doctor said, "He has passed the crisis. The 'transfusion' has been a success. The boy will live!"

In-depth faith is a profound healing power. Longer life can result from the kind and quality of the thoughts we think.

Ralph Waldo Trine, popular writer of "In Tune with the Infinite," said, "Would you remain always young, and would you carry all the joyousness and buoyancy of youth into your maturer years? Then have a care concerning one thing—how you live in your thought world." I would add that the thought most important to health and energy is the thought of God, our Creator and Re-Creator.

Repeat aloud the following health- and energy-giving affirmation:

> The life-force of almighty God, my Creator and Re-Creator, is now pouring through my being, from the crown of my head, to the soles of my feet. The inflow-

> ing powerful life-force is cleansing my mind, soul, and body. It is filling me with newness of life, health, and energy. For this wonderous benefit, I thank God through Jesus Christ.

May health, happiness, and God's peace be yours, now and always.

Since positive thinking is so basic in our daily living and in our search for health and energy, people sometimes ask me, "How can one be a positive thinker?" Some answers to that question are in the next chapter.

10.

How to Be a Positive Thinker

Some people, it seems, are just naturally positive thinkers. Others come by it the hard way. There is, I believe, much to be said for the theory that we are all born positive thinkers. I cannot recall ever having seen a negative baby, unless perhaps one that was ill. But some, perhaps many, babies are born into negative families. Infants are highly sensitive to their atmosphere and tend to take on and absorb the prevailing mental and emotional characteristics of the family. Hence, if the family atmosphere is negatively conditioned, they become unconsciously negative in their thought processes.

They grow up to have negative mental attitudes. If later, at age twenty or thirty or so, they want to be positive thinkers, they face the problem of unlearning long-held habits of thinking, and that relearning process can take some doing. But a human being is endowed with habit-breaking power the same as habit-forming ability, and any habit can be changed. Though sometimes the cerebral grooves made by habitual thought processes run deep, they are nevertheless subject to revision if the desire to do so is sufficiently intense, the will to do so strong, and the imagination acute.

Human beings, made in the image of their Creator and possessed of His characteristics, are by nature positive because He is positive. The Creator has an astounding confidence in His creatures, for He confers upon them the right and privilege of choice. They are granted the right to choose error instead of truth, evil instead of good, wrong instead of right. They can be negative instead of positive in their thinking. But having chosen one set of values and having lived by that pattern for years, they may at any time exercise their right of choice again and choose opposite values. Christianity calls this conversion, the process by which one converts or changes the essential being. "If anyone is in Christ, he is a new creation; old things have passed away; behold, all things have become new" (2 Cor. 5:17).

So, I wish to emphasize this basic fact—you can change from negative to positive thinking and enjoy all the blessings that follow such a change. This is possible no matter how long and how completely you have been a negative-thinking person. How may I say this so confidently? I experienced this change, and if I could revamp my thinking from negative to positive, I believe sincerely that a similar change can happen to anyone who will pay the price in effort and persistence.

Since a personal experience is worth a thousand unsupported assertions, I will remind you I was badly afflicted with a horrendous feeling of self-doubt and inferiority when I was a young boy. Along with this misery was the haunting doubt about whether I could ever achieve my dreams, for I had them, or realize my goals, for I had them also. I was reared with and by people who were active mentally. But I was also surrounded, it seemed, by quite a few habitual worriers. It was always touch and go financially in our family, a situation which no doubt helped develop my sense of insecurity. Apprehension of vague but dire outcomes was in the mental atmosphere of my youth. But whatever the cause, there was added to my feelings of inferiority and inadequacy a negative attitude generally. Despite my dreams of the future, I was a negative thinker. I continued in this unhappy state until my sophomore year in college when in a miraculous way God turned around my negative pattern of looking at the world.

The number one priority in becoming a positive person is desire. You must want to be a positive person so intently that you determine to start at once the process of change in yourself. And let me assure you that if you believe you can change from negative to positive, you will do so.

There is a curious side to this changeover from negative to positive. If you are a positive person today, you may not realize just how you got to be that way. As you struggled to believe, all that time you were in the process of becoming positive. The very moment you tried, you were in the power flow of new and dynamic thought.

I was speaking along this line at a convention for the top-producing agents of a large national insurance company. An attractive young couple, all excited, came up to me after my talk, and the man said, "I never knew before how I became a positive thinker. But in your message today you described exactly what happened to me. I just want to tell you that now I know how I achieved the success that has surprised me and that brought me to this conference as a winner. Thank the Lord," he concluded fervently, "for God did it."

He explained that he developed an intense desire to bring an end to his negative attitude which he had suffered from childhood. Though he had not been reared in a religious family, indeed quite the contrary, he nevertheless got the definite belief that only by faith in God would he ever overcome his sense of inferiority and self-doubt. He tried to hide this belief from his father who was a fanatical anti-Christian, but the older man saw through his son. "I don't believe in this God stuff, as you well know. And I've tried to rear you as an objective thinker, free of all that religious emotionalism. But, Son, if God can remove the failure-producing feeling of inferiority from you, as a fair-minded man I'll give Him the credit He deserves."

"Well, what does your father think now that you have become one of the top producers of your company and are a recognized positive thinker?" I asked.

He chuckled, "Well, Dad says if God could change me from a defeated negative thinker to a successful positive thinker, maybe he better get acquainted with God. And he tells people, 'God did something for my own son which I was never able to do myself.' Anyway," concluded the young man, "I see clearly that what happened to free me from a deadening negativism was a spiritual process. And believe me, I'm going to stick with it."

In October of 1952 I published my book *The Power of Positive Thinking*. It was the first book ever to bear that title. It sold over fifteen million copies in forty-five languages. Since its publication, many authors have written on the same theme under various titles. But that one phrase "the power of positive thinking" has become a basic concept in the English language and culture and, by translation, in many cultures of the world.

That positive thinking works as described, I have no doubt whatsoever. A vast correspondence with readers, which began when the book was published, each letter telling how positive thinking turned a life around and lifted a person from failure to success, is evidence that millions have found new hope and new life through the principle of positive thinking. In short, it gave each person a joyous fulfillment.

To satisfy the oft-repeated demand, "I want to know more about positive thinking," I organized a Positive Thinkers Club, and every month I write a lesson on positive thinking that is mailed to every member of the Positive Thinkers club. (For further information about the Positive Thinkers Club, write to the Foundation for Christian Living, Box FCL, Pawling, New York 12564.) Thousands receive these lessons. Thousands of young people—teenagers and those in their twenties who were not born when my first book was written—are asking, "Tell me more about positive thinking." They want to know what it is and how they can become positive thinkers because they are convinced that this is the best of all ways of life.

Answering these questions and helping as many people as I can to live creative, happy, effective lives I take to be my mission on earth. The Lord apparently wants this mission to be fulfilled. I have been given the strength to speak constantly about positive thinking to audiences around the world, to write books on the subject, to publish *PLUS: The Magazine of Positive Thinking* ($7.00 per year—write to the Foundation for Christian Living, Box FCL, Pawling, New York 12564), and *Guideposts* magazine ($6.95 per year—write to *Guideposts*, Carmel, New York 10512), one of the phenomenal, successful publications of our time. In addition, we have two nationwide radio programs carrying the message—the Positive Thinkers Network and the American Character.

This current book was written in part to answer many questions, especially how people may become positive thinkers and continue to be positive in the ups and downs of life. So, how can you become a positive thinker and remain one?

As I have mentioned, the number one priority is desire, but even that is not enough. Intensity of desire is required. To become a positive thinker, you must want to be, not halfheartedly or wistfully, but intensely with all the wanting of which you are capable. If you do not have intensity of desire, the chances of your succeeding are minimal. But with intense desire, if it is sustained, you have the basic ingredient for becoming a positive person.

I must point out once again that some people are positive thinkers by nature, and fortunately they were never subjected as children to a prevailing negativism. For some reason, probably because of heredity or strong family influence, they proved impervious to the predominantly negative attitude all around them in the world. It seems that natural positive thinkers are less numerous than negative thinkers. However, since the positive-thinking concept came upon the scene in the 1930s in the time of the Great Depression, this type of thought and action has become immensely popular. As a result, the number of persons attaining a positive attitude has greatly increased.

One night after I had spoken to a rally of several thousand sales personnel in Atlanta, a young man approached me and said, "Keep on underscoring the idea that intensity of desire is basic to gaining and maintaining a positive attitude."

He seemed so earnest about the matter that I asked, "Why, have you had experience in this connection?"

He then told me he came from a very poor rural family, that his father could never make a go of his little farm. The farm equipment, already second- or even thirdhand, was always breaking down. And since his father was constantly short of cash, hand repairs were necessary. He added, "None of us were handy. As a result of always being on the edge of poverty, conversation around home was always negative: 'We can't. We'll never get anywhere. Things are hopeless.' So ran the same old dismal outlook. I never heard any optimistic statements. Then one day some fellow spoke to our school assembly. I still don't know who he was, but vaguely I heard later that he was from the National Cash Register Company at Dayton. We lived down on the river in southeastern Ohio. He gave a talk on positive thinking, and he said if you develop the habit of thinking positively, even about the most negative conditions, you set in motion creative forces that will counteract any negative.

"This speaker was down-to-earth, had a lot of humor, was convincing, terrifically persuasive. He showed me that there could be a brighter outlook. And I wanted to be different, to get away from all that gloomy thinking and talking.

"I don't know how I ever figured it out by myself because there was no one to teach me, but I began to realize that I had to want positiveness with everything I had. I was smart enough to go to our little local library and look for a book that might help me. I found one of your books, *You Can If You Think You Can*. Then I realized the truth that what you think, if you think it hard enough, will ultimately come to you. If you think you can move up to a higher level, then with God's help you can.

"So," he concluded, "as you go around making speeches, always remember that in every audience is someone like me who, as the Bible says, hungers and thirsts for righteousness (Matt. 5:6)."

He defined *righteousness* as "right-mindedness." This earnest young fellow had experienced both a mental and a spiritual change. He was changed in his mind and in his soul. He discovered that hungering and thirsting after something greater, call it intensity of desire, led inevitably to that which is intensely desired.

Naturally you need to know exactly what you desire so intently. Just what is positive thinking? Let me define it by describing a positive thinker. He or she is a person who is strong, tough, and rugged mentally, one who sees every difficulty but sees it straight. This person is not dismayed by any adversity, setback, or seemingly impossible condition, knowing that he or she is able with the help of the good God to see through, think through, pray through, and overcome any difficulty. To the positive thinker, there is always a way, always an answer. To every tough problem, the positive thinker says quietly, "Yeah, I know, but ——!" And he may add, "The things which are impossible with men are possible with God" (Luke 18:27), or "I can do all things through Christ who strengthens me" (Phil. 4:13). Then do you know what? The positive thinker then just goes ahead and accomplishes his goals.

One thing is sure, positive thinking is not, as some negativists assert, a Pollyannish, sweetness-and-light concept. Nor is it an unrealistic, easy philosophy. On the contrary, positive thinking is for strong people: strong in faith, strong in thought, strong in character. And if they are not so when they embrace positive thinking, the struggle to become positive will make them strong.

Positive thinking is the direct opposite of negative thinking. The negativist is a disbeliever; the positive thinker is a believer. The one is full of self-doubt; the other is endowed with self-confidence. The one gives up when confronted with difficulty; the other rises to the occasion when the going gets tough. The negative thinker, by hopelessness, shuts off the flow of creative power. The positive thinker, drawing upon faith in God and self, opens wide the channels of inflowing power and creativity that produce amazing results. In short, the negative thinker tends to see, and thereby to cause, failure. The positive thinker images the possibles and attracts success to himself and his projects.

Effecting change from the negative to the positive requires, at first, beginning to entertain positive ideas about small things. Bombard your long-established negative mental attitude with small positives such as the thoughts "I can," "It's just possible," "That's going to turn out well." The mere passage of such fragmentary positive thoughts through the mind will start a fresh, though small, mental track. Repeated daily over a period of time and followed by stronger thoughts, this practice will ultimately deepen the channel forming across the mind and eventually undercut the old negative thought channel, causing it to cave in. Then the dominant thought of your mind will be a positive mental attitude.

One may become a positive thinker not only by having intense desire and by retraining the thought processes but also by learning a new manner of speech. Speech is the audible articulation of an idea formulated by thought in the mental process. And repeated statements of a thought tend to imbed it ever deeper in subconsciousness to the extent that it eventually assumes the permanent form of a habit. Habit is determined by constant repetition of instinctive, intuitive and, sometimes deliberate, action. The ultimate of what a person becomes is a combination of thought, speech, action, and attitude, which combination develops into habit and finally, by reception into the deep subconscious, solidifies one's values or point of view. This is the process by which a person becomes either a negative or a positive thinker. It is the method by which the mental attitude forms.

In this mind-revamping process, what you say daily in normal conversations has a more powerful influence on the total attitude than might be considered possible. If your usual speech is filled with negative remarks, it indicates that your thoughts are negatively conditioned. However, when an increasing number of positive statements are spoken, it clearly indicates that you are attempting a mental revamping, trying to shift from a negative to a positive mental attitude. When the ear constantly hears a positive thought which has been formulated by the mind and spoken by the mouth, three powerful forces—the mind, the ear, and the mouth—are united in a campaign to change that individual from a negative to a positive thinker.

I used this idea of a combined attack on the negative habit by the mind, the ear, and the mouth in a speech to a national sales rally in Kansas City. Months later I returned to that same city to speak to the Kraft salesmen from the middle western and western states but did not include this idea in the talk that day.

On the way out of the Music Center where the meeting was held, a man intercepted me. "I barged into the Kraft meeting. I saw that you were billed to speak and figured they wouldn't mind my gate crashing. You see, I heard you when you were here some months ago when you spoke of that mind, ear, and mouth bit. Thought you might develop it further for this crowd."

Then he went on to say that he had made use of this technique because, as he put it, he was trying to work his way out of negativism. "But," he said, "I improved on your idea. I added the eye to the mind and the ear and the mouth. Then I stopped reading all the negative junk in some newspapers and magazines and books. I figured I could take in positive ideas through my eyes. So I've been reading every motivational and positive book I can find. I've got a positive-thinking library started. Anway, I think positive, speak positive, listen positive, and see positive. Every avenue into my personality is being worked."

"And what is the result?" I asked.

"Boy, I'm so packed full of the positive that all that old negativism I went along with for years is being crowded out." He hesitated. "Hey, say a prayer for me sometime, will you?" Then suddenly he seemed to get another thought. His mind was working at full capacity. "Maybe we should add the soul to the mind, the ear, the mouth, and the eye. I'll tell you something. You just can't go with this program without the Lord going along with you." Then he shook my hand. "Got a business appointment. See you." And he was off, going strong.

Becoming a positive thinker when one has long been negative is essentially an educational process. And in that learning experience, thinking, hearing, speaking, and growing (especially spiritually) have important roles. The truth is that an individual can be what he wants to be if he knows what he wants to be and if he desires with intensity and utilizes all the forces of mind and spirit inherent within him. Then he can attain his goal of becoming a positive thinker.

It is conceivable, I suppose, that one can become and remain a positive thinker in spite of all the difficulties experienced by all men and women without emphasis on the spiritual. But I cannot imagine anyone fully overcoming negative thinking and action without the benefit of prayer and faith, without what we call spiritual experience. To overcome a profound inferiority feeling, I have personally used every method suggested in this book and in all my other ones. I must say that without spiritual help I would never have made it and been freed from negativism. The Lord saved me from myself, and if I have been able to do anything at all of a constructive nature in life, it is because He has helped me all the way. I owe everything to Him.

In the first place I finally had to admit, as a teenager, that I was never going to be able to overcome self-doubt and inferiority without help, that I simply could not do it on my own. Years later a superbenefactor of mankind named Bill Wilson, whom I had the privilege of knowing, founded a tremendous organization called Alcoholics Anonymous. Bill had tried every possible means to overcome the disease that was destroying him, but he had no success whatsoever. He told me that finally he went to the top of a high hill. There he poured out his feelings and voiced his longing for deliverance and victory. Aloud he cried out, "Help me, dear Lord, oh, please help me. I am powerless. I can do nothing on my own. Oh, please help me." He stood for a long time alone on that hilltop. But he was not alone. Presently it seemed that a strong, fresh, clean wind started blowing, and it seemed to be blowing through him, blowing him clean. All his weakness was swept away. Power flooded into him. He was re-created.

The validity of this remarkable experience is attested by the fact that Bill Wilson walked down the hill determined to bring to others the same incredible release from the destructive disease he had experienced. So it is that in every Alcoholics Anonymous headquarters, I am told, are the words, "There but for the grace of God, go I."

This particular problem was not mine. But negative thinking was and inferiority was and self-doubt was. To get over them, to be cured, I needed the same treatment Bill Wilson had, namely, a power beyond human power, the incredible power of God which is freely offered to anyone who won't quibble about it but who will humbly ask for it and receive it.

Some weaknesses fasten themselves like barnacles upon human beings. I have labeled two of them alcoholism and negativism, and both are deeply rooted in the unconsciousness. Nothing superficial will work successfully on them. They must be pulled up from the roots, their roots killed, and a profound healing method applied, a curative process that reaches to the essence of one's nature. Only the re-creative power of the Creator, almighty God Himself, can effectively deal with diseases so basic.

Therefore, if you have some intellectual notion or dilettantish idea or emotional resentment toward religion and expect to eliminate the deep roots of a negative attitude without religion, try it if you will; but I warn you that if you really want to become a positive thinker with extra power, you will have a very difficult time. I suggest that you overcome your antireligious antipathy and humbly ask God, in your own way, to help you throw off the destructive habit of a negative attitude. He likes you even if you may not like Him, and He stands ready to help anyone who asks for help.

I will never forget the irate man who walked into my New York office one bitterly cold winter afternoon and demanded to see me. "Have you an appointment?" my secretary asked politely.

"No, I have no appointment; but I need to see Dr. Peale. And get this straight . . . I'm *going* to see him."

"Just a moment," she replied and came in to tell me of my "tough oddball, would-be visitor."

"Okay, bring him in," I said, aware that this man's angry actions indicated a mixed-up condition of spirit. The interview proved to be one of the most curious I ever had, and I have had many strange ones.

He seemed a well-educated, substantial man in his thirties. "Look," he said, "I would not have barged in on you if I were not in a pretty bad state, and I've just got to talk to someone. You don't know me, and I have seen you only once when you spoke to a real estate convention. Have you time to listen to me talk my trouble out?"

"Well," I replied, "it so happens that I do have scheduled appointments, but I'll give you an hour. If you organize your story, that should be sufficient time for a first interview. So go ahead."

Immediately he plunged into an angry dissertation about himself. That he was seething with self-hate was evident. His lifelong shyness and self-doubt had taken their toll. Everything was always bound to go wrong for him. He was born to lose. This was his ingrained self-image, and had he not had some inherited wealth, he would have been destitute. Of course, he was a thoroughgoing negative thinker, and he admitted being an alcoholic.

But he had a lingering hope and a flickering desire to change and become a normal person. "I know that you teach the positive-thinking idea, that you invented positive thinking. What is wrong with me anyway? What do I need?"

"Well," I replied, "it is self-evident, I think, that you need God. Only God can unravel your complicated mix-ups."

At this he became red in the face. "Is that all you can say? I expected something better of you, a well-educated man. So you're just like the rest of them. You too start talking God. God. God. God. That's all anyone can come up with. I tell you, I'm sick of all this God stuff." He jumped up and stomped angrily from the room. He did not have the politeness to thank me for my time. All I could do was send a prayer after him that in some way peace might come to this distraught fellow.

A half-hour later my secretary called on the intercom, "That man is back. I think you had better see him. He looks terrible."

I explained to the person with me that our conversation must be terminated. The man came in. He paced up and down. "Whatever has happened to me?" he asked repeatedly.

"Calm yourself, my friend, and tell me what is troubling you now."

He then explained that upon leaving my office, he walked through the streets muttering, "God. God. It's always God . . . God . . . God." Then he said it seemed that suddenly a bright light flashed up everywhere. Winter twilight had faded into darkness, but for him everything was brilliantly lighted. People's faces were alight, the buildings shone in white light. The usually dirty littered streets of Manhattan were clean and illuminated. People passing by seemed beautiful. He stared at them, but they gave no sign of seeing what he was witnessing. "Even the sidewalks seem to emanate light. I'm out of my mind. I'm going nuts!" he exclaimed. He did the only thing he could think of. Bewildered, he headed back to my office.

He turned a pathos-filled face upon me. "What has happened to me? Have I gone balmy?"

"No," I said, "you are in your right mind all right. Perhaps the rightest it's ever been. You have been given a rare experience, one that we call mystical. God had burst into you with power. I think you are healed. I believe you have been re-created. Don't ask me why, for I do not know why. I guess that God wants you to do something special with your life."

The outcome was that this man became a totally different person, peaceful, happy, normal, and definitely positive. In the years that followed this amazing experience, he helped many people find themselves in various ways.

In all my time of working with human problems, this man's experience was unique. The wise God's method of making positive thinkers out of negative thinkers and good people out of bad ones is usually a quieter and more evolutionary process of growth. But in whatever way He may work, one thing is sure—if you seemingly cannot make a personality change on your own, the Lord God is always there to help if you ask for that help.

Inherent in positive thinking is the positive image. The next chapter tells more about this important new ability and how you may acquire it.

11.

Happiness at Last

It is difficult to imagine anyone lower in spirit and in prospects than Ken Butterfield as he dragged himself down Second Avenue that dismal February morning. He had breakfasted frugally on toast and coffee at a joint a few blocks back, and he had exactly seven soiled one-dollar bills left in his pocket. He had spent the night in a shelter for homeless men. But he had one thing going for him, a rather decent suit of clothes, a holdover from more prosperous days. And he was fairly neat and clean.

His had been a fast spiraling comedown. His deceased father had left him about forty thousand dollars. Never having had so much, he had blown it first in posh lounges and finally in cheap bars. "I am entirely out of hope," he had told someone.

"Better see Norman Vincent Peale," that someone advised.

"Who's he, and what can he do for me?"

"Maybe give you a new idea about yourself. Anyway it might be a good idea to see him."

Thus it was that he showed up at my office that winter morning. "Tell me all about it and leave nothing out," I said.

Thus prodded, he gave me a brief life history and ended, "I'm no good at all. I'm a total flop, an absolute failure. In fact, I'm not worth a dime." So ran his complete self-depreciation.

Despite the thorough negativism of his self-evaluation, I noticed that he did not ramble or repeat but tied it all up in a neat and succinct summary. This indicated to me that he had some ability to think and express his thoughts in an organized manner.

"Smart guy," I broke in.

"What do you mean smart?"

I explained my admiration of his ability to tell his story coherently. "You've got a good mind, and anyone with a good mind can get out of any hole, however deep, providing he really wants to and is humble enough to take advice."

"No one ever told me before that I have a good mind," he grumbled.

"So what! I'm telling you now."

He took his seven dirty one-dollar bills out and laid them side by side on my desk. "That's all I have in this world," he announced solemnly.

"What do you expect me to do, cry?" I asked. "I'm not at all impressed. You've got a lot more than those seven dollars. For one thing there is that head on your shoulders we've been talking about. Then you have youth. And if you would stand up straight, you would be a rather impressive fellow. You just told me that you have a college degree and that you graduated with honors. What do you mean that seven dollars is all you have in the world?"

I pointed out that all he had done in our conversation was to lay out his negatives. "Let's go for your assets," I said. It wasn't long before I had Ken feeling so much better about himself that he actually told me of a few ideas he had had in the past.

Unmarried, he had been assistant manager of a store before he began drinking heavily. As a result, he lost a good job, one that promised advancement. Then he really hit the toboggan. But only now was he really aware of it and ready to do something about himself. He was intelligent enough to realize that a first step was to reverse his negative thinking, drop his attitude of hopelessness and self-depreciation, and look for all the positive factors in his situation.

"Why was I so dumb as to run through that forty thousand dollars my dear father had scrimped and saved to accumulate?" he asked.

"Oh, even the smartest people do dumb things. But one of your assets is the intelligence to know when you've been dumb. You have had a very expensive lesson in how not to handle money. In the future, when you have a lot more than the inheritance you sent down the drain, you will be much wiser and more circumspeect. Charge it up to education."

"Yeah, I know that makes sense, but if only I hadn't been such a dope."

"One of the greatest of all futilities is 'if only'," I said, and told him what I had learned from Dr. Smiley Blanton. Dr. Blanton said that many of his patients were emotionally ill, even physically sick, because they would not let go of the "if only I hadn't done this or had done that." Mental health is regained when the patient is able to substitute the thought of "next time" for the impotent regret of "if only." It is the "next time" concept that leads away from life's stupidities and failures and helps get creative things going again.

Despite his negative attitudes, Ken reached for positive thinking as a drowning man for a floating log. He was naturally bright, and he showed it by responding to the suggestion that a successful life-style was not at all impossible. He did not again call attention to those lonely seven one-dollar bills. But I did. It so happened that I had access to a discretionary fund, supplied to me by some generous persons for use in providing temporary help to those in need.

I said, "Ken, look, let's stop fooling around with failure. We are going to get you organized, starting now. First, I'd like you to begin the practice of affirmation. In your present condition you need a big buildup of positive thinking. So here is what you do. Use the affirmation I'm going to give you at least thirty times a day for a while. As it begins to take effect in your system, we can reduce it. But for now, take this thirty times daily. Say aloud:

1. I am in the process of creative change.
2. I am becoming better every day in every way.
3. I am firmly on the success beam.
4. My own is coming to me now.
5. God is guiding and helping me daily.

"Now, Ken," I added, "I'm going to invest a little money in you. Go to the YMCA and get a room. Go out of my office today affirming, 'There is a job for me somewhere in this big city.' Believe that. Definitely image or visualize that job. Then go out and get it and do it better than anyone ever did it before. Thank God constantly for what He is doing for you. And you are on your way."

He found the job, counterman in a small West Side restaurant. He gave the job all he had, which was plenty.

When he came to me that day, he was hopeless. He was at the bottom which, as I have pointed out, is actually a favorable spot to be since one cannot go lower than the bottom. The only direction left is upward. He reversed his thinking, canceled out the word *hopeless*, substituted for it hope and faith and positive thinking. Result? He conquered the alcoholism. He gradually moved up from counterman to manager and ended a successful, happy man.

Instead of a miserable and futile "if only," he experienced a succession of exciting "next times." The process of thinking, which brought about this happy result in the life of Ken Butterfield, can do the same in the life of Mr. or Ms. Anybody. Oh, yes, Ken paid back every cent pronto. And those seven dirty one-dollar bills? He saved one and had it framed to hang on his office wall. His name really wasn't Ken Butterfield, but all other facts in this story are accurate. The important fact is that this man achieved happiness at last.

Two important ideas are inherent in all improvement, in all progress. One was suggested by my friend James R. Knapp when Ruth and I were having dinner with him and his wife Sally one night in Los Angeles. We were talking about how one can always do a better job and reach an improved level of personal achievement. Jim said, "It's basic to take corrective action when things are not going right." That truly lays the matter on the line. Decide to get through with what you currently are doing incorrectly. Take corrective action at once, for only then can you begin the move up to a superior performance.

Corollary to that procedure is an idea that is constantly stressed by another friend, W. Clement Stone, well-known philanthropist and publisher. "Do it now," reiterates Clem Stone. These two ideas taken together will bring about remarkable change and improvement: take corrective action and do it now.

We hear much about timing, that mystic moment when all elements are just right or the sudden awareness that corrective action is needed. Just how can a person who has been muddling along on the edge of failure or living with a feeling of inadequate fulfillment suddenly become so acutely sensitive as to know when the right time comes for taking corrective action?

In some cases a person has the power to create the correct timing. If change is to be considered, it must be right, it must be sensible, it must be within the realm of possibility. The steps are simple: stop, think, visualize, pray. If all the elements are positive, the individual can force the timing by assertive control.

I have discovered that a lot of people are doing things and doing them well, but in their hearts they would rather be doing something else. Now and then we are surprised when some very successful person suddenly changes career in midlife and becomes equally successful in a new role.

Take William Howard, for example. Again I am using a fictitious name, because this man is quite well-known. Only by promising to withhold his identity would he give me permission to tell his story. As a young boy in a small midwestern town, he was fascinated by printing shops and newspapers. He hung around the press room after school, watching compositors make up the paper, and he was thrilled by the excitement of getting the evening edition onto the streets. As a newsboy, expertly sailing his papers onto the doorsteps along his route, he dreamed big dreams of that exciting time when he would be a reporter on a big city daily or top editor of a small town paper. He got printer's ink on his fingers, and as they say, it can never be rubbed off.

But his parents had other dreams for him. They wanted him to be something else. They did not pressure him, but he well knew their desires, and so it was that he turned his back on the world of publishing to enter an entirely different line of work.

William Howard proved to be very good at it too. He became rather famous in the field of endeavor his parents wanted for him. People generally said that he was cut out for the job in which, over the years, he distinguished himself. But as he grew older and received many honors in his profession, he still dreamed of publishing. He learned that some dreams never die. At heart he was an unsatisfied publisher. Even after many years, the ink had not rubbed off.

Did what he was actually thinking make sense after all those years? Could he even contemplate leaving all he had done and actually abandon a brilliant career in one field to return to his boyhood dreams? He studied his fingers. Unlike those of the boy, they were now gnarled a bit. But the printer's ink was still there. His first love was still strong in his heart. For months he vacillated. But he had fulfilled his parents' desire, and they were long gone from this world. So why not? Then one night as he walked under the ancient maples on his farm, he made the decision. He made the turn back to boyhood dreams. He took corrective action on his career. "Do it now," something whispered. That is how he left the career of a lifetime and embarked upon a new old one. William Howard went back to publishing. And happiness came to him at last, quite like it was in boyhood's happy hour.

Every one of us is entitled, I believe, to find his or her true self in this life. If you have run a drugstore for years but have wanted to be a musician, let's say, why not shift gears and give it a try? Or if you have been a musician but would rather run a drugstore, you are entitled to realize your dreams and be yourself. Deep inner dreams are never to be discounted in the fulfilled life. Since the Creator undoubtedly put those dreams in your heart in the first place, they have to be treated with respect. In all of this, of course, you must take your responsibilities into account.

My cousin Philip Henderson was a very successful educator. For some years he was an executive at Mount Holyoke. Later he served as president of Western College for Women at Oxford, Ohio. His father, my uncle, Hershel Henderson, was a building and loan executive, a banker and farm owner. He became a wealthy man, a leading businessman in Highland County, Ohio. He wanted Philip, his elder son, to follow in his footsteps, but the son was not made of the same stuff. He became a student, a thinker, a teacher, and in those activities he found peace and happiness as well as success. His younger brother, Howard, took over their father's business affairs and handled them very successfully. Both boys seemed to have found themselves—the one in education, the other in business.

I became a public speaker and for years have spoken almost everywhere to all sorts of public gatherings. One night Philip attended one of my speeches in a large hall in Cincinnati. Afterward in my hotel room we sat relaxing. The conversation proved memorable for me. "Norman," said Philip, "you must be pretty satisfied with yourself. You received a standing ovation from that big crowd before you spoke and another afterward. The people liked you. In fact, they thought you were great. But would you like to know what I, your cousin who has known you all your life, think about your performance tonight?" (I might say that I have an autographed picture of Philip on which he has written, "From your cousin and your best friend.")

I was prepared for a pretty forthright remark, since he has always been direct and honest. "I think," he said, "that you did not give that speech all you've got. You were coasting. All you wanted was to get it over with. Don't you really like to speak?" he asked. "I know you are completely sincere and believe what you say, but the all-out eager enthusiasm doesn't come through because somehow you don't seem to take entire joy in speaking."

His insight was accurate. I have a message of positive thinking or positive faith in which I believe with passionate fervor, but the technique of communication is always difficult. I can do it better in writing, perhaps. Speaking has always been a rather painful effort for me, and I took on a mild dislike for it which Philip picked up on.

I am very lucky to have such a good friend, someone who devotedly loves me and can, therefore, lay it out forcefully for my own good. I never forgot this conversation with my cousin who was as close as a brother. He made me see that I must love people to be effective as a speaker and I must also try to rid myself of the dislike of public speaking itself. As I have sought to achieve a more positive attitude toward public speaking, my total happiness has increased.

It is important to love what you are doing, to like your job. When you do, you are bound to give it more of yourself. And the more you give of yourself, the more life will give back to you. As someone said, "Love life and life will love you back." So, let me be your friend. If, as my cousin said, you are coasting, I urge you to release yourself more completely to give yourself, really give yourself. To the extent to which you do this, the deep happiness inherent in your nature will surge through you. After all, the important thing is to find yourself, know yourself, believe in yourself, and give yourself. Then and then only will your life become what it was meant to be, a glorious and satisfying experience every day.

As I think about the happiness I have experienced, it seems that it has come in its most acute and pleasing form when I have received a kindness or when I have given kindness. I have concluded that kindness received and kindness given are basic factors in happiness attained. Recall little acts of kindness that you have received or given, and note that they are still capable of stimulating a happy feeling even though they may have occurred long ago.

I shall never forget the morning I received word that my mother had died. I was devastated. At first I was of a mind to cancel a speaking engagement scheduled for that day on the Jersey shore. But my mother had always taught her children to carry on and fulfill their duties. Disconsolately I boarded a train. Looking out the car window and remembering life with her from the earliest years, I suddenly felt a hand on my shoulder. It was an old friend, Colonel Myron Robinson.

"Where are you going?" I asked.

"Oh, some of the boys are having a clambake down at Cape May." He was an aide to the governor of New Jersey at that time. He sat down beside me. Then seeming to detect something amiss, he asked, "What's the matter? You don't seem your usual cheery self." I told him of my mother's death. Making no response beyond placing a hand on my knee, he sat silently and, to my surprise, left the train with me at my stop. "I really don't like clambakes. So if you don't mind, I'd like to hear you speak," he explained.

Myron stayed with me all day long. When we arrived back in Penn Station, New York, he said, "I'll have to leave you here." Then he added, "You've helped me over some rough ones, son. I love you and know how you feel about your dear mother." Patting me on the back, he turned to leave, but as he did, I noticed tears in his eyes.

Myron didn't say much during that day. A long while later Myron Robinson said, "You know something? I have a happy feeling every time I think of that day we spent together." Of course he did because he gave of himself to a friend who will ever think of him as one of the kindest men he ever knew. He is gone now, but I shall never forget him. He brought peace and comfort to a friend simply by showing love. Even in sorrow, happiness began a return.

As I write this chapter, Ruth and I are in Hong Kong. Recently we were walking on a crowded high overpass, and we came to a steep flight of steps leading down to the street. Not looking too well where I was going, I suddenly stumbled and fell. Ruth was dragged down with me since she was holding my arm. We were surrounded by hundreds in the hurrying throng, and though we struggled to rise, no one came to our aid until I heard the sweet voice of a young Chinese girl saying in clear English, "Let me help you, sir." Slight though she was, she gave both of us strong assistance and then insisted upon escorting us down the precipitous flight of stairs.

We protested that we were quite all right, but she made sure of that before she would leave us. "You are very kind," I said, to which she replied, "You must know, sir, that it gives me pleasure to help." I noticed that she had a happy look on her face as she said that.

Since it appears that helping someone produces a feeling of happiness, it follows that you can increase your happiness by simply adding to the number of times you perform an act of kindness. You will discover that happiness will be your primary state of mind if you can multiply the number of kindnesses performed. A person is fortunate to make such discovery.

Quite inadvertently I participated in a small way in opening up a happier life for a stranger on the streets of New York when I took another tumble. The streets were thick with ice following a bitter cold spell. To get in my daily two- to three-mile hike, I walked this day to an office I had on lower Fifth Avenue. At one crossing on a sheet of glare ice, my feet suddenly went out from under me, and I slid on my back across the intersection, ending up prone in the gutter. I can't imagine a more helpless situation than skidding over glare ice in such a position.

Soon, bending over me was a young man wearing a parka. He hoisted me to my feet and guided me to the sidewalk. Solicitously he asked how I felt, whether there were any indications that might mean broken bones. Assured that all was well, we proceeded along the avenue together. As we came to the next street, I saw that the crossing was equally icy. The young man took my arm, and we traversed the intersection safely. "You look familiar to me," he said. "What is your name?" When I told him, he chuckled. "Wait until I tell my friends that I picked Norman Vincent Peale up out of the gutter." We parted after that cheerful banter, and I felt it was a happy episode for us both.

Very frequently happiness eludes those who are emotionally disorganized or filled with anxiety. Anxiety is a dark, mostly irrational, sometimes terrifying mental thought that something bad is going to happen. Anxiety, long-held, discolors thought processes to such an extent that happiness can scarcely develop. And so prevalent is anxiety currently that a distinguished psychiatrist has labeled it "the great modern plague."

Achieving a calm, secure mental attitude is basic to the attainment of happiness. And as you develop such a serene mental attitude, the assurance that comes from faith is most important. It is, I believe, a well-established fact that where faith is weak, anxiety will be proportionately strong; where faith is strong, anxiety will be less of a problem. As the Scripture says, "If you have faith as a mustard seed, . . . nothing will be impossible for you" (Matt. 17:20). When you know that you can handle anything that comes up, you are very likely to be a serene, happy person. Therefore, if happiness is to be yours, you must not allow anxiety to dominate you.

How can you get the kind of faith that rids you of fear, worry, and anxiety? Start thinking faith, affirming faith, and acting on the basis of faith. Practice the "as if" principle because it is very powerful. By acting as if you have faith, your consciousness will accept the idea that you do, for a fact, have faith, and you will have it. I gave this advice once to a New York business executive, and it brought him out of a breakdown and restored him to good health. He had the capacity to believe, the mental power to accept a positive idea and go with it.

This man's wife asked me to see him after his doctor told her that the illness was thought-induced. The doctor believed that fear had so gripped this man that he was actually ill as a result. He was afraid, even terrorized, of a sudden heart attack. This fear was brought on by the sudden death of three rather close business associates, and it happened that all three were in the late-forty age bracket, the same relative age as himself.

Suddenly he began to picture himself as the next victim of such a devastating attack. He developed an acute anxiety neurosis. Despite medical assurance that his heart was sound and that there were no symptoms suggesting a problem, his fear produced powerfully adverse reactions.

Before seeing the patient I discussed the case with the doctor, and in our conversation I quoted the words from Job 3:25, "For the thing I greatly feared has come upon me."

The doctor nodded. "That is a true insight. A person can greatly fear something so strongly as to actually create the condition feared or bring about a similar result," he said.

"How may it be counteracted?" I asked.

He considered that question thoughtfully, then said, "Put against that scriptural statement a similar truth that what I greatly believe can also come upon me. In other words, if fear can make you sick, a strong faith can make you well. So," he concluded, "let's prescribe faith to our friend." Both of us, the doctor of medicine and the doctor of the Spirit, each in his own way, administered a healing therapy.

"I began taking huge doses of faith" is the way the man described his changed attitude. It was not easy going because fear is difficult to dislodge. But faith is more powerful than fear, and when one is determined, as he was, to get rid of the fear destroying him, he ultimately becomes a well man. He became a daily reader of the Bible, and he found one statement he credits with his healing: "I sought the LORD, and He heard me,/And delivered me from all my fears" (Ps. 34.4). "I believe that," he said," and that did it. I found happiness at last."

Attitude has so much to do with whether we are or are not happy persons that in all my books I have stressed positive thinking. The late William Lyon Phelps, famous professor of English at Yale University, used to say that "he is the happiest who thinks the happiest thoughts." It is true that our thoughts determine whether we are miserable or happy in life. We create the world in which we live by the thought patterns that activate our minds. It follows, therefore, that if we are to achieve lasting happiness, we will have to cultivate the thoughts that produce happiness. If we permit ourselves to nurture critical thoughts, hateful thoughts, and mental attitudes other than those of goodwill and generosity of spirit, we will develop into unhappy people. We become, to a great extent, like the thoughts we habitually think.

As I said earlier, it so happens that I am writing this chapter in the city of Hong Kong where I am on a mission for *Guideposts* magazine. I remember a man I met in a hotel elevator in this city years ago. He asked, "Are you Norman Peale?" When I admitted my identity, he said he was a reader of my books and wondered if he might make an appointment to discuss a personal problem.

When I met with this man later, he told me he was the Far Eastern representative of a business headquartered in the United States. Though he had achieved a good post in his business and should be a happy person, he wasn't happy at all. On the contrary, he was "pretty disgusted." Could I make any creative suggestions? He wanted to be a positive person and get some happiness in his life.

In an effort to appraise the nature of his thoughts, I encouraged him to talk. I have found that happiness or the lack of it quite often lies in the quality of a person's thinking. It came out in conversation that he had an enormous number of dislikes of people, of groups, and of business organizations. Many of these were people he did not know personally and organizations with which he had no contact. For example, he had a strong dislike of several retail shops, whom he termed "smug stuffed shirts." I asked if he knew the managers personally, and he admitted that he did not even know their names. He had a similar feeling for the *New York Times* newspaper which he said he "wouldn't be caught dead reading." Certain people whose names appeared often in print had his antipathy, although he did not know them personally. He was a victim of strong dislikes that verged on hate, all of them irrational.

As he expressed his negative attitudes, I realized that he actually seemed to dislike himself to some extent. It occurred to me as we talked that perhaps to the next person with whom he discussed his problem, he might very well express dislike of me as well. He was pathetically mixed up, jealous, critical, totally lacking in understanding, compassion, and respect for personality.

I suggested that he take hold of his thoughts and drill himself in appreciation, in respect for all people, in seeing the best at all times. Furthermore, I urged him to change his attitude in human relations. Only then could he develop the quality of human respect that could create within his mind a spirit of happiness. He was so very unhappy that I found him ready to undertake any reasonable program. I suggested a plan for thought reversal which proved effective.

* * *

1. He was to look for the good points in the retail shops and the *New York Times* daily paper. He was to find some positive good in the organizations he hated and speak about them only when he could emphasize the positive.
2. When he found himself irrationally disliking persons, he was to deliberately invest them with the good qualities they doubtless possessed.
3. He was deliberately to send out, by thought vibrations, good concepts to cancel out the dislikes he had previously expressed so freely.
4. He was to develop the qualities of respect, compassion, and goodwill to everyone.
5. He was to believe that by a program of spiritual healing of his thoughts, he would become a caring, generously disposed human being.

In the years following he reported now and then on his "personality rebuilding," as he called it, at which he worked in all sincerity. Most recently he wrote me, "With God's help I believe I am a different man from the one you talked with in Hong Kong and," I was pleased that he added, "I am really finding happiness at last."

Perhaps the summation is best expressed by the great German philosopher Immanuel Kant (1724–1804), "It is God's will, not merely that we should be happy, but that we should make ourselves happy."

P.S.

Some letters have a P.S. because the writer wishes to add a further word. Why not a P.S. to a book also? So here is my P.S. and a few personal words as well.

Have you wondered why I included the modifying word *Some* in the title? Positive thinking can definitely help anyone, and millions of people have creatively adapted into their lifestyle the idea of positive thinking with positive—and often dramatic—results. But some positive thinkers get more powerful results than others.

Why do these positive thinkers get results that justify calling their outcomes powerful? They get powerful results because they study and believe and practice the principles outlined with deep desire, intensity of purpose, and a persistence that sets them off from the average.

These *Some* positive thinkers have lifted themselves into

an upper category of human beings called *believers*. They are a rare kind of folk who are activated by a realistic faith in their own potential. As children of God in whose image they were created, they accept positive principles as fact. They resolutely put these principles to work and thereby achieve powerful results.

Thomas A. Edison said, "If we were to do all we are capable of doing we would literally astonish ourselves." And so *Some* positive thinkers do actually astonish themselves, and they also accept as fact the promise of Jesus Christ, "If you have faith as a mustard seed . . . nothing will be impossible unto you" (Matt. 17:20).

So I urge you to be a believer, an all-the-way believer in God, in life, and in yourself. I might add, the flip side of this advice is to urge you also to be a follower, a listener, a disciple under His Lordship. In so doing, you will experience life to the full and extend yourself far beyond what you may have dreamed possible. Continue to study and practice until you become one of those achieving positive thinkers who go beyond the mediocre, who surpass the average, and who, as wholehearted believers, get powerful results.

Part II POWER of the PLUS FACTOR

Sincere appreciation to
my longtime friend Arthur Gordon
who lent his great skill
and dedicated thought
to the creation of this book.
And to Sybil Light, my secretary,
for her valuable assistance
in the preparation of the manuscript.

Contents

1.

The Challenge of the PLUS FACTOR

W*hat* if I were to tell you that there is a power within you that can revolutionize your life. A power that is invisible, intangible, but completely real.

A power that can transform you so dramatically that under its influence and guidance you can become an entirely new person, stronger, more confident, better balanced, more energetic, more resilient, more capable of coping with the ever-increasing complexity of modern living.

Suppose I added that this remarkable force could lift you from failure to success, from illness to health, from self-doubt to self-assurance.

And then, if I assured you further that it could help you find congenial friends, solve problems, break out of stale habits, fairly explode into a world totally different from the world you have known before, a world of enthusiasm and exhilaration and understanding and joy—what would your reaction be?

I think you'd want to find out about this power. What is it called? Where does it come from? How do I find it? What must I do to make it operative in my life?

My answers might surprise you because basically they are so simple. Everyone knows that there is a life force that sustains and animates every living thing on this planet of ours. With it, you are alive. Without it, you are dead. This life force was put into all of us by God Himself. What I'm writing about here is a special manifestation of it, a special concentration of it that will do remarkable things for those who understand it and reach for it and allow it to function in their lives.

I call it the Plus Factor.

It's the quality of *extra*-ness that we see in certain people.

People who live with more eagerness, more energy, more enthusiasm than others.

Who set higher goals and achieve them more often.

Who keep going despite adversity and hardship.

Who shrug off misfortune and give out warmth and caring and encouragement wherever they go.

People, in short, who have, in themselves, a marvelous Plus Factor at work.

Well, you may say, I know such people, but what about me? How do I get hold of this extra-ness? Where can I find this Plus Factor?

The answer to that is simple, too. You will find it in the last place you might think of: within yourself.

When the good Lord fashions a human being like you or me, how does He go about it? I like to think that first He arranges all the intricate parts of the body so that they are in balance and harmony with one another: the skin, the bones, the nerves, all the elements that go into a marvelous machine designed to last a lifetime.

But He, who created us "a little lower than the angels," adds one thing more. He gives each of us a power that I call the Plus Factor—that extra something in the spirit.

There it remains, deep in the personality of every individual. You don't have to search for it; it's already there. But there is one thing you must realize about the Plus Factor. Its power is potential, but it is not self-activating. It is latent in human beings and will remain latent until it is activated.

That is why it manifests itself more strongly in some people than in others. They are the people who have learned how to call it forth.

If you want this wonderful stream of power to be activated in you, there are four preliminary things you should do.

- First, make the key discovery that the Plus Factor is no myth, no abstraction, but a reality that has been recognized and used by wise men and women for centuries.
- Next, you accept the fact that it is already planted inside of you, waiting to be released.
- Then you decide you want it to become operative. There can be no maybes, no hesitancies, no halfheartedness about this. You must want it intensely, urgently, ardently. And you must want it *now*.
- You decide to face the fact that this marvelous potential built into you is not being fully realized. You admit that in the past—partly through ignorance—it has been blocked, ignored, neglected. You make a promise to yourself to rearrange your thought patterns so that the blocks are removed, and the power can come surging through.
- Finally you do the thing that gives power to your life—the Scripture method, "To as many as received him, to them gave he the power to become . . ." (see John 1:12).

We live in a universe of laws that operate in the spiritual as well as the physical world. And here is the crucial thing to remember: *The Plus Factor makes its appearance in a person's life in proportion as that person is in harmony with God and His universal laws.*

If you want the Plus Factor to operate in your life, if you want to be on the receiving end of the extra flow of power, you need to learn to think a certain way and act a certain way and be a certain kind of person.

This learning process is well within the reach of all of us, and this book is designed to help you master it. But don't expect that mastery to come easily. The Plus Factor is implanted in all of us. But it is planted deep.

It is almost as if the Creator knew that a degree of struggle is good for His children. He also knew that they value most what they have to work for. Consequently, He arranged things so that the Plus Factor is not going to emerge spontaneously in a person. It has to be understood and activated. The Lord installed this hidden dynamo, but it's our job to remove the blocks and hindrances that short-circuit the emergence of power. It's our job, to open the doors of our inner selves and let this force, this Plus Factor, come through.

You can often tell at a glance whether the Plus Factor is working in people or not. You see a young woman walking down a city street, bright hair blowing in the wind, an almost tangible aura of health and vitality about her, confidence in her clear eyes, a sense of purpose in her stride, and you say to yourself, "Yes, there it is. She has it. She has the Plus Factor and the Plus Factor has her."

Then you come upon some unfortunate derelict slumped against a wall, head sunk on chest, eyes staring vacantly into space, and you know very well that the Plus Factor is not operative. It has been blocked by some or all of a whole series of minus factors: alcohol, drugs, fear, anxiety, guilt, disease, negated to the point where the individual is no longer able to cope with even the most elementary challenge of existence. Or there may be a person of obvious ability who is not living at a level of creativity that his aptitudes indicate he should attain.

I do not believe there is any exact blueprint or precise formula for the release of the Plus Factor. If there were, we would all have it to a far greater extent than we do. But the more we learn to believe in it, trust it, and open ourselves to it, the more we find that goals are achieved, ambitions are realized, high energy levels are maintained, fears and tensions subside, and spiritual growth becomes not just possible but almost inevitable.

In this book I shall indicate some of the key areas of living, and show how the Plus Factor has helped people in times of difficulty or distress, and offer suggestions that will help the reader find it and use it. The purpose of this book is to make possible a better understanding of this inner potential and make it begin to operate in people.

Let's begin where the Plus Factor impinges on an intangible and remarkable aspect of human existence: the area of dreams.

2.

The PLUS FACTOR and Creative Dreaming

Do you sometimes feel that you are living below your potential?

Are you ever troubled by the thought that greater energies, more creative ideas, and problem-solving capacities are locked away inside you?

If so, you are not alone. We *all* have such feelings from time to time.

I think such feelings come from an awareness that the life force in each of us is a fraction of the great universal Life Force that we call God. Since we are made in His image, as the Bible says we are, then we should have access to all the power we need to live successfully and triumphantly. The Plus Factor should operate in us, not just now and then, but all the time.

Why don't we have it every minute, every hour? Because we let certain things block it. Ignorance can block it. Fear can block it. Hatred, envy, anger, anxiety, negative thoughts, selfish actions . . . all these things can keep the Plus Factor from functioning. Some of it may get through, enough perhaps to keep us going, barely. But it will be only a trickle instead of the powerful force it is supposed to be.

Fortunately, just as there are attitudes and actions that narrow the flow of power, there are some that widen the channel and let more of the power through. The first step to be taken in order to start the Plus Factor operating is to learn to be a creative dreamer.

When I use the word *dream* the reference is not to those shadowy images that flicker through our minds when we are asleep. No, the dreams I'm writing about are the indistinct hopes, the far-off visions, the first faint stirrings of the imagination that come when we are in the earliest stages of planning something worthwhile. And there's a wonderful thing about such dreams. In some uncanny way that no one fully understands, they seem to contain the seeds of their own fulfillment. If you dream something long enough and hard enough, a door seems to open and through that door come mighty forces that will guide and support you in your efforts to make the dream come true.

Creative dreaming, in other words, activates the release of power that we call the Plus Factor.

Hard-nosed, practical people sometimes scoff at such a notion. To them the term *dreamer* implies vagueness and impracticality.

I remember vividly a conversation I had as a young man with my crusty old Uncle Herschel. He was a top businessman and a pillar of his community, but he could be gruff on occasion.

To get through college I had to borrow money. Since Uncle Herschel was the one member of the family who had any money, I borrowed from him. Then after college, when I wanted to go to graduate school, I needed more money; so I went to see Uncle Herschel again.

"Uncle Herschel," I said, "I know I still owe you some money, but now I'd like to borrow some more."

Uncle Herschel did not look exactly overjoyed. "What do you want more for?" he demanded.

"I want to become a minister," I said. "The world is full of people who need help. I'd like to do something about people's problems. I have a dream of helping people."

Uncle Herschel gave a loud snort. "Dreams!" he said. "Dreams won't get you anywhere!"

Right behind him on the wall was a framed copy of the Declaration of Independence. I knew he thought a great deal of it, so I pointed to it. "That was made by dreams," I told him. "The men who signed that piece of paper had a dream—a dream of a free nation, under God. That document is the embodiment of their dream. Because they had a dream, you and I are living here in freedom today."

Uncle Herschel mumbled and grumbled for a while, but he let me have the loan. And I guess he dreamed that I would pay him back, because eventually I did. I cherish the memory of the good man.

The world has always been full of dramatic examples of what can happen when one determined man or woman locks his or her mind around a dream and lets the Plus Factor begin to come through. Almost two centuries ago William Lloyd Garrison was living in a nation where human slavery was accepted as a natural and even desirable state of affairs. But Garrison decided that it was a monstrous crime against God and humanity. He began to dream of a nation where slavery no longer existed. He began to dream that he—one lonely individual—could actually help make this stupendous change come to pass. He said to himself, in this impossible dream, "I am going to destroy slavery in this land."

The odds against him were overwhelming. The general assembly of a church had stated that slavery was ordained by God. Prominent statesmen insisted that the whole edifice of our country rested on slavery.

Such was the status of slavery in the United States, economically blessed by the North as well as the South, when William Lloyd Garrison dared to dream his dream. But with a tremendous surge of power from the Plus Factor he forged his dream into a "hammer," and he pounded it against this great rock of slavery. People jeered and laughed, but year after year Garrison continued to beat with his hammer, until the hammer grew and became a mighty sledge whose thunderings could be heard throughout the land. Finally a crack appeared in the solid monolith of slavery, and the thrilling fact is that, finally slavery was outlawed in the United States.

Remember, too, what Martin Luther King said a hundred years later, when he talked of a world in which the remnants of racism and prejudice would be abolished? He said, "I have a dream . . ."

Dreamers are always optimists. A pessimist—someone who sees only negative possibilities—believes that nothing good is likely to happen. But dreamers believe that nothing is too good to be true. They live with excitement, because their dreams help them generate it. My mother was a dreamer: She saw romance and poetry in everything. I remember one foggy night on a Hudson River ferryboat when she spent half an hour trying to make me see and feel the thrill and mystery of great ships passing one another in the darkness, lights glowing dimly, whistles bellowing hoarsely. And I guess she succeeded, because after all these years I remember it still.

Sometimes that marvelous mechanism, the unconscious mind, will use an actual dream—the kind that comes while we're sleeping—to send a message to someone who has been wrestling with a problem. A few years ago in Texas an unemployed salesman named Jim Head, unable to find a selling job, had been trying to earn a few dollars by making cheesecakes—his mother had been a notable cook—and selling them to friends. But the income from this fell far short of his needs. Then one night he had an astonishingly "real" dream in which he saw himself baking a cake, using all sorts of unusual ingredients. So clear was the dream and so detailed the recipe that he even remembered when he woke up how much baking soda he had used.

Amazed by the vividness of this dream sequence, he went into the kitchen, and concocted a cake exactly to the dream specifications. When a neighbor came in later Jim offered him a piece. "Yahoo!" cried the visitor. "It's teriffic!"

Thus was born the Yahoo cake. Baked in the shape of the Lone Star State, it has sold tremendously. Jim Head had little experience as a baker; he knew nothing about food distribution. But the Plus Factor that came surging in on the heels of that compelling dream gave him the energy and the optimism to overcome all such handicaps and limitations. Today he is a happy and successful man.

Dreams know no boundaries of age or race or nationality. Not long ago in Japan, we were staying in a lovely new hotel on a hillside just outside the center of Tokyo. The management was very kind to me, and so when time came to leave I asked to see the owner to express my thanks. He was a dignified Japanese gentleman at whose hotel in Kyoto I had stayed several times. He was now eighty years old but still full of vitality and animation. I asked him how he came to be in the hotel business, expressing admiration for his enterprise and energy in building and running a big, new hotel at an age when most men would long since have retired.

"Oh," he said, "as you know, this is not my only hotel. I have four others. All my life I've dreamed of being a good innkeeper. As a child, I set that goal for myself. I dreamed it would happen. I believed it would happen. And it did happen. To be successful you must first have a dream. Then you must work very hard. Finally, if you dream hard and work hard, the dream comes true. Isn't that so in your country also?"

I assured him that it was. I told him how my friend Bill Marriott, who built a great hotel empire, started with a little root beer stand and no money at all. I also told about another friend, Dave Thomas, the president and founder of Wendy's restaurants, who started out as a dishwasher in Annapolis, but this did not stop him. Why? Because he had a dream—a dream of a restaurant that offered only one item: a superb hamburger. He had the dream and he had the willingness to work, and again, when those two explosive ingredients were mixed together, the Plus Factor was liberated and swept him to astonishing success.

I believe the long dreams we dream as children have a lasting effect upon our lives. Once I asked Dorothy Draper, one of the foremost interior designers in America, to decorate our Institutes of Religion and Health in New York City. Dorothy had a genius for combining colors in a most arresting and dramatic way. She told us that color can either elevate or depress the spirit. So she used bright colors to uplift and stimulate emotions, and soft colors to reduce tension. She also told me that as a little girl, living in poverty in a very plain and drab house, she used to lie in bed and in her mind endow her room with the radiance of all the colors of the spectrum. Her dream was that some day she would lift the spirits of thousands of people everywhere by her infusions of color. And that is exactly what she did.

A well-known writer and storyteller once told me that when he was a very small child of five or six he had a game he would play on cold winter nights. He would crawl under the covers to the foot of his bed, peer out, and watch the embers of the coal fire in his room slowly die away. Deep in the glowing embers, his imagination would see the towering battlements of flaming castles, burning caves where fiery dragons hid, villages swept by the winds of war.

Then, when the fire was out, he would play another game. He would throw off his covers and imagine that he was a poor lost waif shivering alone on an icy street. When he really did begin to shiver, he would pretend that some kind traveler came by and covered him with a cloak (here he would pull up one blanket). Then a fairy godmother would come and add another covering. A whole procession of good-hearted, imaginary passersby would cover him. Then he would fall asleep, and in the morning his parents would wonder why he was sleeping upside down in his bed.

"I never told them," he said with a sheepish smile. "But you know, those dreams came true. All through my life I have had kindly people come to my aid whenever I was in trouble, or needed help or protection."

An example of the Plus Factor in action? He believed it was.

The most memorable song in the musical play *Man of La Mancha* is the one where Don Quixote urges all who will listen to him to "dream the impossible dream." It's a song based on the old knight's burning conviction that the Plus Factor will come to the aid of anyone who does. In fact, the more impossible the dream, the promise says, the greater is the power that will come.

In Chicago years ago there was a ragged newsboy who used to huddle on a sidewalk grating near the *Chicago Tribune* building because the flow of heat from the presses operating in the basement of the building kept him warm. From that vantage point, the boy could see well-dressed men and women going into a theater across the street where brilliant lights on the marquee spelled out the evening's attraction. He decided one cold night that some day he would be that attraction himself, and to record the birth of this impossible dream he took a rusty nail and scratched his name and date on the concrete of a windowsill behind the grating. And the years passed, and the dream did not die, and the day came when the ragged newsboy, now attired in white tie and tails, held the crowds that came to the theater spellbound with the most astounding array of magical tricks the stage had ever seen. He was Howard Thurston, the great magician, and sometimes he would take his friends and show them the name and the date dimly scratched on the concrete windowsill so many years before.

A dream just as impossible as that once came to a little black child living in an orphanage in Troy, New York. Her name was Dorothy Brown. When Dorothy was five years old, she was taken to a hospital for a tonsillectomy. Most youngsters would have been frightened, or at least apprehensive, but Dorothy wasn't. She was fascinated by the wondrous world of medicine in which she found herself. People helping other people by relieving pain, setting broken bones, curing diseases. Then and there, Dorothy Brown decided that some day she would be part of that world. She was only five years old, but she set a goal for herself: Eventually she would become a doctor.

It was a dream that seemed absolutely hopeless. Born out of wedlock, she had been placed in the orphanage because her mother could not afford to keep her. It was understood that when she reached the age when other children enter high school, she would have to go to work. She had no friends outside the orphanage, no family, no connections of any kind. And yet . . .

And yet, something flickered inside this child, a tiny spark that became a flame. A flame that ignored all the odds, all the laws of probability. A flame breathed on by the Plus Factor, and consequently a flame that didn't go out.

One day this little girl, Dorothy Brown, asked the superintendent of the orphanage why she never had any visitors, as some of the other children did. That kind man mentioned this to some of his friends at the church he attended. The result was that a white family named Coffeen came to see the child. When Dorothy told them she intended to be a doctor, they listened and they didn't laugh. They felt her chances were nonexistent, but still they gave her attention and affection and encouragement.

As was the orphanage custom in those days, at the age of fourteen Dorothy went to work as a maid, earning $14 a week. Two dollars a day. There were many books in her employer's home, and she was allowed to read them. In two years, she saved $500, and decided to register for high school. When the registrar asked for her home address, she had to admit that she had no job, no home, no address.

But when a person has the aura of the Plus Factor about her, other people step forward to help, impelled by impulses that they may or may not understand. The principal of the high school listened to Dorothy's story. Then he found a couple who agreed to take her in as a boarder. She paid for her room as long as her money held out. When it ran out, the couple kept her anyway.

When she graduated from high school, she went back to being a maid in order to earn money for college. At the wages then being paid, she figured it would take her eleven years. But her faith in her dream never faltered. Every night she asked God to help her turn it into a reality. She worked extra hours. She took on extra jobs. Something gave her the endurance and energy she needed. I'm convinced it was the Plus Factor.

One of her employers, hearing her talk of becoming a doctor, told her of a scholarship being offered by a small Methodist college in North Carolina. She applied for that scholarship and won it. She took all the science and premed courses that were offered. But when finally she graduated, there was no money for medical school.

When you are really in the flow of the Plus Factor, when its invisible current is supporting and sustaining you, it sometimes seems that even the mighty sweep of world events reaches out to help. The onset of World War II caused a shortage of manpower, and the army turned to women with a background in science to work as inspectors in ordnance depots. In two years, Dorothy Brown saved $2,000. It still wasn't enough, but she could wait no longer. She entered Meharry Medical College in Nashville, Tennessee. When her funds ran out, friends came to her aid. And the day finally came when the friendless little waif from the orphanage in Troy, New York, was a doctor at last.

What does Dr. Brown herself think about all this? She believes quite simply that now she is living the dream that entered her mind when she was five years old. She believes that just as God gives each one of us our special talent, so He gives us dreams to make us aware of that talent. "It doesn't matter," she says, "how farfetched or unattainable the dream may seem. If we remain steadfast, if we have enough faith in God and in ourselves to go to work and stay at work trying to make the dream come true, then God puts into our lives the people who, out of their love for Him and for us, will do for us what we cannot do for ourselves."

A dream vividly imagined. A goal tenaciously pursued. A faith that God will help you with a worthy ambition. An unshakable determination to work and work and keep on working. These are all keys that open the door to the power that we call the Plus Factor.

Dreams are not just idle nothings. They are the parents of possibilities. Possibilities are the descendants of dreams. Without the one, there can never be the other. Dream, therefore. Dream big, dream long, dream strong. And remember . . .

Sometimes the Plus Factor is only a dream away.

3.

The PLUS FACTOR and Setting Goals

Let's assume you have begun to liberate the Plus Factor in your nature by the process of creative dreaming.

Now what must you do?

Since the Plus Factor is to function with ever-increasing power, you must work on those dreams.

You need to shape them, focus them, hammer them down to their essence.

You have to build a viaduct over which they can pass from the world of dreams to the world of reality.

In other words, you have to learn to set goals.

Four centuries ago the great French essayist Michel de Montaigne wrote these words: "No wind favors him who has no destined port."

He meant that a person without clear-cut goals in life is forever doomed to sail in circles, always frustrated, always rudderless, never getting anywhere.

Montaigne's words were true then and perhaps they're even more true today, because the world has become a more complex and competitive place. In this fast-moving, super-specialized century, unless you are able clearly and calmly and deliberately to set goals for yourself, you are becalmed in indecision and inertia.

When people set goals for themselves that are clear and distinct; when they hold tenaciously to those goals through times of disappointment, frustration, or even apparent failure; when they image themselves progressing steadily toward those goals and finally achieving them, then a force emerges from deep within them so powerful that it is virtually irresistible. That is the Plus Factor.

Once the Plus Factor makes its appearance and really takes hold, the surge of energy and confidence becomes so strong that it overcomes all obstacles. Let me give you an example from a small farming community in eastern Pennsylvania.

Walter Harter, just graduated from high school in that small town, seemed like quite an ordinary young man. He had a slight limp caused by a badly broken leg in childhood. Otherwise he seemed like an average young fellow, unable to go to college because his family couldn't afford it.

As any farmer can tell you today, things can get very tough in a farming community. Certainly there were few openings for any kind of work in Walter Harter's area. But a dream and a plan had been stirring in the back of this young man's mind. And when a dream and a plan get together, the result can be a goal . . . sometimes a goal that opens the door to the Plus Factor.

In Walter Harter's case, the goal was to find work in New York City, which he had never visited, and where he didn't know a soul. Only one thing could have given him the unshakable conviction that he could achieve such a goal: the Plus Factor within.

Walter Harter went to the local telephone office and borrowed the New York City telephone directory. He looked up the listings of various stores in the metropolitan area. Finally he decided to concentrate on a well-known chain of stores. There were addresses for 393 of them scattered over Manhattan, Brooklyn, Queens, Long Island, and the Bronx. Walter Harter told himself that among all those stores there had to be an opening for him. He made up his mind to write a letter to every single one of them.

This was a big undertaking for a teenager with no resources, no help of any kind. He composed a letter expressing his desire to become associated with any store in the chain in any capacity from floor sweeper on up. He had no typewriter so wrote by hand to 393 managers of the various stores. He set himself a quota of fifteen letters a day, and he stuck to it, day after day.

No replies came back. Not a single one. Of all the various forms of rejection, silence can be the most devastating. But something was pushing—and sustaining—Walter Harter. He kept doggedly on.

Finally, Walter Harter asked his parents to let him leave home and try his luck in the Big City. They were apprehensive because he knew no one there. But they agreed to let him go and scraped up enough money to sustain him for a few days. They figured he'd be back soon.

In Manhattan, Walter went to Times Square and there found one of the chain's large stores. He asked for the manager, who explained that even if the store had received a letter from Walter, it would have been sent to the personnel department of the chain.

Walter wasn't even sure what a personnel department was, but he followed directions to a huge building on Park

Avenue. There, when he identified himself, he was taken to a stern-faced man behind an enormous desk who seemed to be in charge of everything. The man stared at Walter for what seemed like a long time. Finally he stood up, smiled, and pointed to a table holding stacks of letters. "Your applications are there," he said, "all three hundred and ninety-three of them! We knew that some day you would walk in here. We have a clerk's job waiting for you. You can start this afternoon."

An amazing story? Yes, but a true one. Walter Harter eventually became a store manager. And even after he moved on to other things, he carried with him the momentum that the Plus Factor, in the form of initiative and perseverance, had given him.

This process of aligning yourself with the inner flow of power and becoming a true goal setter isn't easy. Like any other skill it has to be studied and practiced before it can be mastered. It comes by developing a positive attitude and imposing certain disciplines on yourself. If you are suffering from aimlessness and a sense of defeat, especially negativism, here are five suggestions that will help you. I know, for at different times in my own life they have helped me.

1. *Sharpen your thinking about goal setting*. Give it some real thought. Obviously, goals range all the way from very broad life goals to small specific goals. Learn to distinguish between long-term and short-term goals. Decide how many you can handle. Be realistic about the amount of time and effort that may be necessary. The objective is worth the price. One must not drift in vague circles but use the compass of the brain, and chart a course, and follow it.

2. *Make a commitment to excellence.* Sometimes people say, "Well, I really don't know yet what I want to do with my life." Okay, perhaps not. But while you're waiting for that

goal to come into view, or into focus, there is nothing to stop you from choosing one supremely important goal: the determination to do *everything* as well as you can, to make the most of whatever the Lord put into you in the way of talent or ability.

A few years ago, I remember, I met a lady who had been in high school with me. She looked at me pensively for quite a while. Finally she said, "Well, I guess you've done pretty well with what little you had!" People always laugh when I tell this story, but in a way she was paying me a great compliment. At least, I like to think so. I hope I took that little and tried to make the most of it. That is what we are supposed to do.

Actually, my long-term goal in life has been a clear and direct one ever since I left the newspaper business many years ago to enter the ministry. That goal is to persuade the greatest possible number of people to commit their lives to Jesus Christ. To get people to know that He is just as alive today as He was two thousand years ago in Judea and Galilee. That He can bring peace and power into their lives. That is my goal today and for as long as I live. I have pursued it with every ounce of determination and energy that I possess. More than once I have run into difficulties. But always the Plus Factor has come to my aid and pulled me through dark periods.

3. *Learn to distinguish between a goal and a wish.* There's an old saying, "If wishes were horses, beggars would ride." That's just a way of saying that simply wishing for something isn't going to make it happen. The fairy tales we all loved as children are full of spells that bring instant happiness and charms that make dreams come true; but they are fantasy, not reality. The reason such stories have had such appeal through the ages is that they promise glowing rewards without effort. Life isn't like that.

Quite often, I think, people cling to wishes that are really just fantasies. I used to stay sometimes at a certain hotel in the Midwest. Whenever I did, the young manager always assured me that his ambition was to become governor of that particular state. He was an affable and likable fellow, and he met a lot of people in his role of innkeeper. But nothing ever happened to change his way of life.

I finally discovered that this amibition of his dated from the time when the governor had stayed at the hotel. All the pomp and ceremony surrounding him impressed the manager a great deal, and he decided that it would be nice to be governor himself some day. This concept made him feel important, so he clung to it, magnified it, talked about it. But it was just a wish, a daydream akin to the vision I used to have as a small boy when, growing up in Ohio, I dreamed of playing shortstop for the Cincinnati Reds. It was a glorious idea, but it was just a wish and so not a realizable goal.

Compare the daydreaming hotel manager with a young couple I knew who wanted a home of their own. They couldn't afford to buy a house, but they did manage a down payment on a lot. Once they had the lot, they drew some rough plans on wrapping paper on the kitchen table of their little rented apartment. Then they went out with stakes and string and paced off an outline of their dream house on the lot. They discussed what every room would contain, what it would look like. Whenever they wanted more of a house they would change the stakes and the string. This went on month after month.

In the meantime, they set themselves the discipline of a double tithe. Both had jobs. They set aside 10 percent of their joint earnings for their church, and another 10 percent for their "some day" house. If either of them took a moonlighting job, that money went into their building fund. They denied themselves a lot of minor pleasures to keep the fund growing.

At the end of three years they took their plans and their savings to a mortgage company. By this time there was a kind of momentum, a quiet confidence, an aura of determination about them that impressed even the hard-boiled loan officer. Call it the Plus Factor, call it what you will, they got their mortgage, they built their dream house, they're living happily in it today with two attractive children.

Why? Because they didn't sit and vaguely wish. They had a definite plan. They had a timetable. They had a goal, and they went for it, and they got it.

4. *Prepare for ultimate goals by achieving interim goals.* If you learn to do this consistently, you won't even have to overtax yourself for your ultimate goals; they will come to you in due course.

Often I've seen this happen in industry. Once I asked a bank president how he got his start in banking. "By cleaning things," he said with a smile. "My first job was sweeping up in a little small-town bank. It wasn't much of a job, but I cleaned everything as if my whole future in banking depended on it. Which of course, at that point, it did.

"Finally, I became an errand boy, then a teller, then a cashier, and so on. At every stage, I tried to do everything well. By the time they needed a president to clean up some really big financial problems, I knew every step of the banking business. And so they called on me." That man rose from a menial position to a top post, and I have no doubt that the Plus Factor was aiding him all the way.

Hotelman Ed Leach, who was president of the Jack Tar chain, did the same thing. His first job was as a gardener's helper, spreading manure on the flower beds of a hotel in Galveston. His goal was to manage that hotel, and in time he did, but not before he himself had filled every post in the chain of command. He knew when a waiter was efficient or inefficient, because he had been a waiter. He knew when a desk clerk was courteous or discourteous because he had been one too. Finally, when he was ready and *because* he was ready, the goal he was seeking fell into his hands.

The principle involved here is completely logical and completely sound: The training and experience you acquire in attaining a lesser goal leaves you ready to pursue a greater one. I knew a young man once who had considerable potential as a writer. His long-range goal was to be a novelist, but he knew that called for more maturity and more craftsmanship than he had. So he set himself a progression of separate but related goals. He got a job on a magazine that enabled him to observe how short stories were constructed, why some were successful and others were not. Then he became a writer of short stories himself. Next, he became associated with a television network and learned how dramatic scripts were put together. Finally he did begin to write novels and, not instantly but eventually, met with considerable success. Why? Because he didn't leap for a goal, he worked toward it; he prepared himself step-by-step for success. Then he was ready.

5. *Choose goals that will benefit others as well as yourself.* A goal that involves concern for other people seems to liberate the Plus Factor much more readily than one that doesn't. It's not enough for a person entering medical school to want to be rich and successful; his or her basic goal should be the desire to help people. The same is true of lawyers, businessmen, or whomever. You'll find it helps to have the concept of service embedded in the goal.

I know a young man, Isaac Tigrett, who summoned up all his courage and opened a restaurant in London. He called it the Hard Rock Cafe. It was very loud, very brassy, very exuberant, and very American, and many people thought it would be a resounding flop. On the contrary, it was—and is—a huge success. Long lines of people are always "queued up," as they say in Britain, waiting to get in. Now there is a

Hard Rock Cafe on West Fifty-seventh Street in Manhattan, and another in Stockholm and another in Tokyo and another in Dallas. And what is Isaac Tigrett's motto? "Love all; serve all." And he is just that kind of person.

I once asked John Johnson, publisher of *Ebony* magazine, the secret of his great success. "By small realizable goals," he replied. "In time they added up to the achievement of big goals."

This is the attitude that underlies some of America's greatest success stories. A number of years ago, a young man, the son of a midwestern college president and preacher, was flailing around at various jobs; his problem: "None of them really seemed to serve anyone." Since childhood he had been imbued with the Christian ethic, which involved, among other things, the concept of service, of the improvability of the individual, the value of time, the importance of attitude. Even as a seventeen-year-old, he had begun the habit of writing on slips of paper the gist of his daily reading in magazines and books; just before sleep he would repeat what he had learned that day, referring to his slips of paper if he forgot anything.

Finally, in 1921, pushed out of his job at Westinghouse in Pittsburgh because of a recession, he decided to push ahead with his idea that had been born of that early reading: to publish a Reader's Service, consisting of articles of value, condensed to save time, and issued in a small, pocket-sized magazine that the reader could carry around and refer to at odd moments. Then the young man had approached existing magazine publishers of the time; they had all turned down his idea. Even the great William Randolph Hearst told him it would never sell enough to succeed. But, as the young man said some years later, "I didn't care if I made a penny, as long as the magazine served the reader."

Already the Plus Factor that comes to the aid of people with altruistic goals was coming into the picture. With faith in his idea, DeWitt Wallace and his wife, Lila, started putting out their little magazine. That was in 1922. When the Wallaces died, the little magazine had 100 million readers, 30 million subscribers, 18 million in the United States and the rest worldwide. The *Reader's Digest* was, and is, the great publishing success story of our time.

I knew the Wallaces well, and whenever I was with them the focus of the conversation always was, "How can we help young people? How can we help older people? How can we help anyone anywhere who needs help?"

So if you have a goal that includes helping people in some way, don't let anyone talk you out of it. Don't believe them when they say, "It can't be done." Miracles can happen when you set clear, worthwhile, useful goals and go after them with belief. So aim high. Put all negative or defeatist thoughts out of your mind, and give it all you've got. When you do, great forces will come to your aid.

Among them will be your inner Plus Factor.

4.

The PLUS FACTOR and Two Magic Words

We have written about the importance of creative dreaming.

We have stressed the necessity of setting goals.

Is there a logical third step in this process of liberating and activating the Plus Factor in human beings?

Yes, there is. It consists of just two magic words.

Let me digress for a moment. Have you ever thought about the power inherent in certain combinations of words? Shakespeare tells in ten words how a person's future is determined: "To be or not to be; that is the question." Of course it's the question! Is the Plus Factor to be a force in your life, or is it not? Are you going to set goals and reach them, or are you not? Is success something you will achieve, or isn't it? Is happiness going to come to you, or will it ever remain just beyond your grasp? Are these things to be, or are they not; that is indeed the question.

Then there is an even shorter combination of words than that given by Shakespeare. These words are credited to Henry Kaiser, the great industrialist, and they accurately describe many successful enterprises. Just six words: "Find a need and fill it."

And now we get down to two magic words that tell us how to accomplish just about anything we want to accomplish, two powerful words that can change any situation, two dynamic words that all too few people use. And what are these two amazing words?

Do it!

Have you got an idea? Do it!

Do you have a dream? Do it!

Do you have an ambition? Do it!

Have you some great impulse, some burning desire? Do it!

Are you defeated by something? Are you afraid of something? Are you hesitant to try something? Many people spend their lives being afraid to do what they really want to do. But if they stand tall and say, "I will do this thing!" then the Plus Factor is liberated and power begins to surge into them.

That power begins to flow at the moment one takes the first step even when the first positive thought comes. No matter how intense your dreaming, no matter how clearly defined your goals, nothing is going to happen until you *make* it happen by taking an active step toward the fulfillment of those dreams, a decisive step toward the realization of those goals.

Back in 1912 when Juliette Low returned from England to her hometown of Savannah, Georgia, she brought with her a dream, a spark of an idea that had been planted by Sir Robert

Baden-Powell, the British hero of the Boer War, who had started an organization in England called the Boy Scouts. If scouting was good for the boys of England, Juliette Low asked herself, why wouldn't it be good for the girls of America? A dream, you see; a creative dream. All the way across the Atlantic she thought about the dream and shaped it and honed it until it became a goal, a difficult far-off goal, but still a goal.

With that dream and that goal in her mind she went back to the town where she was born and picked up the primitive telephone—a replica of which they still have on display in the old house on Bull Street—and called her friend Nina Pape, who was headmistress of a local school.

"Nina," she said, "come right over. I've got something for the girls of Savannah and the girls of Georgia and the girls of the whole country and the whole world *and we're going to start it tonight!*"

There it was, that crucial third step. And as millions of Girl Scouts past and present can testify, they *did it*. It took many years before Girl Scouting became a great national movement, but as the old Chinese proverb says, the longest journey begins with a single step.

I have seen that single step summon the Plus Factor so powerfully that the person taking it was released from a paralysis of fear. Emerson said, "Do the thing you fear, and the death of fear is certain." I thought of that prophecy a number of years ago when United States Senator Warren Barbour of New Jersey became a friend of mine. We first met one night at a banquet in Newark where we both were speakers. We sat next to each other at the speakers' table, and he said to me, "How do you feel when you are about to make a speech? Are you ever scared?"

I admitted to him that often I was. I don't know about all public speakers, but I'm sure that most never overcome a certain fear of facing an audience. Maybe that's a good thing, because the adrenaline keys you up and makes your mind work a little better.

Senator Barbour told me that there had been a time when public speaking was sheer agony for him. "I used to be an amateur boxer," he said, "and I was never afraid of anyone in the ring. But when I got up to make a speech my mouth got dry, my hands shook, I went hot and cold all over. Finally I decided I wasn't going to live with a fear like that. So to overcome it I announced my candidacy for the Senate." (He *did* it.) "I announced with no idea that I would win, really, but I knew that running for office would force me to go out and make speeches. The only way I could overcome this fear of speaking was to do it."

So what are you afraid of? What is holding you back? What is it that stands in your way? Do it! I have seen this simple rule work so many times. When I can persuade someone to *do* it, they become victorious instead of defeated.

Usually it is fear of failure that is blocking the flow of power from the Plus Factor. That fear leads to inertia, sometimes a real paralysis of the personality. And the longer the inertia persists, the harder it is to break through it.

Sometimes it can be literally a matter of life or death. I remember an incident that took place a few years ago in North Carolina. A young man named Samuel A. Mann was tramping through the countryside and decided to go through a swamp rather than make a wide detour. He had on high hip boots and was slogging through the wet ground when he came to what looked like an area of dry sand. As he tried to cross it, suddenly he sank down to his knees; and as he tried to get back, a powerful suction gripped his legs like a vise, dragging him down deeper. In a moment of complete horror he realized he was in a great pocket of quicksand and he remembered, that the natives always said, "Nobody ever gets out of those quicksands alive."

For a moment he was paralyzed by panic, sinking deeper and deeper. To his left he saw some marsh grass growing, each blade perhaps half an inch wide. He thought to himself, "If I could just reach that grass, perhaps a handful would have the strength of a rope." He reached out his hand, but there was a gap of about three feet between his fingers and the marsh grass. He knew that if he lunged for the grass and missed it, he would disappear under the treacherous sand. But if he did nothing he was doomed also.

By now the sand was almost over the top of his hip boots, and he realized suddenly that the sand wasn't holding him but rather was holding his boots, which in turn were holding him. With shaking fingers he undid the straps that were holding his boots to his belt. Then, taking a deep breath and asking God to help him, *he did it.* He flung himself full length across the deadly sand. His fingers touched the marsh grass, grasped several strands. Then slowly, carefully, inch by agonizing inch, he pulled himself out of his boots onto the solid earth.

He saved himself because *he did it.*

Do you want power in you? Do you want peace in mind and heart? Do your want to reach for success across the quicksand of timidity and doubt? Then take these two magic words, say them to yourself again and again. Ask God to help you—and DO IT. And not tomorrow or next week or next month or next year.

Now. Do it now!

5.

The PLUS FACTOR and Persistence

In the pages of this book so far I have suggested methods to activate the Plus Factor . . .

Dream creative dreams.

Set high and worthwhile goals.

Take the first decisive step toward your goal.

And then what?

Then take another step, and another, and another, until the goal is reached, the ambition realized, the mission accomplished.

No matter how long it takes, *persist*. No matter how discouraged you may get, *persevere*. No matter how much you want to quit, *hang in there*.

President Calvin Coolidge, known widely as "Silent Cal," may not have talked a lot, but when he did say something it was usually worth listening to. Here's what he said on this subject:

> Nothing in the world can take the place of persistence. Talent will not; nothing is more common than unsuccessful men with talent. Genius will not; the world is full of educated derelicts. Persistence and determination alone are omnipotent. The slogan "press on" has solved and always will solve the problems of the human race.

Winston Churchill said the same thing in different words. Where any worthwhile endeavor was concerned, he said: "Never give up. Never, never, never . . . give up!"

Why is persistence, why is perseverance of such enormous importance? Because so little of consequence is achieved without it. And because lack of it leads so often to failure. We've all heard the story of the rusty old pickax stuck in the rocky wall of an unproductive mine, left there by a miner who had given up in disgust and walked away from it. Years later another miner idly swung his pick against the same wall and broke through into the fabulous Comstock lode. Untold wealth had been waiting for the first miner if only he had persisted a little longer. A few more swings of the pickax would have done it. But he gave up too soon . . . and never knew what that negative decision had cost him.

Contrast that with the job-hunting young man in Boston who saw a want ad in the local paper. He wrote to the post office box number that was given, but received no reply. He wrote again, and yet a third time. Still no answer. So he went to the post office, located the box, and waited until someone came to collect the mail. He followed that person to an office, went inside, and told the office manager what he had done, adding that he still wanted very much to have the job that had been advertised. The manager looked at him in astonishment. "Well," he said, "we are always looking for people with perseverance and determination. You seem to have both; we'll take you on." That was how Roger Babson, who later became a famous financier, got his first job.

Sometimes we see people persevering in the face of what seem to be insuperable odds. When that happens, I can't help but think that through their Plus Factor information has been conveyed to them that even they are unaware of.

One of the most remarkable men I ever met was a native of Lebanon, Musa Alami. He had been educated in England, and his family had been quite well off until in one of the disturbances that periodically convulse Lebanon they lost everything. Musa Alami found his way to the bleak desert country of the Jordan River valley not far from Jericho.

This sun-scorched land had probably not changed much since the days of John the Baptist. No crops could grow because of lack of water. On one side of the valley the mountains of Judea shimmered in the heat waves; on the other side were the mountains of Moab. There were no funds or equipment to dam the River Jordan. But somehow Musa Alami, who had read of successful irrigation in other areas using subsurface water, became convinced that there might be water underneath the burning sands. And he announced that he was going to dig for it.

Jeers and scornful laughter greeted this announcement. The old Bedouins of the area pointed out that the desert had been there from time immemorial. The water of the Dead Sea had once covered the region; the sand itself was full of salt. Musa Alami was a fool, or perhaps a madman. And it wasn't only the Bedouins who laughed. Government officials and scientists from abroad were equally scornful. No water was there. No water could be there.

Nevertheless, aided by a few poverty-stricken refugees

from the nearby Jericho refugee camp, Musa Alami started to dig.

With well-drilling equipment? With steam shovel or earth removers? No. He and his motley crew dug by hand, with pick and shovel. Down they went under the blazing sun. Day after day. Deeper and deeper, while onlookers jeered. Down they went, this dauntless man and his ragged friends, week after week.

What kept them going? Hope kept them going. And with hope they had perseverance, just plain persistence.

I'm sure it came from the Plus Factor.

One day, six months after they started digging, the sand became damp. And a little deeper it was wet. Finally water, fresh water, began to fill the hole. And Musa Alami and his friends did not laugh or shout or cheer. They wept. An ancient Bedouin man said, "Musa, now I can die. I've seen water come from the desert."

That's quite a story, isn't it? I know it's true because I knew Musa personally and saw the great stream of water gushing out of the parched heart of the desert, and Musa himself told the story to my wife, Ruth, and me. Today thousands of acres are yielding fruits and vegetables of all kinds . . . all because one persistent and determined man was convinced it could happen . . . convinced and sustained by his Plus Factor.

Some years ago in Dallas, Texas, before the Salk vaccine was available, a young man named James C. McCormick was stricken with polio. He was totally paralyzed, totally helpless, and in great pain. He could not move; he could not swallow; he could not breathe; he had to stay in an iron lung. He wanted to die. He prayed, saying, "Lord, I'm so helpless that I can't take my own life. Please take it for me."

But God chose to ignore that prayer.

Then he prayed, "If I can't die, please take away this awful pain."

The doctors gave him drugs that did ease the pain, but he was becoming dangerously dependent on them.

So he prayed, "Lord, please take away this craving for drugs."

And gradually the craving left him.

Then he prayed, "Please let me be able to swallow again. Let them take this tube out of my throat and these needles out of my arms. If I can just drink a swallow of water, I'll try not to ask for any more favors."

And he became able to swallow, but he was not able to stop asking God for favors. The Plus Factor wouldn't let him.

So he prayed, "Lord, let me be able to breathe a little bit on my own. Let me be able to get out of this iron lung just for a little while."

And this too came to pass.

After a while he prayed again, "Heavenly Father, I'm so grateful for all Your favors. Can I ask just one more? Let me be able to leave this bed just for an hour and go in a wheelchair to see the world that lies outside this hospital room."

This request, too, was granted. Then James McCormick asked to be given strength enough in his arms to move the wheelchair himself. And after that he asked for the ability and stamina to walk on crutches. And finally, after a twenty-year struggle, James McCormick could walk with two canes, and he was able to marry and have children and lead a very-close-to-normal life.

What did it? The doctors helped. But, supremely, prayer did it—and persistence. But it was prayer of the most intense and most persistent kind. I'm sure that God is not annoyed by such prayers. He doesn't grow impatient or weary of hearing them. His great compassionate heart is touched by such faith and such perseverance. Ask James C. McCormick. He'll tell you the same thing.

Here's how my dictionary defines these two important words:

> *Persist:* To continue steadily and firmly in some state, purpose, or course of action, especially in spite of opposition, remonstrance, etc.
>
> *Persevere:* To persist in any undertaking, maintain a purpose in spite of difficulty or obstacles, continue steadfastly.

Note that last phrase: *continue steadfastly.* It makes me think of an Ohio housewife and mother named Alice Vonk. She lived in a small town in that rich farming country, and she loved to plant things, especially flowers. She had a little private custom that she always observed. Whenever she put a seed into the ground, she would murmur a little prayer. She figured that human beings could plant the seeds, but it took God to make them grow.

One night Alice Vonk read in a seed catalogue about a prize being offered for a pure white marigold. She loved to grow marigolds herself, but they were always yellow or orange or rust colored. The seed company wanted a pure white marigold because that would enable them to develop hybrids of many colors through cross-pollination, and they were offering a prize of $10,000.

Now Alice Vonk, mother of eight, was no expert on the genetics of flowers, but she did know a little about hybrids, and something inside her said, "Why not try it?" She was impelled into action by her Plus Factor.

So Alice Vonk started out with the largest yellow marigolds that she could find in the seed catalogue. As was her custom, she said a little prayer as she dropped each seed into the rich soil. Then she waited.

Finally up came the marigolds, yellow as sunlight. Alice

Vonk chose the palest ones, let them die naturally, gathered the seeds and planted them again the next year. "Somewhere," she told her skeptical family, "is a pure white marigold and I am going to find it!" No discouragement there, you see; no doubts, no hint of failure. She was going to persist. She was going to persevere. No matter how long it might take.

And she did, year after year. Gradually her marigolds grew paler and paler, but none was the pure white marigold she was seeking. Her children grew up, some of them married and moved away. Her husband died, and for a little while Alice Vonk gave in to sorrow. But then she took a deep breath and went back to her marigolds. By now the grandchildren were coming along, and they were eager to help her. "Flowers and children are a lot alike," she said. "You have to understand them—and never give up on them."

For almost twenty years she kept planting and praying, always persisting. And then one morning she looked out at her garden and saw, in full glorious bloom, a pure white marigold! Not almost white. Not nearly white. Pure white!

Alice Vonk sent 100 seeds from this marigold to the seed company. There was a long wait while the seeds were tested and grown under laboratory conditions. But the day came when the president of the seed company called on the telephone. "Mrs. Vonk," he said, "I'm happy to tell you that you have won our prize!"

And indeed she had.

What was the inner voice that said to Mrs. Vonk, "Why not try?" What kept her going year after year when most people would have become discouraged and given up? I can only believe that it was the quality we have been writing about all through this book. It was her Plus Factor at work.

Does this unseen quality, the Plus Factor, activate and strengthen the capacity for persistence in a person, or does a display of perseverance in an individual call it forth? I think it probably works both ways. If you make a determined effort on your own, the Plus Factor will come to your aid. On the other hand, there seem to be times when the Plus Factor is manifested in a most unlikely way. It causes that person to choose an almost unattainable goal, and persist against almost insuperable odds until a hopeless hope becomes an actual reality.

Do not minimize the power of persistence. Just hang in there always, always. And never, never give up. Realization and achievement come to those who persist.

"The kingdom of God is within you" (Luke 17:21), Jesus told His disciples. He also said, "If ye have faith . . . nothing shall be impossible unto you" (Matthew 17:20). The Plus Factor is a reflection of eternal truth.

6.

How the PLUS FACTOR Begins to Work

Does one always know when the power of the Plus Factor begins to work? No, not necessarily. Just recently I watched on television as Boris Becker, the brilliant young German tennis player, defeated Ivan Lendl in the finals at Wimbledon. Boris and Ivan put on a tremendous match, but there was no doubt as to who was superior that day. The eighteen-year-old youngster with the carrot-colored hair defeated the world's number-one player in straight sets. Lendl, of course, played well, but Becker was in control, and you could tell that Lendl knew it.

Afterward a reporter was asking Becker the usual postmatch questions, and the young man was replying with suitable modesty. No, he said, he didn't consider himself the best player in the world. The best on grass, maybe, but not necessarily on slower surfaces.

"You played with great confidence," the reporter said, "almost as if you felt you owned the center court at Wimbledon. Is that right?"

Becker nodded slowly, a serious look on his boyish face. "When I came out to play my very first match in this tournament on this court, I had a strange sensation. It's hard to describe. I felt it in my feet and in my ankles and in my legs. . . . It gave me a great feeling of confidence and strength. I was sure that on this particular court I would go all the way. I was sure that I would win."

A strange sensation? Almost indescribable? A tremendous feeling of power and assurance?

Was it an expression of the Plus Factor? Who's to say that it wasn't?

Hearing Boris Becker describe the strange feeling that came to him on a tennis court reminded me of a story Michael Landon tells about himself. Today Michael Landon, a television superstar, is famous for his roles in *Bonanza, Little House on the Prairie*, and *Highway to Heaven*; but in those days he was a scrawny tenth grader in New Jersey named Eugene Orowitz . . . called Ugy by his friends.

Ugy was not a good athlete; he was shy and self-conscious. He had no confidence at all until one day, when he was watching some older boys throw the javelin, the coach half-jokingly asked him if he'd like to try. To the amazement of everyone, when Ugy did try, the javelin soared all the way into the grandstand, where it came to rest with a broken point. The coach told the boy he could keep the broken javelin, and from that moment on he began to practice day and night. Before he left high school he had thrown the javelin 211 yards, a national record that year for high school students. His skill brought him a college track scholarship in California, and he thought seriously about the Olympics. As it turned out, a torn muscle in his shoulder eventually put an end to his javelin-throwing career.

But he never forgot the strange feeling that came to him the first time he ever held a javelin in his hand. "I felt like a Spartan warrior. I had this terrific sense of excitement and confidence and power. It was amazing. And then, years later the same feeling came to me in another area altogether. My javelin-throwing career was over; I was just getting by with odd jobs when a friend of mine who had a part in a play called *Home of the Brave* asked me to rehearse his lines with him. We started reading the script together, and all of a sudden the same sense of excitement and confidence and *rightness* came to me. I knew I wanted to get into dramatics. I knew I wanted to be an actor. I knew I was *supposed* to be an actor. So I enrolled in acting school at Warner Brothers and was on my way."

How did Michael Landon know he was supposed to be a javelin thrower? How did he know he was supposed to be an actor? Something spoke to him, something deep inside. I think it was the Plus Factor.

Or consider another man, John Holmes, who wrote to me from England. He told me about himself and his childhood in Australia. His parents were farmers who suffered considerably during the Great Depression. "I was not aware of this as a child," he wrote, "because I had space and freedom, care and attention from loving parents." But life was hard there in the Australian outback.

Gradually it improved so that eventually John was able to borrow some money, buy a small farm of his own, marry, and start raising a family. By the early 1960s, he wrote, things were going pretty well and the Holmeses seemed to have everything they needed. "But from time to time vague inner stirrings disturbed me. It was like a distant voice telling me there was a bigger and better life for me somewhere. But I ignored it as just a dream."

Children were born. The "something" continued to agitate John's mind, kept on whispering that somewhere great things awaited him. But he didn't know what—or where—those things could be.

"By the end of the 1960s I had decided that I must seek opportunities elsewhere. If such opportunities were not to be found, I could always return to what I knew best: farming the land. In 1970 I sold most of the property I owned, settled my debts, which were considerable, and with my wife and children set sail for England. We had no idea where we were going to stay or what we were going to do."

Now, on the face of it, this was madness. To travel thousands of miles, with few or no resources, to an unfamiliar land where he had no friend or contacts, with five dependents, with no experience or skills except farming . . . one might well say to John Holmes, "What on earth possessed you?"

The only answer that makes any sense at all is one that would never have occurred to John. It was the Plus Factor that was motivating him, like a whisper in his ear for all those years. The Plus Factor that impelled him to leave his native land and go far across the sea. And it was the Plus Factor, springing from some deep reservoir inside him, that was going to provide him with the energy and the determination to overcome whatever obstacles stood in his way.

"Although it took us more than four weeks to reach England, within ten days of our arrival I had acquired a position as a salesman. I tackled my task with great determination and enormous enthusiasm. My new trade was learned, often with great difficulty, but with the sincere belief that I would eventually succeed."

Well, succeed he did, so much so that today his business firm has franchises in several cities. When he wrote to me, he was asking if I would meet with him and six of his top salesmen who were coming to New York with their wives.

This I was glad to do, and I was tremendously impressed by the caliber of these people. You could tell that the Plus Factor was energizing all of them.

Sometimes, I think, a single action on the part of an individual can open the door to the Plus Factor. The long-term results of the action may not be fully apparent for years, but the process has begun.

Consider the case of a young immigrant, Bernard Castro, who came to this country from his native Sicily while still in his teens. Go back through the years to the night when he stood at the grimy window of his cheap room on New York's East Side, staring at the snow that was whirling down, blanketing everything. Already it was a foot deep in the streets; traffic had come to a complete halt.

Still struggling to learn English, young Bernard Castro had signed up for a night course at DeWitt Clinton High School. But that was far away on the west side of the city. Outside the wind howled; the storm was reaching blizzard proportions. Should he try to fight his way through on foot, or should he stay where he was?

Young Castro had found a job as an upholsterer. It paid very little. His mouth was sore from holding the tacks that he hammered into furniture all day long. He was tired. His shoes were thin and his overcoat was thinner. Would it make much difference if he missed one evening's classes?

Standing there before the window Bernard Castro remembered something he had read in a newspaper column. The columnist had said that the margin between success and failure was often simply the willingness to make the extra effort, go the extra mile, endure the extra hardship. Either you had this quality, the columnist said, or you didn't. Abruptly Bernard Castro turned from the window, picked up his shabby overcoat, wound a scarf around his face, and plunged into the storm.

On he plodded through the dark, block after block, hands

and feet growing numb, until finally he came to the high school entrance—and found it locked. A custodian peered out at him. "Are you crazy? No one's going to come out on a night like this! The school is closed!" And the door swung shut.

Back through the storm went Bernard Castro, chilled to the bone, head bowed against the icy wind. But as he walked, he felt a little spark of warmth begin to glow inside him. It was the knowledge that out of two thousand students he was the only one who had fought his way to the entrance. He was the only one who had made the extra effort, who had gone the extra mile, and even though his effort was unsuccessful, he knew that the invisible power that had impelled him to make it would support and sustain him in all future endeavors.

He did not know what to call this power; he did not know where it came from. But when at last he came to his little room and fell into his narrow bed, he knew that the force would never desert him—and it never did.

It was the Plus Factor.

Later on Bernard Castro's energy and determination carried him through the Great Depression. He advanced from being an apprentice upholsterer to opening his own interior-decorating business. Nothing very remarkable about that, you may say—lots of people weathered the Depression. But the mysterious force that led young Bernard Castro to plow through the blizzard that bitter night in Manhattan continued to guide and influence his life as the years went by.

One gift that the Plus Factor brings out sometimes—and a very valuable gift it is—is the ability to see the hidden potential in apparently unrelated things. Sometimes it's a new use for a familiar object. Sometimes it's a hitherto untried combination of ideas or theories. Sometimes it's the unexpected answer to a puzzling problem.

The time came in Bernard Castro's life when he needed this gift. He was struggling to design a streamlined sofa bed, something slimmer and more attractive than the clumsy davenports that took up so much room. There seemed to be no solution. Nothing worked.

Then one day on a small cabin cruiser Castro watched the owner convert a seat into a bunk by sliding out the lower part of the seat frame and putting cushions down flat. The frame consisted of slats that fitted together like the teeth of two combs. Open, it could sustain the weight of a sleeper. Closed, it took up half the space. There, staring him in the face, was the answer to the design problem that had been baffling Bernard Castro. Using it he designed the Castro convertible sofa bed that made him famous—and rich.

Luck? Alertness? Imagination? Inventiveness?

Yes, certainly, all of these. But when you put them all together, when you add them all up, I think you have to look for something deeper.

You have to credit the Plus Factor, plus stick-to-it-iveness, hard work, hard thinking, and a powerful lot of faith.

7.

The PLUS FACTOR and Mental Attitudes

Thinking back to my school days there is one experience I shall never forget. In the fifth grade I had a teacher who was a confirmed positive thinker. His name was George Reeves and he made an unforgettable impression on his students. He stood over six feet and weighed more than 200 pounds, a towering man.

George Reeves was somewhat of a character, full of vitality, often doing things that were entirely unpredictable. For instance, he had a habit of suddenly shouting, "Silence!" and believe me, when he demanded silence, there was silence! Then he would go the blackboard and in big letters print the word C A N' T.

"Look at that word," he demanded. "What shall we do with it?"

We knew the answer he wanted and the whole class would chant: "Knock the T off the CAN'T." And with a sweeping gesture, George Reeves would erase the T, leaving the word CAN standing out impressively. Dusting the chalk from his hands, he would face us. "Let that be a lesson to you and never forget it. You *can* if you think you can." Glaring at the boys and girls looking wonderingly up at him, he would allow a smile to come over his face. "Listen, young ladies and gentlemen" (for some reason he never called us boys and girls), "listen, really listen! You are greater than you think you are! You can, if you believe, really believe, that you can. And," he added, "that is the one important thing I want to teach you in this class."

Through the mist of years, I can see that strong, wise, good man standing there trying to make a class of American youngsters realize what they could do with their lives—what they could become. And the lesson he taught is as right today as it was then. "You can, if you think you can!" So let's really believe that we can reach our goals, achieve our objectives, be what we want to be.

One reason we can achieve is that built into every one of us is something I have been calling the Plus Factor. And this power or energy, this motivational quotient, can lift us out of the ordinary and above the mediocre. It is the Plus Factor that helps a person handle all the problems of life. This Plus Factor can make achievers of you and of me and of everyone who lets it take over.

The Plus Factor is closely allied to the mental attitude which I have called positive thinking. And just what is positive thinking? Well, naturally, it is the opposite of negative thinking. It is the "I can" principle as contrasted with the "I can't" way of thinking. It is believing in your possibilities and disbelieving in your doubts.

Positive thinking is not just a matter of "thinking big." It may express itself in small ways, but these add up to something big. For example, you may awaken in the morning and your first thought is, *This is going to be a lousy day.* Your wife, already cheerily getting breakfast, asks, "And how are you this morning, Honey?" And the negative thinker comes up with the habitual reply, "Oh, I don't feel good. I'm just all out of energy. I'm pooped!" The trouble with such a response is that it really isn't true. He is just *thinking* "pooped."

Perhaps you are a salesman and on your schedule for that day is a really tough buyer. "I can't get through to that guy. He won't buy." So it goes. "I don't feel good." And "I can't." Two self-defeating negatives. So the negative thinker goes his uninspired way throughout the day, thinking and talking himself down—the victim of the three pernicious "L's"—lack, loss, and limitation.

By and large, there are two basic types of thinking. One is negative thinking; the other is positive thinking. And negative thinking is a very hazardous procedure, because it blocks the flow of the Plus Factor.

There is a law called the law of attraction—like attracts like. Birds of a feather flock together. Similarly, thoughts of a kind have a natural affinity. If habitually we send out negative thoughts into the world around us, into our personal world, into our business world, we tend to draw back negative results to ourselves. Thoughts spoken, or even unspoken, possess strong vibratory power. They set forces in action which, inevitably, produce outcomes precisely as conceived, articulated, and affirmed. It is a law of mind that negative thinking, negative attitudes, negative mental pictures are bound to result in negative outcomes.

If you are currently experiencing negative conditions in your life or career, such a situation did not just happen, nor is it necessarily due to "bad breaks." It just might be the natural and inevitable result of the nurture and projection of negative mental attitudes. This defeatism may have been germinating in your mind for a long time. Perhaps it has made a negative thinker and receiver of you.

But I have good news for you, *great* good news, and it's this—you can change and become a positive thinker with the positive good of the Plus Factor flowing into your personality, into your business, into your relationships. And I hope you realize that the time for this personal change is now. For if you don't do it now, there is a danger that you may never do it.

The positive thinker is an optimistic, faith-motivated person who habitually projects positive images and attitudes—every day sending creative and positive thoughts into the world around him. These strong thought waves condition the surrounding world positively and positive outcomes are activated. What you send out mentally over a long period of time will return to you in kind, precisely and inevitably. So, if you really want to succeed, or having become successful want to move further on, it is crucially important to change radically from destructive negative thinking to creative positive thinking.

Sometimes, seeking excuses for their negativism, people tell me, "I'm just a born negative thinker. My father was a negative thinker, so was my grandfather. It runs in the family." Well, it is a fact that it can run in the family and often does, but the assumption that one was born a negative thinker will not hold up.

The Creator made each one of us in His own image and breathed into us the breath of life. That means energy, enthusiasm, optimism. I can't remember ever seeing a negative baby. They seem to be positive by nature. But some are born into negative families, and since babies are sensitive to the atmosphere in which they are reared, they take on negative characteristics. Such babies grow up with low opinions of themselves, putting themselves down as natural-born failures or losers.

Once walking through the twisted little streets of Kowloon in Hong Kong, I came upon a tattoo studio. In the window were displayed samples of the tattoos available. On the chest or arms you could have tattooed an anchor or flag or mermaid or whatever. But what struck me with force were three words that could be tattooed on one's flesh, *Born to lose*.

I entered the shop in astonishment and, pointing to those words, asked the Chinese tattoo artist, "Does anyone really have that terrible phrase, *Born to lose*, tattooed on his body?"

He replied, "Yes, sometimes."

"But," I said, "I just can't believe that anyone in his right mind would do that."

The Chinese man simply tapped his forehead and said in broken English, "Before tattoo on body, tattoo on mind."

He qualified as a philosopher, I thought. For what a person becomes is what he or she tattoos on the mind over a long period of time. But the fact is, it need not be "Born to lose." It can be "Born to win."

George Hallas, famous coach of the Chicago Bears, of the National Football League, had a slogan prominently displayed on his office wall, "Always go to bed a winner." A wise thought indeed. During sleep the thoughts of the conscious mind may permeate the subconscious. And George Hallas did not want his players to think losing thoughts. So never take defeatism to bed with you. Image yourself winning as you drift off to sleep, and let the image of success germinate. It will have a wonderful effect. Take the advice of one of the most successful athletic directors of our time.

Coach Hallas was on sound psychological ground too. It is a fact that there is a deep tendency in human nature to become precisely what we image ourselves as being over a long period of time. The image of ourselves that we hold in consciousness strongly tends to reproduce itself as fact. If, for example, you suffer from an inferiority complex and constantly image yourself as inadequate, in effect disbelieving in yourself, this process will ultimately make you exactly as imaged.

You can, however, get your self-image normalized and begin to think of yourself as an adequate and capable person. Do this and you will become as visualized.

This is not just theory. This is a fact, as I know from personal experience. As a young boy I had an acutely painful inferiority attitude. I was shy, timid, and *bashful*. That word means abashed. I shrank from going among people. I imaged myself as being very short on ability and totally lacking in any talent. I saw myself as a nobody. Then I found that people were agreeing with me. It is a fact that others will unconsciously take you at your own self-evaluation.

But new self-knowledge came one day during my second year in college in a course in economics. The professor, Ben Arneson, later became a lifelong friend. As the class session closed he said, "Peale, stay a few minutes." He looked searchingly at me, "What's the matter with you? Just why are you such a worm? You go skulking around like you're scared. When I ask you a question in class you get red in the face and tongue-tied when I am sure that you know the material very well indeed. And," he added, "why don't you get over this inferiority complex and act like a man?"

Though angered by this seemingly ruthless treatment, I had to admit he was right about me. "I don't know," I said, "I guess I'm just a failure."

"Don't ever say such a negative thing! Never even think it," he thundered, "Draw on your faith. Ask your Heavenly Father, who made you, to change you," he said more kindly.

I stumbled out of the classroom, along the hall, and out of the building down the long flight of outside steps. On the fourth step from the bottom I stopped. And on that particular step one of the greatest things in my life happened. There I started on the road to believing in myself.

This is how it happened. I stood completely discouraged and hopeless. Then I did what I had been taught to do. I prayed! It was a simple, desperate prayer. The poet James Russell Lowell in "The Cathedral" has a passage:

> I, who have ever prayed at morning and at eve,
> Thrice in my life perhaps have truly prayed.
> Thrice thrust beneath my conscious self
> Have felt that perfect disenthralment which is God.

Well, anyway, this time I meant the prayer with all my mind. "Look, Lord," I said, "You can change a thief into an honest man or a drunk into a sober person. Why can't you change a mixed-up defeated guy like me into a normal person? Amen."

I guess I expected a miracle, but nothing happened right away except that I felt peaceful and sort of happy.

Subsequently, another professor started me reading Emerson and Thoreau, Marcus Aurelius, and William James, writers who taught what could happen when a person learns to think right. I learned that I could alter my life by altering my attitudes of mind. Gradually I came to have a normal belief in myself, discovering that the Plus Factor will come to our aid if we let it. I made the most important discovery of all: that we can if we think that we can.

8.

The PLUS FACTOR: Source of Courage

One human characteristic that has been admired since the dawn of time is the ability to face danger or suffering bravely. And closely related to this ability is the capacity to make right decisions when facing difficult moral choices. We call these special qualities *courage*—and very few among us can afford to be smug or contented about our possession of it. The truth is, most of us are afraid of something, and we're never quite sure how we'd react if suddenly we were called upon to face that which we fear.

Fortunately, there is inside each of us a hidden power that can and does help us respond to such emergencies. I have been calling that power the Plus Factor, and many times I have heard or read about extraordinary happenings where this power flowed into the lives of people in dangerous or desperate circumstances, supplying them with almost incredible strength and stamina as well as the resistance to fear that we call bravery or heroism.

Consider what happened a few years ago at a Pacific Coast beach near San Francisco. It was early in May. Two freshmen at San Francisco State College, Shirley O'Neill and Albert Kogler decided to take a swim. They plunged into the rough surf with Al in the lead, swam out beyond the breakers, and floated lazily in calm deep water about fifty yards from shore. "Sure beats sitting in the library, doesn't it?" Al said and Shirley nodded contentedly. What neither of them knew was that homing in on them out of the depths was the most terrifying and deadly of all living creatures, a great white shark.

The great white is the most fearsome killer in the animal kingdom. Often it reaches a length of fifteen feet, a ton or more of streamlined muscle, its great jaws with triangular razor-edged teeth capable of snapping a sea lion in two or cutting a man in half. As it drives through the water its round black eyes seem devoid of any sort of intelligent purpose, just a blind malignancy with one fixed intent: to rend and destroy.

Shirley heard a scream as a giant gray form suddenly seemed to rise into the air and hurl itself upon Al. His head disappeared under water suddenly crimsoned with blood, then reappeared, his face contorted with agony. "Get away, Shirley," he shrieked. "Get away! It's a shark!"

Shirley O'Neill felt as if her heart had stopped beating. For half a second, she could not move. *Get away*, every fibre of her being screamed, *get away!* She turned toward shore, seized with a terror beyond description. Death was there in the water with her. Death would choose her for its next victim. She was sure of it.

But then she stopped swimming for shore. Something

made her stop. Something made her turn back, back into the crimson water where the shark was still thrashing, back where the water boiled and churned, now blood red. Back toward her friend she swam. She reached for his hand, and drew back in horror. His arm had been torn from his shoulder.

Surely the shark would return. Surely it would attack again. Surely this young girl had every excuse, every reason to try to save herself.

But she did not try to save herself. Instead she swam close to Al and put her arm around his chest. "Lie still, Al. Don't try to swim. Lie still!"

On her back, stroking with her free arm, kicking with her legs, slowly she began to tow him toward the beach. Slowly, slowly, with a plume of blood trailing behind, blood that could attract other man-eaters, or the same one. Waves washed over her head. Al's body seemed to grow heavier, second by second. But he was still alive. She would not abandon him. She would not let him go.

Now they were in the breaking surf, and her feet touched bottom, but she could go no farther. She could only call feebly for help, and the roar of the surf drowned her cries. But miraculously, farther down the beach, a surf fisherman saw her. In a flash, Joe Intersonine was racing down the beach. With a perfectly aimed cast, he dropped his line close to Shirley. She wrapped it around her waist. He reeled in, dragging her and her torn, bleeding burden into shallow water.

Now people came running from all directions. One laid a blanket over Al. He was still conscious, but just barely, and Shirley O'Neill, a Catholic, who knew that Al had never accepted any form of religion, asked if she might baptize him. When he nodded in assent, she ran to the ocean, dipped up sea water in her bathing cap, knelt beside Al, drew the sign of the cross on his forehead and baptized him "in the name of the Father, and of the Son, and of the Holy Ghost." Then a stretcher was brought, and Al was taken to the hospital. Two hours later, he died.

So the earthly life that Shirley O'Neill was trying to save ended. But believers would say, I think, that for Albert Kogler, eternal life began. The question is, what was the power that came to a young college freshman in the face of the most terrifying of all possible threats and gave her the courage and the selflessness to act as she did?

I think it was the power that God has planted deep in all of us. I think it was the Plus Factor.

Sometimes in an unforeseen crisis like the one faced by Shirley O'Neill there has been no previous fear, no built-in dread. So perhaps the reservoir of courage has not been drained. But can the Plus Factor make its appearance where there is a long-standing, deep-rooted fear that has saturated the whole personality of a person? I think it can. Consider the case of Naomi Clinton of Camden, South Carolina.

Some people go through life with a terrible fear of fire, usually the result of some traumatic experience in childhood. Naomi Clinton was such a person. When she was three years old, her family home burned to the ground. She was carried out safely by her sister, but she remembered looking at the flames and screaming in terror. Years later the family home was again destroyed by fire, leaving everything in ashes. Whenever she left her own home and her children, Naomi Clinton worried about their safety. Fear of fire was never far from her mind.

Driving home from a business convention in Florida one day, Naomi Clinton saw a pillar of black smoke rising above the highway a short distance in front of her. As she drew nearer she saw several cars on the side of the road and a handful of people staring in horror at a truck that had overturned and had burst into flames. Drums of oil that had fallen from the truck were scattered about. Naomi Clinton wanted to avert her eyes and drive on, but the flames were leaping higher, blocking the road. She had to stop. She could feel the familiar terror building up in her, but she got out of her car and joined the onlookers.

That was when she saw what looked like a heap of burning rubble near the truck. As she stared, she saw the rubble move. It wasn't a heap of rubble. It was the driver of the truck, lying there in the fire. As Naomi Clinton watched she saw one hand rise above the flames, waving, flapping. Then, somehow, the burning man raised his head and looked through the smoke at her.

It was a sight Naomi Clinton would never forget. "I could see his eyes. They were filled with anguish, so big and staring. And his mouth was moving. I could see the cry on his lips, so faint and weak that I could not hear it. The roar of the fire blotted it out. Everyone else was just standing there, looking.

"At that moment an uncontrollable feeling came over me. Before I thought, or let anything enter my mind, I began running toward the burning man. Somebody shouted, 'Don't be crazy. Those oil drums will explode any second!' The burning man's arm flopped down, then rose again. It seemed to say, *Help me, I'm burning*!

"My dread of fire tugged at me, telling me 'No! No! No!' But a Power much greater than fear, a Power that I can't understand, took control of me. I shook off the man who was trying to hold me back and ran through the burning grass to that blackened, outstretched hand. The truck driver's clothes were on fire. He was trying to lift himself up, but he couldn't."

Naomi Clinton weighed only 111 pounds. Somehow she got her hands under the man's armpits and started to drag him away from the blazing truck. Heat was scorching her bare arms and legs. There was fire everywhere. A tire exploded with a roar and showered her with chunks of burning rubber that bit into her neck and singed her hair. She kept dragging the man off the burning grass and onto the roadway. When she got him there, she beat at his smouldering clothes with her bare hands, then threw herself upon him trying to smother the flames with her own body.

When the police and an ambulance finally came, Naomi Clinton was in such a state of fear and shock that she could barely answer questions. When she tried to go back to her car, her legs gave way, and she sank to the ground.

The truck driver, though terribly burned, did survive. Mrs. Clinton was given a special award for heroism by the governor of South Carolina, and later received a silver Carnegie Medal.

How did she do such a thing, this tiny woman who was so petrified of fire? She was able to do it because, to use her own words, "a Power much greater than fear took control of me."

Naomi Clinton believed that Power came straight from God. And I think she was right, because that's where the Plus Factor comes from.

It's strange how often people who react wisely and strongly in an emergency feel that the wisdom and the strength came to them, not from an act of will or determination on their part, but from some mysterious source that they cannot identify. They are quite candid about this; usually they are the first to admit it. Such was the case with John Skerjanec, a power-line foreman for the Southern Colorado Power Company.

Skerjanec had been checking power lines in the mountains west of Red Canyon Park and was headed back to the company offices, driving a half-ton pickup truck over the winding mountain roads. Early in the afternoon he came to U.S. 50, a two-lane macadam road, not far from the point where it begins a steep descent in a stretch called Eight Mile Hill. That was a very dangerous piece of road; five people had been killed there in the previous three years.

As Skerjanec stopped at the intersection, a car flashed past him, going downhill so fast that he knew something was wrong. Two women were in the car. One was clutching the wheel. The other was waving her arms and screaming. It was obvious that the brakes on the car had failed, and the gears had been stripped also. It was hurtling down the mountain completely out of control. Ahead of it lay at least five miles of steep grades and hairpin mountain curves.

Skerjanec swung his truck onto the road behind the runaway car and stepped on the gas. "And it was a strange thing," he said later. "I was already planning exactly what I was going to do. The idea just seemed to come to me from nowhere. I don't know how I thought of it, because I had never heard of it being done before, but it seemed the only possible way I could keep those women from flying off the road."

The runaway car was going seventy-five miles per hour. It took a mile for Skerjanec to catch up with it. He knew that just ahead was a relatively straight stretch of road perhaps a mile long. If he was to pass the car, it had to be then. He floored his accelerator; the truck shot forward; the needle on its speedometer registered eighty-five miles per hour.

Now they were roaring down the road side by side. The danger to both vehicles was enormous. If they so much as touched fenders all the occupants would be dead. But Skerjanec's mind was locked around "the idea that came from nowhere." He pulled in front of the runaway car watching it in his rearview mirror. When it was directly behind him, he began to slow down, hoping that the woman driver would not panic. He waited until her front bumper touched his rear bumper. The cars bounced apart, but he knew the woman understood what he was attempting to do, and was trying to help him. The bumpers touched again, solid contact this time. Gingerly, gradually, Skerjanec began to apply his brakes. As the speed lessened, he threw his truck into second gear. Ahead loomed a sharp curve. But the combined drag of brakes and engine was enough. Just before they reached the curve, both cars shuddered to a stop.

Where did the "know what to do" come from? And the determination? And the driving skill? And the courage? The courage that made it possible for John Skerjanec to risk his life in an attempt to save two total strangers? No doubt about it. The courage came from the same source that Naomi Clinton's courage came from. It came from the God-given gift that I call the Plus Factor.

Courage isn't always a physical thing. There is such a thing as moral courage, too. This is the kind of courage that enables an individual to do what he or she knows is right, even when—especially when—it seems expedient to do something else. Many great men have displayed it—that's why they were great. Martin Luther facing his detractors at the Diet of Worms and saying, "It is neither wise nor prudent to do aught against the dictates of conscience. Here I stand; I cannot do otherwise." Abraham Lincoln facing the crisis of civil war. Some of his advisors thought he should not resort to force. Horace Greeley said to him, "If you lose, you drench the country with blood; if you win, you only pin the country together with bayonets." But Lincoln had a vision of a united land, and the moral courage to fight to preserve it. Because he persevered, this country is what it is today.

Sometimes moral courage enters into the highly physical realm of sports. One December evening a young football coach stared through a Birmingham hotel window at the dark Alabama night outside. This was a situation he had hoped he would never have to face. He had been head coach at Georgia Tech for only seven years. In that short time he had reversed a long losing trend in Tech football. His Yellow Jackets had battled hard all season long, finally winning the chance to play favored Michigan State in the post-season All-American Bowl on New Year's Eve. Tech was the underdog, but Coach Bill Curry had a lot of confidence in his young players. At least, he had had a lot of confidence in them . . . until now.

Word had come to him that four of the key players on his team had broken training. All players had been told that physical conditioning was of the utmost importance; they were expected to abide by training rules at all times. Failure to do so, they were warned, would bring swift disciplinary action. They were asked if they understood this. All said they did.

Nevertheless, with the all-important game just forty-eight hours away, four of the players had failed to observe the curfew deadline. After a team dinner designed to ease tensions and relax taut nerves, they were supposed to be in bed at a certain time. But a bed check by assistant coaches had revealed that the first-string quarterback, a flanker back, a split end, and the reserve fullback were not where they were supposed to be—in bed.

What should the penalty be? If the coach disqualified them from playing in this crucial game, Tech would almost certainly lose. The first-string quarterback had completed passes during the regular season for 1,557 yards and 10 touchdowns. The back-up quarterback had thrown only two passes—one an interception, the other for the loss of a yard. The split end was Tech's leading receiver with 29 catches for 645 yards and 6 touchdowns. If the coach sent them back to Atlanta, he would be sending 2,202 yards and 16 touchdowns worth of offense with them. How could Tech possibly win under those conditions?

Nowhere is winning football games more important than in the deep South. If Curry suspended his players and lost, the storm of criticism would be furious. If he announced his intention of suspending them, the pressure to rescind the order would be enormous. All the acceptance and popularity that Curry had built up during the year would be on the line. The most important game Tech had played in years would be in jeopardy. And yet . . .

And yet, the players had known the rules. They had broken them. How would they ever learn the importance of self-discipline, self-control, if they were given a tap on the wrist and allowed to play? How would the players feel who *had* obeyed the rule? What was the *right* thing to do?

When he asked himself that question and when he prayed about it, Coach Curry knew the answer. He issued the orders: The offending players would not be allowed to play in the game.

Was the Plus Factor operating here? Of course it was. It is always operating when a person making a difficult decision chooses the one that is morally right. And when the Plus Factor is thus injected into a situation, remarkable things can happen.

Take that football game, for example. The back-up quarterback, Todd Rampley, was only a sophomore. The pressure on him was terrific; he might have made all sorts of mistakes. Instead, he played the game of his life. Linebacker Ted Roof, Tech's defensive captain, said, "It's time to circle the wagons and play harder." Incredibly, in the closing minutes, Tech scored a touchdown that gave them a sensational 17-14 victory.

If you had been in the stadium at Legion Field in Birmingham that night, you would not have been able to see the Plus Factor, because it is always invisible. But you could have felt it, as an underdog football team, crippled by the loss of its key players, rose up with a mighty surge of courage and determination and won the game.

Courage, says my big Webster's dictionary, is "the firmness of spirit that faces extreme danger or difficulty without flinching or retreating." It points out that the word itself is derived from the Latin word for heart; brave hearts have the courage to endure, and I think it is often the Plus Factor that provides such courage. Let me end this chapter by telling you of an episode that happened a few years ago in the forested hills of Kentucky.

As he pushed through the thick brush that sunny day, Marshall Clouse was a happy man. He was seventy-nine years old and blind in one eye, but he carried his chain saw and woodcutting tools easily, and he was doing what he liked to do, cutting trees to be carted back to the little sawmill he had owned for the last twenty years. He had parked his pickup truck a hundred yards away, just off the old dirt road. He expected to be home by suppertime. No one knew exactly where he was.

He felled a couple of trees with no difficulty. Then, as a tall poplar toppled, it caught in the branches of another tree. Marshall Clouse cut through the trunk of a third tree, hoping it would knock the stuck tree loose. It didn't, and so he turned away—just as both trees fell suddenly with a thunderous crash, hurling him to the ground unconscious. When he awoke, his face lacerated and bleeding, both legs were pinned under one of the fallen trees, the bones smashed, the pain almost unbearable.

Probably Marshall Clouse had never heard of the Plus Factor. But all his life he had believed in a Power greater than himself, and now he called on this Power for strength and courage. Somehow, with a screwdriver that was in his overalls pocket, he dug his shattered legs out from under the tree. He tried to move them, but they were useless. When he tried to crawl on his face, his feet caught in the vines and twigs, causing him excruciating pain. The only way he could move, an inch at a time, was on his back, dragging himself along by his elbows.

Many men half the age of Marshall Clouse would have been defeated by pain and shock. They would have decided that the truck was hopelessly distant, out of reach. They might well have chosen to lie still rather than incur the agony of moving at all.

But something inside Marshall Clouse refused to give in. Inch by agonizing inch he dragged himself, on his back, over sharp stones, through the tangled underbrush, blood flowing from his forehead, shirt ripped to shreds, useless legs trailing behind him. Inch by inch, hour after hour, as the sun dropped steadily and the chill of nightfall fell across the silent forest. On and on, biting his lips to keep from screaming, until—four hours after the trees fell on him—he was alongside the truck.

He opened the door and reached up to grasp the steering wheel so that he could pull himself into the cab. The wheel was just beyond his quivering fingers. Again he tried, gasping with pain. He could not reach it. At this point a lesser man, a man unsupported by an unconquerable determination, would have given up. But the brave heart of seventy-nine-year-old Marshall Clouse did not give up. Slowly, painfully, he began to build a little mound of leaves, dirt, twigs, anything he could reach. He built the mound and he dragged himself to the top of it. Then he reached up, grasped the steering wheel, and calling on some final reserve of strength pulled himself into the cab.

Even then, he was in a terrible predicament. His legs were useless. He could not use them to touch the brakes, or the accelerator. All he could do was start the engine, put the truck in low gear, and try to guide it as it rolled slowly downhill to the main road, back to someone who could help him. And that is what he did.

Marshall Clouse spent weeks in a hospital, then months convalescing at home. Doctors told him he would never walk again. But today, being the kind of man he is, Marshall

Clouse is walking again. Not very well, perhaps. But walking.

What brought a seventy-nine-year-old through an ordeal like that? Marshall Clouse, who has been a committed Christian for over sixty years, would tell you that the Lord Jesus did it. And he would be right. But would it not be fair to say that the Lord Jesus came to his aid by liberating in his mind and in his body the Plus Factor and the extra strength within that enabled him to rise above shattering injury, massive shock, blood loss, agonizing pain, and apparently unsurmountable obstacles?

There is no doubt at all in my mind that the Plus Factor was liberated in Marshall Clouse by a Power greater than himself. And the courage and strength it gave him saved his life.

9.

The PLUS FACTOR and Peace of Mind

Peace of mind is important to well-being, to successful achievement and happiness. How is it attained? One of the greatest passages in the Bible says, "Thou wilt keep him in perfect peace, whose mind is stayed on thee . . ." (Isaiah 26:3). The word *stayed* is a reference to the ropes and stays that hold a ship's mast upright, even in the worst of storms. So it means that if your mind is braced on God—the vast, immovable, unchanging, everlasting God—the anxieties and confusions and tensions that surround you will not penetrate the peace that enfolds you. You will be quiet and controlled, without strain or stress. And this is the kind of spiritual climate in which the Plus Factor is able to grow.

Crises are going to come into every human life; that's reality. But it was a great American psychiatrist who said that attitudes toward facts can be more important than facts themselves. Thomas Carlyle had this same truth in mind when he spoke of "the calm superiority of the spirit over circumstances." You can react to a problem or a crisis with fear and tension and panic. Or you can follow the advice of an old Chinese philosopher who said, "Always take an emergency leisurely." The person who masters this art—and it is an art—will know how to overcome stress and tension.

The everyday American phrase that sums up this attitude is "easy does it." All great athletes have this relaxed control of themselves. The late Branch Rickey, one of the greatest baseball men this country has every known, told me once that he wouldn't hire a player, regardless of how well he could field or hit or run, unless he was "loose as ashes." Now there's a picturesque and vivid phrase! Can you imagine anything looser than ashes?

Of course, I suppose there's a point where creative relaxation can turn into inertia or even laziness. I remember a story I heard about a tourist who came upon an old Indian sitting half-asleep outside his adobe home. The tourist, a hard-driving banker from the East, felt a bit indignant about this; so he said to the Indian, "Chief, why don't you go into town and get yourself a job?" The old Indian opened one eye and said, "Why?"

The banker said, "Because they're paying good money these days. You might make as much as two hundred dollars a week." And the old Indian said, "Why?"

The banker said, "If you started earning two hundred dollars a week, you could save your money and invest it. Then you could retire and not work anymore."

Then the old fellow opened both eyes and said, "Not working now!"

Was the Indian lazy—or was he right?

Well, this is just a droll little story that I like. Peace of mind, indeed the peace of God that passeth all understanding, as Saint Paul said, is something all of us can achieve if we will just let calmness enter our minds. This is the ultimate control of tension.

There is a passage in the fourth chapter of Saint Mark's Gospel that anyone who suffers from tension or anxiety should read. Those verses describe Jesus asleep in the stern of a small boat on the Sea of Galilee when a storm arose. Storms come up quickly on those inland seas, which, since they are relatively shallow, can become extremely agitated and rough.

The Bible account vividly portrays the fear and distress of the disciples. They knew they were in a highly dangerous situation. They were blinded by rain driven horizontally into their faces. The sail may well have been torn away. Lightning was blazing, thunder was crashing all around them. They groped their way to the stern of the lurching boat where Jesus was lying asleep, head pillowed on His arm, relaxed as healthy people are in slumber. They shook Him awake, calling out in terrified voices, "Master, save us! We're all going to die!"

He opened His eyes and looked at the storm-lashed sea, at the frightened faces around him. I can imagine His smile as He stood up, crossed the wet planking, clasped the mast, a tall, broad-shouldered figure, hair soaked, drenched to the skin. Then He raised one arm aloft and in a voice that carried above the shrieking of the wind uttered just three words: "Peace, be still!"

And as the writer of the Gospel says with such simplicity, "There was a great calm."

I have wondered sometimes where that calm was. In the actual waves of the sea? Yes, undoubtedly. But wasn't it even more significantly in the minds of the disciples? Fear was driven out. Panic was gone. In their regained calmness of spirit the waves must not have looked so terrifying.

What a sensational example of Christ's power at work! His was a tremendous Personality, so strong, so compelling that it brought calm to the raging seas and peace to the terrified minds of His companions! No wonder they whispered in awe to one another, "What manner of man is this, that even the winds and the seas obey him?"

I think we ought to remind ourselves that Jesus rides with us in the small boats which are our lives, boats often beset by tempests and stormy seas. Let Him hold up His hand and say to us, "Peace, be still." And then we can say, "And there was a great calm."

My mother used to say, "Turn your troubles over to Jesus. Keep your mind filled with God. Keep it braced on the greatness of God. Keep it stayed on the knowledge that He loves you, and cares what happens to you." She was so right, for that is the fundamental secret of having a peaceful mind, one in which the Plus Factor can flourish and grow. As you keep yourself attuned to God's will and God's laws, the Plus Factor will operate in your nature.

It calms and soothes the spirit to read the Bible, to pray, to meditate on the goodness of God. It helps to affirm that the power of God resides in you and is available to you. Not long ago I found it helpful to write an affirmation along these lines that I keep in my wallet and repeat to myself now and then. It is a statement that I have found both tranquilizing and strengthening. Here it is:

I affirm that the Plus Factor, a manifestation
    of God's power, is rising in me,
  Renewing and healing my body,
  Bringing power to my mind,
  Giving me success in my work.

I affirm health, energy, enthusiasm, the joy of life.
All this I owe to Jesus Christ, my Lord and Savior.
He has given me the victory principle
For which I thank Him every day.

Here is another powerful idea that can be of tremendous value to anyone who wishes the Plus Factor to operate with strength and efficiency. The Bible tells us that Jesus gave His disciples authority over evil spirits. Why, then, shouldn't we, who are also His disciples, take authority over the devils of doubt and fear and anxiety and tension that block the flow of the life force in us?

Imagine those negative forces arrayed against you like an enemy army, threatening, malevolent, poised to attack. Then, in your mind's eye, see yourself putting on your spiritual armor, drawing your sword, charging headlong into those hostile ranks, confident that God Himself is on your side.

Summon up this image, not just once, but over and over again. Gradually, if you are truly determined to establish your authority over these destructive elements, the powerful, creative forces of the Plus Factor will begin to work unhindered through your being.

Modern science is just beginning to understand the power latent in a relaxed and peaceful mind. It is also beginning to understand the importance of a relaxed body. Almost everyone, by now, is aware of the benefits of simple muscle control. It can be practiced quite easily. To achieve a state of physical relaxation, begin by getting into a comfortable position. Then you say to the muscles controlling your face, "Let go," and image serenity stealing across your countenance. Then you say to your lungs, "Breathe deeply and tranquilly; let go." Go down to the muscles of the legs, the toes; say "Let go." Stretch out your hand slowly, palm upward; then turn it over and say, "I am now pouring all my troubles, all my tensions, all my anxieties into the great, all-powerful hand of God." *Let them all go.*

Muscle tensions can tie us into knots; but muscle tensions are created and controlled by thoughts. When you can get your mind into harmony with God's power, it can direct the muscles of your body to relax and function smoothly.

Of vast importance in achieving peace of mind is dealing with the contents of the mind itself: the mass of ill thoughts you have stored up over the years, all the regrets, all the futilities, all the hidden sins, all the hates, all the grudges, all the vindictiveness. The minds of many people are filled with pockets of poison. And the poison flows out from these pockets through the whole personality, making fingers tremble, causing the heart to beat more rapidly and the blood pressure to rise, increasing stress and tension.

When your mind is thus filled (clogged might be a better word), you are everlastingly living at too high a tempo because of a deep, subconscious feeling that you should be punished. You are trying to get away from this feeling. But there can be no peace in your mind until you empty your mind by confession and by the cleansing that can come only from God. This is the most healthful experience that can come to anyone.

Not long ago I was preparing to retire in my hotel room in a city where I had just made a speech. The phone rang. A woman's voice said, "If I send a car for you, will you come out and see my husband? Nobody seems able to cure him."

I said, "Madam, I am not a doctor."

"I know that," she said. "But all the doctors say that his illness is the kind that only a spiritual treatment can cure."

"I'm sorry," I said, "but I'm no faith healer. I believe that faith can heal, but if you expect me to heal your husband, I don't want you to be disillusioned."

"My husband has great faith in you," she said.

"Faith in me won't get him anywhere," I said. "Has he any faith in God or in Jesus Christ?"

"He hasn't gone to church very often," she confessed. "I guess he's been too busy making money. Please come. We both need you."

The car came for me. It took me to a large, impressive house, almost a mansion. The man was a big, burly fellow, a hard-driving, self-made type. "What is your trouble?" I asked him.

"I'm nervous," he said. "I can't sleep. I have funny feelings in my arms. This one is so stiff I can't raise it properly." And he demonstrated. "The doctors don't seem to know anything. They tell me that physically my arm is all right. They say my trouble is my mental attitude."

Then we sat down and talked. "How is business?" I asked him.

"Oh, it's all right," he said. "But exasperating things keep happening. Recently I brought a young fellow into the firm and he double-crossed me!"

"How did he do that?" I asked.

He told me at length, ending, "I got rid of him. He still thinks I owe him money. But he will never get it out of me."

"I take it you don't like him much," I suggested.

"I used to like him," he said, "but not now. No more. I hate him. I'd give my right arm to beat him up."

His wife, who was sitting by, said, "That is the trouble. My husband is filled with ill will and hate."

I asked her to leave us alone for a while. When she had gone, I said to the man, "Tell me, have you committed sin? Better get it out. It festers. Perhaps this is connected with how you feel."

He hesitated for a while. Then he said, "Yes, I have done some things I regret. It's strange; I never did want to be a bad person. Some of the things I've done—I would give my right arm if I had never done them." He really meant it.

That he would give his right arm, curiously, the arm he couldn't raise, was recurrent in his speech.

"Listen," I said to him. "I'm no healer. But I am going to put my hand on your shoulder. I probably should put it on your head, because I believe that's where the trouble really is. But I am going to put my hand on your right shoulder. You are filled with all kinds of poison and you must pour it out."

I was there for a long time listening to him.

When he got through he looked up at me and asked, rather pathetically I thought, "Did you ever hear anything worse?"

"Yes," I answered, "but you are now being cleansed, for you have emptied out your mind. Now ask your Saviour for mercy." He did that most appealingly. I prayed, "Come into this man's troubled mind and give him peace."

A few months later I met him again. I hardly knew it was the same man. "Look at this arm," he said, raising it easily above his head. "The pain in my shoulder is gone. My head is all right, too. I have learned to follow Jesus Christ, and He has given me peace as you said He would."

Confession. Repentance. It's as simple as that. Empty out all the pockets of poison in your mind, every one of them, and let Jesus Christ fill your mind with His healing power. That is the secret of having mental peace. That is the way to activate the flow of the Plus Factor.

10.

How the PLUS FACTOR Lends Reality to Hope

Have you ever stopped to wonder what it is that keeps you going from one day to another? What lies behind your ability to fight your way through periods of discouragement or depression? What makes you believe that sooner or later bad times will get better?

It's a little four-letter word that has enormous power in it. Power to bring failures back to success. Power to bring the sick back to health. Power to bring the weak back to strength. It's the word called *hope*.

Saint Paul knew how powerful hope is. He put it right up alongside faith and love as the three great words with power in them.

Most of the memorable people I've known have been strong hopers. Sometimes they had to *learn* to hope; they had to walk before they could run. I had a friend, R. P. Ettinger, who was founder of the publishing house of Prentice-Hall, Inc. He was brilliant, articulate, and forceful, an outstanding businessman. I first got to know him because his firm published my books, and we became warm friends.

Then R. P. Ettinger developed cancer of the throat. It was necessary to remove his larynx, and this man whose voice had dominated so many business conferences became speechless. One day in my office I had a telephone call from his wife. She said, "You know Dick can't speak now. But he's written me a note, and it says, 'Get Norman on the telephone and ask him to speak a word of hope to me.'" She said "You'll hear no answer, because he can't say anything, but he will be hearing you, whatever you choose to say to him."

Right there, with no warning, I had to give this afflicted man a word of hope. I said, "R. P., you and I published *The Power of Positive Thinking* and we are believers." Then I gave him that familiar passage from the book of Psalms: "Why art thou cast down, O my soul? and why art thou disquieted within me? hope thou in God: for I shall yet praise him, who is the health of my countenance, and my God" (Psalms 42:11). "Just keep on believing and hoping and thinking positively," I said.

His wife came back on the phone. "Say that again for him," she said. "He wants to copy it down. Repeat it slowly, please."

So once again I said, "Dick, this is the word of hope that you wanted. I'll repeat it again, and you write it down, and read it and believe it and hang onto it." And slowly I repeated Psalms 42:11.

That little seed of hope took root, and it grew. He began to hope that he would speak again, and thanks to medical science and a mighty effort on his part the day came when he *did* speak again, and he presided once more over business conferences with assurance and power. When people asked him how he did it, he always smiled and said, "Hope turned me around." Or sometimes he would say quite simply, "I was saved by hope."

If you look back through history you will see many shining instances where a single man or woman brought hope and courage and endurance to a whole nation: Winston Churchill in the Battle of Britain; George Washington at Valley Forge; Joan of Arc, that extraordinary peasant girl, calling out to the soul of France. The Plus Factor was surging through the lives of such people, energizing them, sustaining them, filling them with unconquerable hope.

Every time I go to Athens I think of Saint Paul standing almost two thousand years ago on the Hill of Mars, telling the Greeks, who worshipped a whole pantheon of pagan gods, about the ultimate God "in whom we move and live and have our being." The Greeks were not great admirers of hope. They believed everyone's destiny was fixed and unchangeable, and therefore that hope was just a delusion. Here came this fiery little man from some obscure Roman province in the Middle East with his remarkable message that a single God had created everything. Not only that, this omnipotent Creator cared so much about human beings that He had sent His Son to die on the cross and thus redeem them. More extraordinary still, those who accepted the Son and believed what He said would never die, but would have everlasting life.

What a stupendous message of hope this was! The Greeks didn't know what to make of it. The Bible tells us that some of Paul's hearers laughed and mocked him. But others said thoughtfully, "We'll talk again about these matters." Perhaps those were the Greeks who remembered that in their own ancient legend of Pandora, who opened the forbidden box and released all the plagues and miseries that afflict mankind, the last spirit that fluttered out was hope—with iridescent wings.

There's something about hope that makes clear thinking possible. When you're faced with a problem, do you regard it with hope or with despondency? If you hope there is a solution, if you believe that somewhere there's a solution, you are probably going to find it. If you think dismally about it, you're likely to come up with dismal results.

I know a remarkable woman who demonstrates the tremendous power of hopeful thinking. She is living proof that such thinking keeps the mind clear to function at maximum efficiency. At a meeting of the directors of a business organization where she is an executive, a really tough problem was under discussion. They wrestled with it for quite a while. The five men present came to the gloomy conclusion that there was just no solution.

But not this woman. "Look," she said, "what is a problem? Simply a set of circumstances for which there seems to be no solution. But actually there is always a solution. All we have to do is find it. Then there willl be no more problem." The men around the table grinned sadly at what they considered a totally naive remark.

"Now," she continued, "the first step is to start thinking hopefully. Let's get rid of all this dismal thinking, because it's paralyzing us. Let's affirm that there is a solution, and that we're smart enough to find it." This cleared the air, and the minds around that conference table began to do some real thinking. They reviewed the matter step-by-step, found the error, and without too much trouble corrected it. All because one positive person injected hope into what seemed like a hopeless situation.

We should never write off anything as impossible or as a failure. God gave us the capacity to think our way through any problem. The hopeful thinker projects hope and faith into the darkest situation and lights it up. As long as the thought of defeat is kept out of a person's mind, victory is certain to come sooner or later.

Is there a difference between hoping and wishing? Yes, there is. Hope has the quality of expectancy in it. When you hope strongly, something in you *expects* to have that hope realized. And this intangible called expectancy, which is closely allied to the Plus Factor, can affect events in a remarkable way.

All parents know that if you expect your children to live up to certain standards, and let them know that this is what you expect, they are likely to measure up. Football coaches know that if they expect a player to do well, usually he will. On the other hand, if they expect or predict poor performances, they are likely to get it.

Psychologists have labeled this phenomenon, "The Theory of the Self-fulfilling Prophecy." Some interesting experiments have been carried out by Dr. Robert Rosenthal, a Harvard University psychologist, to prove the truth of this theory. This professor went into a ghetto area of San Francisco where school children were undisciplined, nonachievers, poor students. He picked at random twenty-four students and divided them into two groups. He put half of these children in the hands of certain teachers, telling them that these children had tremendous potential. He assigned the other twelve children to another group of teachers, telling these teachers that the children lacked any real potential, that doubtless it would be impossible to accomplish anything with them. Then he prescribed a series of training exercises for all these students to be put through.

Six months later he returned to check on results. The students in the charge of teachers who had been told to expect good things were doing spectacular work, while the other children were, if anything, more listless and desultory than before.

What people think you expect of them, they will usually deliver. And what your own psyche, your own unconscious mind thinks you expect of it, it will deliver. When you hope strongly enough, expectancy goes to work for you. And when expectancy turns the key that we call the Plus Factor, great things happen.

You can tell strong hopers by the way they seem to be facing, psychologically speaking. Hopers look forward. Regretters look back. The eminent psychiatrist Dr. Smiley Blanton, who was a good friend of mine, kept in his office a tape recording of typical problems brought to him by people struggling with frustrations or disappointments. Their identities were concealed, of course, but sometimes the doctor would play the tape for a new patient and ask him or her to listen for a significant phrase that occurred over and over again. That phrase was, "If only . . ." The unhappy people kept repeating it as they reviewed their failures, their broken relationships, their deep unhappiness. "If only" they had made wiser decisions. "If only" they had done things differently. On and on. If only . . . If only . . .

"You see," Dr. Blanton would say, "those people are bogged down in the swamp of regret. They'll never be happy until they change the direction in which they're looking. The phrase they should be repeating over and over again is not 'If only.' The phrase should be 'Next time.' 'Next time' I'll avoid all those mistakes and errors and come out with a success instead of a failure."

Now what was Dr. Blanton saying? In one word, he was counseling *hope.* That was his prescription for dazed or despairing minds. "Next time . . ."—that phrase is packed with hope. It lets the Plus Factor begin to stir in persons from whom it has been excluded by pessimism, fear, gloom, despair.

Some years ago I spent a few days in Jamaica. It's a lovely tropical island, lush and mountainous, set like a jewel in the jade and turquoise waters of the Caribbean. At the hotel where we were staying, an old map hung in one of the hallways. Looking at it, I noticed some very faint lettering that ran across an almost uninhabited part of the island. I had to look close to make out the words, but finally I did. They said: "The Land of Look-Behind."

Intrigued, I asked the owner of the hotel what those words meant. He told me that in the days of slavery, runaways from the sugar plantations sometimes escaped into that lonely and barren territory. They were often pursued by slave owners or other authorities with guns and dogs. The fugitives were always on the run, always looking over their shoulders. So that was where the term came from: The Land of Look-Behind.

I never forgot that melancholy term, because my years of counseling people have led me to believe that many of them are living in their own private land of look-behind. They are the ones who dwell endlessly on past mistakes, who let fears generated by old failure rob them of success, who refuse to accept God's promises of forgiveness of sins. When a person lives in the land of look-behind, he or she is really excluding hope from his or her life. They are also making it almost impossible for the Plus Factor to operate. How can the Plus Factor make an entry into a mind that has lost the buoyancy of hope?

Speaking of buoyancy, I remember an old lithograph that a businessman friend of mine keeps in a prominent place in his office. It's not a colorful or handsome print. It shows an old, clumsy-looking scow, about three times the size of an ordinary rowboat, with high sides. From the oar locks, two oars are resting dejectedly on the sand. The tide is out and the old scow is stranded high on the beach; at the side of the picture is a glimpse of the distant water. The whole effect is rather somber; there's nothing more hopeless looking, more inert, than a beached boat. You can't pull it or drag it;

it's too heavy. It's just stuck there on the sand with the water far out.

But down at the bottom of the picture is this caption: "The tide always comes back." And when the tide does come back, that inert thing comes alive. It rises on the mighty shoulders of the sea. It dances on the waves. The tide always comes back! I asked the owner, "Why do you have that picture on your wall?"

He told me that he had seen it in an old antique store at a time when things were going very badly. He had bought it for a few dollars because he was very discouraged, and the message in the caption gave him a lift. It sent a flicker of hope through him every time he looked at it. That was why he kept it: to remind himself that troubles do pass, that storms do blow over, that the tide doesn't go out and stay out forever. Sooner or later it comes back in.

I've gone through some difficult times—who hasn't?—and I know how easy it is to think that troubles have become your constant companions. You let a gray film of hopelessness creep into your mind, where it colors everything. You can even begin to enjoy this sense of hopelessness, in a perverse sort of way. It gives you an excuse for not trying to improve the situation!

The remedy for this state of mind is a good strong dose of hope, given to yourself at least three times a day. Don't ever say to yourself, "I've had it. I'm finished. I can't cope with all this." Never think, "This is more than I can take; it's more than I can handle." Say aloud the words of the Psalm, ". . . hope thou in God: for I shall yet praise him, who is the health of my countenance, and my God" (42:11). Affirm to yourself, "The tide may be out just now, but it is turning and soon it will come back in!"

I remember being taught a lesson in hopefulness very early in life. When we were children, my brother Bob and I used to go every summer to visit our grandparents, who lived in Lynchburg, Ohio. Beside the house, quite close to it, was a great tree. One night, just after our grandmother had put us to bed, a tremendous storm came up. The wind whistled around the house with a sound like a thousand banshees. Lightning flashed and thunder roared. Rain was hurled in sheets against the windows. The whole house shook. Bob and I were scared. From where I lay, I could see the tree, silhouetted against the lightning flashes. Seeing how violently it was being tossed by the storm, I was suddenly filled with terror. "Bob," I cried, "the tree is falling! The tree is falling!" We jumped out of bed and scurried down to where my grandmother was sitting by a kerosene lamp, quietly reading the *Christian Advocate*. We cried, "Grandma! Grandma!"

"What's the matter?" she asked calmly.

"The tree! It's going to fall down on us!"

My grandmother was a very wise woman. She bundled us up and took us out on the porch in the wind and the rain. She said, "Isn't it great to feel the rain on your face? Isn't it marvelous to be out here in the wind? God is in this rain. God is in this wind. You don't have to worry about the tree. The tree is having a good time with this storm. See how it yields to it, bending one way or the other. It doesn't fight it. It cooperates with it. It's playing with the storm. It's laughing with the wind and the rain. It's not going to fall tonight. It's going to be there for a long time to come. Now, you go back to bed, boys. God is in the storm, and ultimately all storms pass."

All through my life the memory of that simple incident has reassured and sustained me. I thought of it again not long ago when I was seated in an airliner in Washington, D.C., waiting to take off for New York. We had taxied out to the runway, when the sky became dark and sinister. A high wind came roaring up the Potomac, and sheets of rain pelted the aircraft. The plane actually rocked violently from the force of the wind. We passengers were getting very apprehensive when the voice of the pilot came on the loudspeaker. He had a soft southern accent. "Ladies and gentlemen," he drawled, "there's a storm center directly above the airport. We can't take off in this weather. We're going to wait it out. Our report is that the storm will pass in about forty-five minutes. So you people who have business engagements in New York, stop fretting and sit back and relax, because we're not going to New York for a while. Meanwhile," he went on, "I'm going to head the plane into the wind so that you'll be more comfortable. Don't worry about anything." And then he added these words: "All storms ultimately pass."

Of course they do. Believing that fact, accepting that fact, is the beginning of wisdom, the beginning of hope.

If your belief in hope includes the conviction that God is for you and will help you through any emergency, enormous power is available to you. You may never know that power is there until you need it and call upon it in some dire situation, perhaps even a life-threatening situation; then you find out. I remember we published many years ago in *Guideposts* magazine, a true story where this power that I'm writing about—the power of hope backed by faith—comes through so vividly that I've never forgotten it.

Lucinda and Charles Sears lived on the edge of Lake Okeechobee in Florida. They will never forget—no one who was in southern Florida at the time will ever forget—that day in September when almost without warning one of the greatest hurricanes in history boiled up out of the Caribbean. The monstrous storm slashed into Miami, then surged up the peninsula, leaving death and destruction behind.

Lucinda Sears stood at the door of her little house with a troubled look in her eyes. The sky had a strange, yellowish look. A mounting wind was whipping the fronds of the palm trees and driving gusts of rain that seemed almost horizontal. Lucinda and her husband knew nothing about the full extent of the storm; this was in the days before there were hurricane warnings. All they knew was that suddenly the nine-foot earthen dike around the lake burst and water began to surge around their cabin. Moments later the roof blew off their small home as if it were a piece of cardboard. They knew they were looking into the blank eyes of death.

They grabbed their three children under their arms and ran outside looking for shelter. All they could see was one bent old tree that had withstood many a storm in the past. Whether it could withstand this one they didn't know, but it was the only hope they had. The rising water from the lake drenched them as they ran to the tree. It made everything so slippery that one of the little boys dropped from his father's arms and disappeared for a moment. Balancing the other boy with one arm, Charles finally pulled the child from the swirling muck. Floating branches and other debris battered the family as they finally made it to the tree and climbed into the sheltering branches.

The fury of the storm grew worse. As the water level rose, the terrified family climbed higher into the tree, until they were clinging desperately to the topmost branches. Water continued to rise until it came to the parents' shoulders. They could climb no higher. They had to hold the children up above their heads. It was the only way to keep them from being drowned.

As the winds lashed them and the rain stung their faces, night came on. Still the water inched relentlessly higher. "Cindy, we're all going to die!" cried Charles.

"Be quiet," Lucinda commanded him. "We're not going to die. The Lord is here with us. You just hold up those children." And the storm continued to rage. Once Charles slipped, and he and the two boys were nearly swept away.

Lucinda made their little daughter, Effie Ann, lock her arms around her mother's neck. Then, with her legs wrapped around a branch, Lucinda reached down and pulled the boys up with her. She held all three children until Charles could get hold of the tree and help her again.

But still the waters reached for them in the blackness with the muddy hands of death. "It's no use," Charles sobbed. "We can't hold on. We'll never make it."

Into the storm Lucinda's strong voice cried. "We will make it!" And then, incredibly, she began to sing, with hope in her heart, above the shrieking of the wind:

> Father, I stretch my hand to Thee,
> No other help I know.
> If Thou withdraw Thyself from me,
> Ah, whither shall I go . . .
> Author of faith, I lift to Thee
> My weary, longing eyes;
> O may I now receive that gift;
> My soul, without it, dies.

As the old hymn was borne away by the wind, Lucinda saw three flashes of light streak across the eastern sky. Perhaps it was only lightning, but to Lucinda it was a sign. "Thank You, God. Dear Jesus, thank You," she murmured. And the wind slackened and the night became quiet.

Slowly the water receded until at noon the next day they were able to get down from the tree, battered, hurt, hungry, exhausted, but still alive. They made their way painfully to an aid station where they found food and shelter. Thanks to the hope and faith in one woman's heart, they had lived through the terror of the night.

We have a marvelous faith by which we triumph over danger, over discouragement, over despair, over everything—a faith of no defeat.

So build hope into your philosophy. Base your life upon it. *Hope* that difficulties will pass. *Hope* that storms will cease. *Hope* that pain will not endure. *Hope* that weakness will be overcome. *Hope* thou in God . . . and ultimately you will find yourself saying, "Praise God, from whom all blessings flow."

11.

The PLUS FACTOR and the Thirteenth Stone

In the ancient city of Kyoto, Japan, there is a famous garden that consists of nothing but thirteen large stones placed in what seems to be a random pattern on a base of carefully raked white sand.

For centuries these stones have intrigued visitors. What do they symbolize in their stark simplicity? One observer may see them as representing thirteen basic problems of mankind, each a unity in itself but also part of a greater whole. Another onlooker may decide that the stones are emblematic of thirteen different forms of happiness, and find himself wondering what those happinesses may be. Yet another observer may become aware that the stones are carefully positioned so that it is impossible to view all of them at once.

One visitor may find that the garden conveys a deep sense of peace and tranquillity. Another may find his mind stimulated and somehow expanded. In a way, the garden is like the famous Rorschach inkblot tests used by psychologists and psychiatrists to gain insight into a patient's thought processes. The inkblots have no intrinsic meaning of their own, but what the viewer thinks he sees in them may give a clue to his mental or emotional condition.

The last time I was at the garden in Kyoto the concept of the Plus Factor was very much in my mind, and I began to wonder if perhaps in some way the stone garden might be a reflection of that concept. Suppose, I said to myself, the white sand symbolizes the universal nature of the Plus Factor, the truth that it is built into all of us.

And suppose further, I went on, that these thirteen stones represent attitudes or states of mind that release the Plus Factor, translating it from the general to the actual, concrete, specific needs of individual human beings?

So, choosing one stone and fixing my eyes upon it, I said to myself, "That represents faith." And of the next, "That's a symbol for love." And then, "That's the quality of persistence." And then, "That one stands for the power of prayer." I went all around the garden, assigning to each stone some positive characteristic of this kind.

The first twelve choices were quite easy, but somehow I got stuck on the thirteenth. Try as I might, I could not think of a suitable identity to bestow upon this thirteenth stone. I wrestled with it for a while and then turned away impatiently. "What does it matter if you can't think of an appropriate name for a rock?" I said to myself. "Who cares?" And like an echo a phrase jumped into my mind. "Caring. Perhaps that's what it represents. The power of caring."

Well, regardless of what the stone may or may not represent, there is no doubt whatsoever in my mind that people who care about other people, and show that caring in loving, unselfish ways, almost invariably have a strong, deep current of the Plus Factor operating within themselves. When we say of someone, "He (or she) is a very kind person," what we are really describing is a person who has discovered a key that unlocks the door to real happiness. And the name of that key is caring, or kindness.

The caring has to come from the heart, though. Helping people in some casual fashion, or because you have some ulterior motive for helping them, won't activate the Plus Factor. Remember how the Good Samaritan in the Bible cared about the man attacked by robbers? The Good Samaritan had nothing to gain from helping the victim, but he helped him anyway. It was the caring principle in action. And I'm sure the Plus Factor in the Samaritan's life was strengthened because of it.

Caring is an extraordinary characteristic, when you stop to think about it. Self-preservation is said to be the first law of existence. But it really isn't; there are times when the power of caring is so strong that the instinct to save one's own life at any cost is simply swept aside.

The other night on television I watched a drama based on the dreadful crash of an airliner in Washington a few years ago, a crash in which seventy-eight persons lost their lives. You may remember that the plane tried to take off in a snowstorm after waiting on the runway for a period of time that allowed ice to form on its wings. It hit one of the twin spans of the 14th Street Bridge with its tail section and crashed through the ice into the freezing waters of the Potomac River. Only a handful of dazed survivors managed to struggle to the surface. The rest went down under the black water with the plane itself.

Rescue efforts were hindered by the appalling weather and by late afternoon traffic that clogged the bridge. A rescue helicopter manned by two skilled and heroic specialists, Gene Windsor, a paramedic, and Don Usher, a pilot with many hours of Vietnam experience, flew through the whirling snow and hovered above six victims who were clinging to ice floes or the wreckage of the tail section that was still above the water. They dropped a rope right into the arms of a middle-aged man with a bald head and mustache. Instead of tying it around himself, he passed it to a woman near him. The chopper lifted her to safety.

Then it flew back and dropped the rope again. Again the bald-headed man passed it to his companions. The helicopter dragged four of them toward shore, but one woman slipped back into the icy water, too weak to hold on. As she thrashed about, a man in the crowd on the shore stripped off his coat and plunged into the freezing river. He was Lenny Skutnik, a clerk in the government's Budget Department. He said later that he had had no training in lifesaving or rescue work. But something in him cared so much that he was willing to risk his life to save the woman. And he did save her.

Meantime the chopper headed back for the bald-headed man, but he was gone. Gene Windsor said, "I'll never forget his pale, upturned face as he watched us moving away with the others, knowing that probably he would not be there when we got back." Twice this man, believed to have been Arland D. Williams, Jr., a bank executive from Atlanta, had handed the gift of life to a stranger at the cost of his own. Jesus had a word for such a person. "Greater love hath no man than this, that a man lay down his life for his friends." (John 15:13).

When Gene Windsor finally called his wife to assure her that he had survived the dangers of the rescue mission and tried to tell her about the man in the water, he broke down and cried.

What is this marvelous intensity of caring that moves us so when we hear about it or witness it in action? Sometimes it appears in flashes of almost incredible heroism, as on that tragic afternoon in Washington. Sometimes it infuses a whole lifetime, as with a Florence Nightingale, or an Albert Schweitzer, who gave up a brilliant career in music to spend his days in the jungles of Africa, bringing the healing gifts of medicine to the primitive people he found living there.

There is a Christ-like quality about such people. I think it was Tolstoy who said of Lincoln that he was a "Christ in miniature." And so he was.

The capacity for caring doesn't always take such dramatic form; it can show through in countless little demonstrations of kindness or concern. The other day I had one of those experiences painfully familiar to air travelers. I arrived at my destination in a midwestern city, but my suitcase didn't. I waited and waited by the carousel as a procession of bags went past, but mine was not among them. I was still waiting when the captain of our flight came through the baggage area. I had exchanged a few words with him during the flight. Now he stopped and asked me if I was having a problem.

When I explained the difficulty, he nodded understandingly. "You made a close connection in Chicago," he said. "Your bag will probably come in on the next flight. But don't worry about it. You go on to your hotel, and I'll see that the bag gets to you as soon as possible."

I protested that I didn't want him to be inconvenienced, but he insisted, so finally I gave in and took a cab to my hotel. I thought the airline would send the bag along by messenger when it arrived. About two hours later there was a knock on the door. When I opened it, there stood the captain himself, gold stripes gleaming, holding my bag. It was amazing that a man in his position would go to so much trouble for a stranger, and I told him so, with profuse thanks. All he said, with a smile, was, "Well, I knew you'd need your toothbrush!"

Caring, that's what he was, a caring person with the imagination and self-discipline to set aside his own convenience in order to help someone else. No wonder he had risen to be the captain of a great airplane. It wouldn't surprise me if some day he becomes chief executive of the whole airline, because the Plus Factor is pushing him upward.

Sometimes the Plus Factor will give an individual the insight and imagination to be helpful and caring in subtle and surprising ways. I once knew a man whose body was painfully twisted and deformed by polio. But his spirit was unconquerable. "My body may be handicapped," he would say, "but my mind isn't."

One day I asked him where this marvelous attitude came from; had he always had it? "No," he said, "not always. As a teenager I was terribly self-conscious and unhappy. I never wanted to undress in a locker room or in a place where other boys could see how I looked. Even the prospect of a routine physical exam left me filled with self-loathing and dread.

"One day I had to endure yet another physical exam by a doctor I had never met before. He was completely impersonal and professional, but I was miserable. Afterward he told me to get dressed. Then he sat at his desk and asked me various questions, making notes on some kind of medical form that lay before him. Finally he stood up and asked me to excuse him briefly. He would be back in about ten minutes, he said. Then he left the room.

I sat there staring at the form on his desk, wondering what sort of grim notations he might have made about me. At last, unable to contain my curiosity, I went over and looked at it. There were some medical references that meant little to me, but then my eye fell on what he had written in the box reserved for "Comments." There he had written five words in a strong, clear hand: *Has a magnificently shaped head.*

"I'll never forget the extraordinary sense of gratitude and relief that flooded me when I read those words. They made me feel that I was not just a cripple, not just a freak; I was a person with compensating features and attributes. Right then and there I made up my mind to look on the bright side of things, to put my handicap in its place, to move forward and make the most of myself regardless of circumstances, regardless of anything.

"And the most marvelous component of that tremendous feeling of warmth and optimism was the knowledge that this doctor, this perceptive, caring man, had staged the whole thing. He had left the room knowing that I would be unable to resist the temptation to look at the piece of paper on his desk. He had written a prescription designed to restore my damaged ego, my shattered self-esteem. What a wonderful thing! What a wonderful happening! It turned me completely around. It has illuminated my whole life!"

Yes, when it works through people like that doctor, the Plus Factor is a wonderful thing indeed.

Becoming a compassionate person isn't easy; sometimes a person has to go through pain and suffering before he achieves it. Certainly that was the difficult road that Detective Richard Pastorella of the New York City police force had to follow.

Detective Pastorella had an assistant in his work named Hard Hat. The most important thing about Hard Hat was his nose. Alert, intelligent, carefully schooled, Hard Hat was a German shepherd trained to work with the bomb squad to which Detective Pastorella was assigned. If his nose detected explosives, Hard Hat was taught to stop patrolling and sit down.

On the night of New Year's Eve, 1982, Detective Pastorella and his partner, Tony Senft, answered an emergency call to the plaza of a federal building in downtown Manhattan, where a bomb planted by a terrorist or a madman had gone off. No one had been injured in that explosion, but soon word was flashed that another bomb had exploded at police headquarters a few blocks away. There a patrolman, badly wounded, gasped to Detective Pastorella that he thought the bomb had been concealed in a paper bag.

Knowing that if two bombs had exploded there could easily be more, Pastorella and Senft began a search of the ground-level area of the police station with Hard Hat pacing alertly beside them. Suddenly, tugging at his leash, the big dog drew the officers to a darkened area near a pair of uprights that supported the building. There in the gloom Detective Pastorella saw, not one, but two paper bags. Each was placed behind one of the support columns.

And at that moment, Hard Hat sat down.

When Hard Hat sat down, Detective Pastorella knew that he and his partner were facing a situation of enormous danger. Curious bystanders were beginning to collect at the scene. He had a uniformed patrolman move them, and move Hard Hat, behind a wall some distance away. Then, with his partner behind him, he inched toward the paper bag over which he had placed a protective device known as a bomb blanket. Slowly he reached out his right hand . . . and the universe seemed to explode in his face.

The blast left him unconscious until the next day. Then he awoke to agonizing pain. His face and right arm were badly burned. There were no fingers on his right hand. One eye had been removed; he was blind in the other. Most of his hearing was gone. His partner's injuries were almost as bad.

His career as a police officer was over. For a year he was in and out of hospitals, fighting against a sense of total despair. What about his wife, Mary? What about their two teenage children? What did the future hold? There were no clear answers to such questions.

For a while fellow police officers came to see him, but eventually their visits stopped, and Detective Pastorella knew why. His plight reminded them all too vividly of the dangers they themselves faced every day.

Sometimes, I think, the Plus Factor uses other people to impart its mysterious design to us. One night after Richard Pastorella's sense of loneliness and frustration found vent in a torrent of bitter words, his wife, Mary, said to him gently, "You're not the only one, you know. There are other cops who have been hurt, too. You're not unique."

All night long those words seemed to dance in Pastorella's mind. The next day he wrote to police headquarters asking for a list of police officers severely injured in the line of duty. Headquarters not only sent such a list, a place was offered where Pastorella and others on the list could meet.

From that beginning came "The Police Self-Support Group," dedicated to helping injured policemen and their families. Now Richard Pastorella works six or seven days a week helping wives with disabled husbands, easing family tensions and quarrels, improving the psychological climate in which the children of such victims must live, helping with specific financial or medical problems, providing transportation, offering a steady source of comfort and support.

Indomitable . . . that's the word that comes to mind when I think of Richard Pastorella. It means undaunted . . . unconquered . . . unembittered. It means a life glorified by . . . the Plus Factor.

Helping someone in trouble, caring about people you hardly know, is almost a form of prayer, when you stop to think about it. It's an offering to God and the benefits flow right back to you.

Years ago I had two friends in Chicago, Gus and Frank Bering, who owned the Sherman House, a fine hotel. I remember Gus telling me about a barbers' supply convention they had in the hotel. Barbers' supply people from all over the United States were there, and some of them decided to stage a dramatic demonstration of the barber's art.

They went down to Halsted Street where derelicts used to gather and they picked out the dirtiest, seediest, most disreputable-looking one they could find. They brought him back to the Sherman House and took off his ragged clothes and gave him a bath. They shaved him, they groomed his hair, they squirted after-shave lotion on him. They bought him a new suit, new shoes, the best shirt they could find, an elegant tie. They even bought him a cane and a fancy vest and an expensive hat. He looked terrific. They presented him as an example of what barbers could do for a man, and he maintained a dignified appearance throughout the convention.

Gus Bering became interested in this man, and when the convention ended he offered him a job in the hotel. He told him to report the next morning. But the man didn't show up. He didn't appear for several mornings, so Bering went down to Halsted Street to look for him. He finally found him under some newspapers in an alley, his fine clothes all torn and dirty, his face covered with stubble, his eyes bleary from drink.

Bering picked him up and put him in a taxi and took him back to the hotel and cleaned him up again. He said, "The barbers didn't do enough for you; in fact, they didn't do anything for you; they just wanted an exhibit and you were it."

Then, Gus Bering told me, he took the man over to the Chicago Temple, a Methodist church around the corner.

I said, "What did you do with him over there, Gus?"

He smiled, because he knew I already knew the answer. He said, "I got some real religion into him and he was changed. He took the job I had offered him, and he succeeded at that, and he went on to other jobs. Eventually he married and had a fine family. He turned out all right."

Yes, he turned out all right because one good and wise man went out of his way to help, truly help him. The barbers were trying to help themselves; they weren't really interested in the man. But Gus saw beneath all the grime and the rags and the despair to the suffering child of God who desperately needed help, and he gave that help because of the caring principle, and a life was turned around. That's what being a helper really means.

What made a smart, big-time hotel owner like Gus Bering such a caring person? It was his total commitment to the greatest Example of caring that this world has ever seen. I have seen countless examples myself where this attitude of caring came into a person's life and changed it completely.

There is a man I have known for more than thirty years, and for many of those years he was an abject failure. You might almost say he was an expert in failure. Every job he undertook went awry. Practically everything he said was the wrong thing to say, and most of what he did was done without skill. Sometimes I would see him staring into space with so bewildered an expression that it haunted me. I tried to help him, but with no success. I knew he wasn't stupid, because from time to time his personality would display flashes of intelligence and even charm.

One night I had to drive nearly a hundred miles to give a talk, and I invited this man to come along with me, thinking we might get somewhere with his difficulties. We talked all the way there and got nowhere. He listened to my speech, but that didn't help either. On the way home he kept repeating, "What's wrong with me? What's wrong with me?" I had no ready answer.

We stopped at a roadside restaurant for a snack. I shall never forget the beauty of that moonlit night. The entire countryside was bathed in silver radiance as we came out of the diner.

My friend was standing beside the car when suddenly he gripped my arm and shouted. "Norman! I've got it!"

I was startled. "You've got what?"

"I know what's wrong with me," he said. "I know why everything goes wrong. It's because I am wrong myself."

I knew that he was sincere. I also knew he had taken the all-important first step in finding himself, so I asked him quietly, "Do you know what can make you right, all the way down to the depths of your nature?"

"No," he answered. "I just know that I'm wrong. Can you tell me how to become right?"

So I told him, standing there in the moonlight. And he listened. For the first time, he really listened. I was reminded of this experience when I saw him the other day. He is now a leader of his community, an elder in his church; he has a wife, a lovely family, a beautiful home. But more important, and beyond all else, he is filled with the joy of living.

"Do you know what happened to me, that night we drove together?" he asked me. "I had been breaking apart, but when I finally listened to you telling me about Jesus, suddenly I seemed to come together."

Of course he came together. He came together because he was touched by the infinite caring compassion of Jesus Christ, who had been waiting all the time to come into his life, just waiting to be invited in. He discovered that Jesus Christ has the power to bring into harmony and into focus all the mental, spiritual, and emotional faculties of a human being and make everything wonderfully better.

You may say that you have observed people who have lived wrong lives and still have prospered. I, too, have observed them. But remember that God does not settle His accounts on the thirtieth of every month, or even this year, or the next, or the next. And I can tell you this: Many people I have known who insisted on living a bad life ended up badly. It isn't always a swift or dramatic occurrence. But sooner or later it comes.

Some years ago I spoke at a meeting downtown in New York sponsored by the Salvation Army. The audience was composed of several hundred of the unhappiest-looking human beings I have ever seen. Many had started out with great advantages in life, but now they were down-and-outers. To be in the presence of these wasted lives was a chilling experience, almost a frightening one.

A man came up to me afterward and told me his name. "Why, Harry!" I said. "What are you doing here?" I remembered him from years back, when we were both youngsters growing up in Ohio. In those days when cars were still far from numerous, he drove the sportiest one in town. He belonged to my father's church, but he didn't attend very often. He was an attractive fellow with a nice personality, but even then he drank too much and seemed concerned about no one but himself.

"What am I doing here?" he repeated. "Well, to tell you the truth I'm here by the natural sequence of events. Cause and effect. It's probably too late, but I realize now that if people will just behave themselves, act decently and honorably, if they are just good rather than bad, abundance will come to them. If not, well . . ." He shook his head. Then he muttered, "There are some of us who need to be saved from ourselves. I've been wrong since back in Ohio as a boy."

"It's not too late, Harry." Sadly he shook his head. "There's no good in me, Norman." But there was. The Plus Factor was there. I'm glad to say that caring eventually released it so that the rest of this man's life was good, very good.

Try caring, the compassionate kind of caring taught by Jesus. It will not only help people; it also does wonders for the person who does the caring.

12.

How the PLUS FACTOR Helps You Handle Trouble

What's the most important thing in this world for all of us? It's learning how to live, isn't it? Life is a priceless gift, but it doesn't last forever. While we have it, our happiness depends on just one thing: how well we learn to cope with the challenges it presents.

When the seas of life grow rough, when troubles come, when problems arise, the Plus Factor, that shining ingredient poured into us at birth, is ever ready to help us, sometimes in surprising ways. For example, have you ever heard of the Law of Challenge and Response? Arnold Toynbee, the great historian, believed that the key to understanding history, with its rise and fall of civilizations, lay in the action of this invisible law. He was convinced that if a civilization faced some tremendous life-threatening challenge, met it head on and survived, the energies released by that mighty effort carried that civilization to new heights of art, of literature, of every aspect of culture.

Centuries ago, when the Greeks were threatened by the overwhelming might of the Persian empire, they responded with courage and determination. They hurled the Persians back. Then they went on to astounding achievements in art, in architecture, in philosophy, in drama. Two thousand years later, the English did something very similar. They rose up to defeat the great Armada that the Spaniards sent against them. The national pride and purpose and energy thus liberated produced such literary giants as Shakespeare, the colonization of the New World, and ultimately the great British Empire on which, it was said, the sun never set.

What does all this have to do with you or me? Simply this: The same law that raised the Greeks and the English to such heights, the law that Toynbee called Challenge and Response, exists in all of us and can operate in all of us as one more manifestation of the great dormant force we have been calling the Plus Factor.

When you get right down to basics, what Toynbee was saying is that trouble can be good for you. When you look it in the eye, when you refuse to be defeated, when you make up your mind to fight back, you discover you have hidden strengths and energies that you didn't even know you had.

Now, I'm not claiming that all troubles should be welcome or that all difficulties are blessings. Some sorrows can be devastating; some troubles can be agonizing.

But you can't deal with human beings and their problems as long as I have without recognizing that a certain amount of trouble is essential for character development and spiritual growth. And this too I have observed through the years: Trouble either makes a person bigger or smaller. It never leaves him exactly the way he was before. Some people break under trouble; others break records.

Sometimes the Plus Factor, called forth by this Law of Challenge and Response, appears in the form of quiet courage that faces up to bitter trials and then carries on undiminished through the years.

Not long ago, filling a speaking engagement in one of our southern states, I went into the motel dining room quite early for breakfast. It was a gray, wet morning with low hanging clouds. Outside I could see Spanish moss dripping from the trees in melancholy streamers. It was not, I thought, a day calculated to raise the spirits.

But this negative attitude was not shared by the waitress behind the counter, a cheerful black lady with a radiant smile. "Good morning," she said. "Sure am glad to see this rain. Yes, sir. Bet those farmers out there are too. I can just about hear those crops a-growing on a morning like this, can't you?"

Well, I had not really been listening for crops growing, but she went right on: "Now what can I fix you for breakfast on this fine day that the Lord has given us?"

"How about a poached egg and a little dry toast?" I asked, adding apologetically, "I'm on a diet, you know."

"Diet?" she said. "Diet? Nobody ought to start a day with one little old sad-faced egg. You just sit there now and I'll bring you a real man-sized southern breakfast, eggs and sausage and biscuits and grits with red-eye gravy. Keep you going all day long!"

And despite my feeble protests, that's what she did.

It was so early that we were alone in the dining room, just the two of us.

"Tell me," I said, "what makes you so happy? No, don't tell me; I'll tell you. You've just got to be a Christian, a real one."

"Yes, I surely am," she said, and there was such a note of gladness in her voice that the whole day seemed suddenly golden, as if a shaft of sunlight had come lancing in. "I started out mighty poorly in this life, but the Lord made me a promise and He kept it, too."

She went on to tell me that she and her husband had been born in abject poverty. Ten years after they were married, he had been killed in a sawmill accident, leaving her with three small children, all girls. "It was hard," she said. "Oh, Lord, it was so hard at times. But I had the Lord's promise, and I believed it. So I started a little dry-cleaning business and I still have it—I just come to work here in the morning because I like to meet new people and tell them about the Lord if they'll listen—and one of my girls is through college, now, and the next one is halfway through. Oh, yes, I'm a Christian, all right. It's the greatest thing anybody can be!"

"You know," I told her, "I've spent my whole life trying to get that message across to people. But tell me, which of the Lord's promises meant so much to you?"

"It's in the Gospel of Saint Luke," she said. "Ninth chapter, first verse, where it says: 'Then he called his twelve disciples together, and gave them power and authority over all devils, and to cure diseases.'" She had been mopping the counter with a rag, and now she stopped and looked right into my eyes. "You see," she said, "there are lots of different devils. I guess every one of us has his own special devil. My devil was poverty, and that's a terrible devil because it will fill you with bitterness and hate if you let it. It will wreck your health, because you are filled with fear all the time. It will warp your mind and your soul.

"But when I remembered that Jesus said I could cast out devils in His name, and when I invited Him into my life, He drove out the fear. And when the fear was gone, do you know what happened? Well, I'll tell you. For the first time I could think. Yes, sir, my mind, free of all that hate, went to thinking. I began to think clearly. That's when I got the idea for starting my little business. And I found I could plan and have hope and move ahead without being chained down and made helpless by that devil called poverty. I cast that devil out in the name of the Lord. So when you ask me if I'm a Christian, you can see why I say I am."

"You certainly are," I said. "You're a great lady. Meeting you has given me a tremendous lift. I just know this is going to be a terrific day!"

And I was so full of enthusiasm that I ate all the eggs and all the sausage and all the biscuits and even most of the grits and the red-eye gravy.

Now there was a case where the Plus Factor liberated energies that sustained and fortified a whole lifetime, and I have no doubt that it spilled over into the next generation too. And what was the trigger? Trouble was the trigger. Trouble that might have crushed or embittered some people, but in this case called forth a valid response, and the strength of mind that was equal to the challenge.

There is excitement in this concept of trouble as a dynamic force in human affairs. But you have to know how to handle it. You have to know how to respond to it. Anyone can sail with a fair breeze. It's when the seas get rough that seamanship—really understanding the sea—counts. When trouble comes in human affairs it's lifemanship—understanding the role that trouble can play in life—that makes all the difference.

There is no doubt that trouble often does burn away undesirable traits or characteristics. Take pride, for instance, or arrogance, or willfulness—these things block us from people and from our most cherished goals. Like constraining fences, they have to be broken down before we can love and be loved, before we can really join the human race. Trouble can do that.

I believe that if trouble avoids a person (or he avoids it) for too long, he may grow complacent and careless and even a bit smug. I can speak to some extent from personal experience in this. For years everything in my life went well, almost too well. People brought their troubles to me, but I had almost none of my own. Then, abruptly, I found myself at the center of a storm of criticism. I became upset and discouraged and very unhappy. Well, I lived through that storm. But now, when people seek my help, I truly believe I'm better qualified to help them. I know how it feels, I know how it hurts, I know how vulnerable and fallible despairing humans can be. That's why I believe trouble can humanize a person. That's why I think the notion that God may use trouble for His own purposes may not be so old-fashioned or out-of-date after all.

Sometimes when I talk to people about the inevitability of trouble and the importance of it, they ask if I have any formula for dealing with it. I usually reply that since no two troubles are alike, there is no magical remedy that will deal with all of them. But then I add that there are five common-sense attitudes that I have found helpful in dealing with trouble in such a way that the Law of Challenge and Response becomes operative and the power of the Plus Factor comes through. Here are those five suggestions:

1. *Face up to the problem.* There's always the temptation to shy away from it, to play ostrich, to bury your head in the sand, and hope the problem will go away. It probably won't. In fact, the longer you hide from it, the more menacing it becomes.

So stand up straight. Look the problem in the eye. Take its measure. Analyze it. Dissect it. Perhaps it isn't as formidable as it looks. Even if it is, say to yourself, "All right. The challenge is here. I am going to respond to it. With God's help, and with the hidden Plus Factor within me, I can handle it."

2. *Having taken a good hard look at the problem, take a good hard look at yourself.* Very often people find themselves in trouble because the trouble is really in them. People have come to me plagued by business or financial woes, only to find on closer discussion that they were carrying around such a load of guilt from moral transgressions that their thinking was impaired, their energy short-circuited, and their business judgment clouded. They were in trouble, all right, but before they could deal with it they had to recognize and deal with the trouble in themselves, the moral trouble that was preventing the Plus Factor from coming to their aid.

3. *Having faced up to the problem and examined yourself, take some kind of action.* Have you ever noticed how many of the majestic healing utterances of Jesus begin with a verb of action? "Go and wash. . . ." "Stretch forth thy hand. . . ." "Take up thy bed. . . ." This surely is no accident. Action is a great restorer and builder of confidence. Inaction is not only the result but the cause of fear. Perhaps the action you take will be successful; perhaps different action or adjustments will have to follow. But any action is better than no action at all. So don't wait for trouble to intimidate or paralyze you. Make a move. The Prodigal Son didn't make his way home by lying in the gutter. He moved!

4. *Don't be unwilling to ask for help.* Some people act as if trouble were a disgrace, something to be concealed at all costs. Others say grimly, "It's my problem. I'll work it out by myself." Such attitudes are a mistake. No one is completely self-sufficient; we all need help from time to time. In just about every area of trouble there are experts who are trained to help you: your doctor, your lawyer, your minister. Is your problem a fairly common one? Then in all likelihood there are organized groups of people who have been through the same mill and are willing to help you. People who have been alcoholics. Or compulsive gamblers.

People who have retarded children. People who have lost their sight or their hearing. These are people who have faced trouble, who have survived it, and who stand ready to help others face it.

Even a sympathetic friend can help just by listening or offering a word of encouragement. Sharing trouble eases the strain and often helps perspective. I once knew an artist who ran into various difficulties. More than a little sorry for himself, he told a friend that he would never paint again, adding, "Don't give me any platitudes or advice. It won't do any good. I'm through as a painter. I have too many troubles. I just can't see around them." "Well," said the friend, "I won't give you any advice, but I'll give you a definition of poetry that I once read. *Poetry is what Milton saw when he became blind.*" That was all the friend said, but the artist went back to his easel. He's a well-known watercolorist today.

5. *Don't fall in love with your trouble.* This last bit of advice seems to startle some people, but they are usually the ones who need it most. Painful though it is, trouble sometimes gives a kind of melancholy importance that can be very soothing to a shaky ego. It can also become a very convenient alibi for all sorts of failure and procrastination. Have you ever noticed how many people "enjoy" poor health, talk about it, dwell upon it, make it the unhealthy center around which their lives revolve? Have you ever known people who, once they've made a mistake, refuse to move on, refuse to forget it?

This is no way to be. Troubles come. They also go. But you have to let them go! William James, the great psychologist, once said that the essence of genius lies in knowing what to overlook. Why not apply that to your troubles? Overlook the small ones, and when the big ones are ready to move on, open wide the door and let them go.

I believe what the Plus Factor is trying to teach us is this: Trouble can be unpleasant and painful and damaging, but it can also be the flint that strikes sparks out of the steel in your soul. The famous actor Walter Hampden once was asked which sentence in the English language he considered the most memorable. He thought for a moment. Then he replied that in his opinion the greatest sentence was in an old Negro spiritual: "Nobody knows the trouble I've seen; glory, hallelujah!"

Hampden was right: There is splendor in those words and wisdom too. They recognize that human life is full of pain and sorrow and suffering, but they don't stop with that mere recognition. They go on to express exultation. Those last two words ring with the magnificent conviction that there is something hidden in the spirit of man which, if called forth, can enable him to surmount trouble and suffering. Something that will turn defeat into victory.

That something is one of God's great gifts to mankind. It's the Plus Factor.

13.

The PLUS FACTOR and the Power of Prayer

What is the greatest power in the universe? Is it the enormous force of the hurricane or the tornado, or the tidal wave or the earthquake, or the exploding volcano? These are tremendous manifestations of nature's strength, but they are not the greatest power.

Is it man's discovery of the immense force that lies at the heart of the atom? This is a great wonder, but when you consider that this planet is just a speck of dust in the vast reaches of space, man's achievements with atomic energy are nothing but a little puff of smoke in the vastness of the cosmos.

What, then, *is* the geatest power in the universe? I believe that it is the mechanism by which man on earth establishes a connection that provides the flow of power between the mighty Creator and himself, between the great God who scattered the stars in the infinite night sky and the creature made in His own image: man. The flow of power between the Creator and man is the world's greatest power. It lies at the heart of the Plus Factor in human beings. And it is released and transmitted by means of a mechanism known as prayer.

Now when I say this, immediately you may feel let down because to you prayer may be nothing but pious words. It may be just a paragraph of sonorous language written in a book, or a string of hollow-sounding phrases uttered by a preacher, or some frantic last-minute plea for help in a crisis. These are superficial forms of this communication. But when this communication truly activates and liberates the Plus Factor in people, it has the power to change them.

In the Gospel of Saint Matthew we read, "All things, whatsoever ye shall ask in prayer, believing, ye shall receive" (Matthew 21:22). The key word, the word involving battle and struggle, is that word *believing*. Belief is hard; doubt is easy. Anyone can doubt. It doesn't take brains or skill to doubt. But to cast your doubts aside and believe—ah, this requires stamina and resolution. And when you do believe, *really* believe, then impossibilities are overcome.

The reason I believe in the power of prayer is that over and over again I have seen what it can do for people. I know what it has done for me. To change a human being is the greatest feat imaginable, because the most complicated entity in the world is man himself. Man is riddled with contradictions, he is shackled with habit patterns, he has prejudices, he has resistances, he has complexities. He is the sum total of countless influences playing upon him since infancy. So when you talk about changing him, you know it will require some force of enormous power to do so.

But prayer has this power. For example, I was speaking one night in a big public hall in the Southwest. I arrived just in time for the meeting and went around to the stage entrance and onto a vast stage. There were some stage-hands there, an electrician, and several other people. I noticed one man in particular. He immediately drew my attention because he was a picture of gloom and discouragement and despondency. He attracted my natural sympathy, so I went over and spoke to him.

He said, "Doctor Peale, I came here tonight because I've read some of your books. I desperately need help. I'm so mixed up and conflicted and confused that I don't know what to do with myself or my problems. May I please talk with you right now?"

"Well," I said, "my friend, I'm going on stage here in about two minutes. But if you'll wait until I finish speaking, I promise you that I'll find time to talk with you about these things."

I went on stage; I started speaking; I could see the man off in the wings. Then I got into my speech and forgot myself and everything else except the people out front.

When the speech was over, I remembered my man backstage. I went back, but he wasn't there. I said to the electrician, "Where did that man go?" He said, "He told me that he had to go home to relieve a baby-sitter." "Well, who is he?" I asked. "I neglected to get his name." The electrician knew his name. He added, "He's quite a prominent lawyer in this city."

I went back to my hotel. The man's number was in the book, so I called him on the telephone. "Oh," he said, "thank you for calling." I said, "It's late, I know, but can't we talk over the phone?" He poured out such an accumulation of frustration and defeat and conflict in the next fifteen or twenty minutes that it would have touched a heart of stone. I could tell that he was an intelligent and well-educated man because of the way he spoke and the orderliness of his mind. Finally he said, "The trouble is, I'm ashamed to admit it, but I can't handle all this trouble. And what is even worse," he added, "I can't handle myself. I'm at the end of my rope. I just don't know what to do."

"Well," I said to him, "do you pray about this?"

"Oh," he said, "yes, I pray all the time. I'm always asking God to help me. I implore Him!" And the very way he said it revealed to me that he was full of fear and tension, he was full of frantic petition, he was hysterically demanding something of God.

I said, "Well, if you don't mind my saying so, I think your prayers are wrong. When you get that panicky in your prayers you're closing off the interrelation between God and yourself. You're praying in such a tense manner that you're not letting go of the problem. The thing that God wants is a humble and a contrite spirit. So," I said, "let's pray right now. You tell the Lord you can't handle these problems so you're going to turn them over to Him."

"Oh," he said, "I hate to be so spineless."

I said, "Be humble. Just tell the Lord you can't handle them. And tell the Lord you can't handle yourself. So, therefore, you surrender the problems and you surrender yourself into His hands." And he said, "Lord, I can't handle these problems. I give them to You. I cannot handle myself. I give myself to You. Thank You very much. Amen."

I never saw the man from that day till this. But I hear from him occasionally. In that moment he found release, he found peace—not a complete answer for every problem, but in the days that followed, his fragmented personality flowed together again. He became master of himself and, therefore, master of his problems. The Plus Factor began once more to work in him. Today he holds a position of trust as one of the honorable judges of his community, and he told me that whenever anybody comes before him who he feels needs this same treatment, he offers it to them. "I give to them," he says, "the greatest secret in the world—that there truly is a power that can heal them and bring them together: 'All things, whatsoever ye shall ask in prayer, believing, ye shall receive' (Matthew 21:22)."

Now what does a person have to do to be on the receiving end of this power? The first step is to humble yourself and let go of the problem, leaving it in the hands of God. This kind of prayer is sometimes called the Prayer of Self-Effacement, and it unblocks the channels through which God's power can reach the person praying. Until you humble yourself and give yourself and your problem to God, you'll never get the answer you are seeking. But when you do, you will.

The second important step is to realize that prayer isn't just some neat exercise in words. It has to be deeper than that. Most people do not pray in depth; therefore, nothing happens.

I remember once being on a train with Roland Hayes, the black singer, one of the finest Christian gentlemen I have ever met. He told me that he'd built his whole life and his whole career on prayer. He was led into this way of life by his grandfather, who wasn't as well-educated as Mr. Hayes, but who had tremendous faith. The old man told Roland that the reason some prayers didn't seem to get anywhere was because "they ain't got no suction." That was the phrase his grandfather used, and that's quite a word: *suction*. He meant that some prayers don't go down to the level where they start pulling on the pray-er, drawing him closer to God.

In my mind there's no doubt about it: the deeper the prayer, the more remarkable the results. A friend told me once of a young American wife who was all alone with her baby in a small manufacturing town in France. She had just gone over to join her husband who was representing an

American company there. She did not speak the language, and she knew absolutely no one.

Just after she arrived, her husband was recalled to the States for an important conference that required an absence of several days. Soon after he left, the baby became ill with an acute respiratory infection. The child's fever mounted very rapidly. As night came on his breathing became more and more labored. None of the remedies the mother tried had any effect. She grew more and more terrified. The house was quite isolated. She did not know how to use the telephone. Even if she had known the name of a doctor, she would not have been able to make herself understood.

As the hours went by she paced the floor, holding the baby in her arms, tears of inner agony streaming down her face. Near midnight the child's fever rose so high that he went into a convulsion, a terrifying manifestation, as anyone who has seen one knows. His breath rattled feebly in his throat. The mother, convinced that her child was dying, fell on her knees by the bed and closed her eyes and cried, "Oh, God, my baby is dying. Please, please hear me. I need Your help. I need it now. Save my baby, Lord; I know You can do it. I believe You can do it. I beg You to do it. Right now. This minute. This second. Please, dear Lord, in Jesus' name. Right now, Lord. Right now!"

She felt as if the prayer had been wrenched from the deepest part of her soul. The room seemed full of a ringing silence. And in the silence she heard a soft, sighing sound. It was her baby, breathing normally. She opened her eyes and looked at the baby's face. The flush of fever was gone. Only a light perspiration remained. The baby was sleeping as peacefully as if nothing had happened. But something *had* happened. The intensity of the mother's prayer had swept aside all barriers and touched the great compassionate heart of the Infinite. It had opened a channel to unlimited power, and as the power coursed through that channel it overwhelmed the disease that had the baby in its grip.

"I believe You can do it," the mother said. *Believe.* That was the crucial element, the operative word that made the whole extraordinary happening possible. A mother fighting for her child's life, praying for him, desperately reaching out for the greatest Plus Factor of all—what greater "suction" can there be?

Well, you may say, others have had serious illness, and others have prayed with deep sincerity and urgency, and yet no such instantaneous cure has been their reward. How do you account for that?

I don't account for it. I am just saying that some prayers seem to be more effective than others, and intensity—or depth—often seems to be present when these miraculous happenings take place.

I recall once discussing the miracles that are said to happen at the shrine at Lourdes in southern France with my old friend and colleague Dr. Smiley Blanton, a psychiatrist. He was also the possessor of one of the clearest and most practical minds that I have ever had the good fortune to encounter. He was a religious man himself; he had been brought up by strong-faithed people in his native Tennessee. So he was always interested in the spiritual aspects of life. He had heard about the miracles of healing reported at the little town of Lourdes, and he decided to make a personal visit there to see for himself. He wanted to observe the whole process from a strictly scientific, objective, medical point of view, and he did. He spent several weeks there, talking to local doctors, to people who had come seeking a cure, to some who were healed and some who were not.

He found, to begin with, that authentic cases of healing—cases accepted by the medical profession and the Catholic Church—were very rare. But he also found that they did occur. Evidence based on diagnoses and X rays before and after the patient's visit to Lourdes showed that in some cases—in cases of advanced tuberculosis and other organic illnesses—instantaneous cures did take place. Sometimes at the moment when the patient drank Lourdes water or was immersed in it, sometimes when no such tangible agent was involved but when prayers were being offered either by the patient or by others.

I remember Dr. Blanton saying that it was as if the time factor in the healing process was enormously accelerated, so that medical progress that might normally be expected to occur over a period of months or even years was somehow condensed into a second or a millisecond of time—a tremendous intensification of the Plus Factor deep inside the sick or dying person.

What Dr. Blanton was seeking, really, was a common denominator that might link these miraculous healings together. What, if anything, did each of these people have in common? That was the question he kept asking himself.

"And did you find an answer?" I remember asking him.

He thought for a moment, then he said, "Well, if there was a common denominator, it was this: All those people were terminal in the sense that mentally and emotionally they had reached the end of the line. They had tried every human remedy, and every medical solution, and none had worked. They were at the point where they said to themselves, 'I give up. I quit. I can't fight anymore. I can't try anymore.' It was this moment of complete and absolute relinquishment that seemed to set the stage for the cure that followed. It was almost as if the struggles and strivings of the patient somehow impeded or blocked the flow of curative power."

I'm convinced that this willingness to let go should be added to the conditions that favor the emergence of the Plus Factor. Maybe we shouldn't wait to be dying or half-dead before we say, humbly and reverently, "I can't carry all the burdens of life by myself. I'm helpless without You, dear Lord. Please take my helplessness and in return give me Your strength." Maybe we shouldn't even wait until things are going badly and problems begin to seem insurmountable. Maybe even on the brightest days, at the brightest times, when the Plus Factor seems strong and success is riding triumphantly on our shoulders, we should still pray that prayer of humility and relinquishment, saying, "I am full of gratitude for all the favors You have granted, all the good things You have given me, but still I know that without You I am ineffective."

The greatest men this nation has ever known have always been quick to acknowledge their dependence on a Power greater than themselves, and quick to seek aid from that Power. Take Abraham Lincoln, for example, in my opinion the greatest of them all, the one through whose life the Plus Factor shone with an unsurpassed radiance.

Where did this homely, gangling, backwoods lawyer get the moral greatness and the unbelievable stamina that enabled him to prevent his nation from being torn asunder and gave him as well the strength to bring freedom to a great race of people? A friend of mine, Congressman Pettingill of Indiana, went down into Lincoln country one time and made an estimate of the height of the primeval trees among which Lincoln wandered as a boy, huge trees, with tops seeming to scrape the sky and, all around, the deep forest silences. Pettingill said that Lincoln went to school to this great environment amidst these silences, and that in them he found God and learned to pray. His were deep, soul-searching prayers with enormous suction in them.

During the height of the Civil War a well-known actor named Murdoch was an overnight guest at the White House. In the dead of night he was awakened by the sound of a voice, a voice in great distress and emotional agony. He crept out into the hall. He followed the sound of the voice and he looked through a door that was ajar. He said that he saw the tall, lanky form of Abe Lincoln face down on the floor, his fingers digging into the carpet as he poured out his sense of insufficiency and inadequacy, asking Almighty God to help him save the Republic. And Murdoch said that at that moment all his doubts about the outcome of the war and about the future of the nation left him.

I believe that when prayer reaches such intensity, even the physical forces of nature may respond, just as Christ stilled the raging waters of the Sea of Galilee in a storm that threatened to sink the boat carrying Him and His disciples. I remember very well a story told a few years ago by Don Bell, a cowboy who lives in Wyoming. He had been brought up by his Aunt Mae, a widow who lived on a homestead in eastern Colorado. Aunt Mae had to fight dust storms and tornadoes and sometimes she and her four children were close to starvation. Grasshoppers came and devoured her small crops. She decided to get some turkeys to eat the grasshoppers, and they did; so she put all her small resources into raising turkeys. She had about two thousand turkeys, and she had to guard them day and night to make sure the coyotes didn't get them. She would take her Bible with her when she went into the fields to watch over the birds.

One day a sudden storm came up, black clouds, a vicious wind, and a hard hail thundering across the plains. Aunt Mae saw it coming. There was no time to drive the turkeys to shelter. She knew that the hail would wipe out the whole flock in a matter of minutes. Her young nephew, Don, was with her, and he wanted to run, but Aunt Mae said, "We're not going anywhere, Don. We're staying with the birds."

Here's how Don described what happened next: "Aunt Mae just stood there with her Bible held to her chest and she watched that storm come on. I kept my eyes on her, watching for a sign that we should run, leave the birds, even if they were our last hope.

"But Aunt Mae would give no such sign, even though the wind threw tumbleweeds and stinging dirt at us. She opened her Bible and started shouting Scripture at the storm. 'Then they cry unto the Lord in their trouble,' she shouted out, 'and he bringeth them out of their distresses. He maketh the storm a calm, so that the waves thereof are still. Then are they glad because they be quiet; so he bringeth them unto their desired haven.' The wind was whipping at her now and the pages of her Bible fluttered, but she went on: 'He blesseth them also, so that they are multiplied greatly; and suffereth not their cattle to decrease.' Aunt Mae was undaunted, defying the storm around her with holy words: 'Whoso is wise, and will observe these things, even they shall understand the loving-kindness of the Lord' (Psalms 107:28-30, 38, 43).

"The sign to run never came. Aunt Mae stood her ground, and in the end the storm passed safely to the north, to an unpopulated area. Only then did Aunt Mae take her eyes off that horizon. She bent her head and prayed. Only then did my fear leave me."

What a magnificent scene, that weather-beaten pioneer woman standing tall in the path of the onrushing storm, clutching her Bible and *praying* that hail away from her precious turkeys!

But the Plus Factor that is released by prayer isn't limited to major crises. It can work in smaller ones no less dramatically. I have a friend, the head of a well-known boys' prep school. He told me that as a boy he worked in a foundry because he had decided to drop out of school. He changed his mind eventually, but by that time he was older than the other boys in his class. He had to struggle to make up the time lost. He said he did it "by study and prayer."

His mother, who was very devout, had made him promise that he would never study on Sunday, and he kept that promise. But the time came when the entrance examination in Greek was scheduled for 11 A.M. on Monday morning "and it was all Greek to me," he said.

He arose at 3 A.M. Monday morning and opened his Greek textbook. He said, "Lord, I have an examination today at eleven o'clock. If you want me to go to college, please help me with this examination. I have only a few hours; tell me what to study."

He said that the number of a page came into his mind. He turned to that page and began to study it. He studied it until he had memorized it. And when the time came, he found that the examination was based almost entirely on the page he had commited to memory.

This struck him as so remarkable that he told his professor about it.

"That's a very curious coincidence," the professor said. "I didn't make out that examination until eight o'clock Monday morning. Apparently you saw the idea even before it was in my mind. Mental transference, no doubt."

"Excuse me, sir," said this boy who was to become a headmaster, "I believe it was more than that. God wanted to use me. He wanted me to continue my education. And so He put into my mind what He was going to put into yours."

Can the Plus Factor do such things? I believe it can, when it is focused and channeled and liberated by prayer.

The flow of power and the release of the Plus Factor that comes from prayer are available to all of us, but they can be blocked by a variety of things. Pride can be a block. Tension can be a block. Fear can be a block. Sin can be a block. Negative thinking can be a block.

Not long ago I gave a talk in a Texas city and afterward a man spoke to me. He said, "Do you believe that prayer can work in practical business matters?"

I assured him that I did.

"Well," he said, "I moved here recently from another state. I own a house up there. I had to buy a house here in this city and I've been trying to sell my former home, but I haven't been able to move it. I've done everything I can think of, and I've asked God to help me, but the house isn't sold."

I asked him what price he wanted for the house, and he told me. Then I asked him what a reasonable profit on the sale of the house would be. He told me, and the price he had placed on the house was a lot higher than that.

I said to him, "I think the problem with selling this house may be that you are concerned only with yourself. How big is this house?"

"It's quite large," he said. "Large enough for a family with children."

"Well," I said, "here's what I suggest that you do. Say to the Lord that He must have a family somewhere who needs this house, and ask Him to bring that family and your house together. You're going to think about that family enjoying that house of yours and you're going to stop thinking about yourself."

He stared at me, and I could tell that he was quite astonished.

I said, "Pray that they will find the house, and when they do, you'll explore their financial situation and work things out so that they can buy the house. When you approach it in this way, you'll eliminate the selfishness that may be blocking your prayers and I think God's will may be done."

The man just nodded his head and went away. About two weeks later I had a letter from him. It said, "Believe it or not, I did exactly as you suggested. The nicest young family you ever saw with three small children loved my house. They said they had been praying and describing the house they needed to the Lord, and suddenly they were led to this house and when they saw it they knew it was exactly what they wanted because it was exactly as they had pictured it in their prayers."

His letter went on: "They didn't have much money, but they did have enough for a down payment. I checked their credit, and it looked good. Anyway, they're happy, and I'm happy, and maybe I didn't make a lot of profit but I discovered something much more important. I discovered that prayer works when you align yourself with the power of God, and that's what I intend to do from now on. Thank you!"

The key to successful living, to happiness, to everything is to saturate your mind and your plans and your hopes and your dreams with prayer. That is what we do at the Foundation for Christian Living in Pawling, New York, which had its start years ago when my wife, Ruth, began mailing out copies of my sermons to a few interested people. Now it reaches nearly one million people all over the world, mailing thirty million pieces of literature annually. *Guideposts* magazine, which we started forty years ago on a wing and a prayer, you might say, is a publishing phenomenon with over four million subscribers and read by nearly sixteen million persons monthly. We saturate these endeavors with prayer, and the good Lord has carried them forward to great success.

Sometimes prayer liberates the Plus Factor in delightful and unexpected ways. I remember once meeting a woman in Pittsburgh who had an interesting story to tell. She said, "I'm thirty-four years of age. My husband died about a year ago from cancer. Not long ago one of my children was badly burned by grease from the stove. I have taken him to doctors of course, but my money is running out." She went on to say that she had worked for a store, but it had gone out of business and she lost that job. And the insurance company had never paid on her husband's death because in the last days of his illness he had neglected to pay a premium and the policy had lapsed. "Now," she said to me, "you always talk about positive thinking. What would you say in my case?"

I said, "The first thing I suggest is that you take all these problems and put them in the Lord's hands and ask Him for guidance, He will clear your thinking and give you creative ideas and restore hope and energy and confidence in you." And I added, "We might as well start right now. Let's pray together about this problem."

She was a good woman. I still remember how earnestly she recommitted her life to Christ. Finally she said, "You know, it's a strange thing, but as we were praying I got the idea that I should go to see the manager of my husband's insurance company."

She tried and tried to see this manager, but the receptionist, who was familiar with the case and who had decided that the manager would do nothing about it, refused to let her in. But she kept trying, and one day when the receptionist was away from her desk, she walked into the manager's office. She sat down and apologized to him for "barging in like this." "But,' she said, "I have prayed most earnestly about this matter, and the Lord told me to come and see you." And she proceeded to outline the case.

The manager got out the file. He said, "I'll study this. Come back tomorrow." When she returned the next day, he said, "There's no legal obligation to pay in this matter. But your husband paid his premiums faithfully for many years, and I think there may be a moral obligation. So I am going to recommend that this policy be paid." Then he said, "And what else can I do?"

She told him about her son, and he went to work on proper hospitalization and care for the boy. And that was taken care of. Then he said, "And what else can I do?" She told him about her unemployment and he helped her get another job. All this took several months. Then again he said, "And what else can I do for you?" "Why, nothing," she said. "You've been very helpful and kind. I do appreciate it."

"Well," he said, "there's something you can do for me. You're a widow and I'm a widower. I would like very much to marry you. Will you marry me?"

And so they were married, and are living happily together to this day—certainly one of the most astonishing results I ever had from praying with anybody!

Do you want this kind of Plus Factor to manifest in your life? Then learn to pray in depth, with "suction," with all the power of belief. And then prepare yourself for great things. Because miracles can happen.

14.

Enthusiasm Activates Your PLUS FACTOR

Enthusiasm is a superimportant, basic element in successful living. The "alive" type of personality always goes places when that aliveness is accompanied by positive thinking and solid faith.

Take, for example, the following letter from a distinguished professor in a leading university:

Dear Dr. Peale:

Through your work you have touched my life. Allow me to expand on this.

Born of European immigrant parents, I grew up in Paraguay, South America. While my schoolmates wore shoes and socks, I wore sandals. But poverty was felt only in material possessions—my parents placed great emphasis on teaching lasting values. During my teenage years my father introduced me to your book *The Power of Positive Thinking,* whose teachings he applied by encouraging me to think big. He scraped up enough money to get me a (one-way) ticket to study in the United States. I would not return home again for another six years.

During the first semester in college I kept in a drawer my entire monetary assets: 5 cents! So, while at the age of 19 I learned English, my third language, I took course work and also worked as a janitor and waiter. But I had a goal, and your work is helping me achieve it.

Today I am married to a wonderful wife, and have three beautiful children. I am professor at a major midwestern university with a Ph.D. in chemistry. The student body of 23,000 has voted me "Top Educator," and I am recipient of the Indiana University state-wide Lieber Award for Distinguished Teaching. I have travelled all over the world serving as consultant to the Ford Foundation and the Asian Development Bank. I operate a publishing firm and own a considerable amount of real estate. I have served my church by leading our congregation through a million+ dollar building project.

I am writing these things not to boast, but to acknowledge the tremendous power locked within human beings, which, when properly catalyzed, will flourish beyond belief. You and your work have served as beautiful catalysts. Thank you!

Cordially yours,
ERWIN BOSCHMANN, PH.D.

Let's look at the factors that worked in this man's personality that contributed to his success. He did not grow bitter in poverty. He was not a griper. Lasting values were taught him and he responded to those values.

He learned to think big and he had a goal which he set out to achieve against great odds: no money and the necessity of mastering a new language.

He possessed boundless enthusiasm and was a committed Christian with the power of faith working in him. Added to all this was positive thinking, and the net result is a great and successful life. Obviously he has the Plus Factor in full measure.

I want to point out that enthusiasm releases and feeds the Plus Factor that is inherent within you. That factor may not be very strong or effective at the moment. But it can become so and one way to activate it into a powerful force is to have enthusiasm going for you, real, contagious enthusiasm.

"But," you may say, "what if you don't have enthusiasm? You can't be enthusiastic if you are lacking enthusiasm. And you cannot buy it in a drugstore in the form of a pill or a liquid. So you are out of luck, for if you just do not have enthusiasm you cannot be an enthusiastic person."

The answer to that doleful complaint and excuse is, "Oh, yes, you can!" All you have to do is practice the "as if" principle. This is one of the most powerful methodologies that can be employed by the person who really wants to do something with himself or herself.

And just what is the "as if" principle? I think it was first stated by Professor William James, sometimes called the father of American psychological science. If you want to cultivate a desired attitude, you may do so by acting as if you had it. If, for example, you are a person of fear and you want instead to be a person of courage, you proceed to act courageously. In due course if you persist in acting as if you had courage, you will ultimately become a courageous person. Now please do not reject this truth and say it isn't so. Remember it was put forth by one of the foremost scholars in American history. And it has been proved to be effective by many people. One of them is the author of this book. I, personally, believe in the "as if" principle because I have used it and found that it works.

In my younger years I was the victim of an enormous inferiority complex. And as is common among people so afflicted, I practiced the "as if" principle, but in reverse; for I acted as if I were a nobody with no ability. And so naturally I developed into a sadly defeated person. I became exactly as I acted. Then through various felicitous circumstances I took on the characteristics of a positive thinker and began to practice the "as if" principle.

When a person develops enthusiasm, exciting things begin happening. From then on that individual is very likely to become different, perhaps markedly so. If previously he or she was lethargic, lacking in drive and forcefulness, the metamorphosis of enthusiasm can be dramatic indeed. A hitherto unimaginative, sleepy man or woman suddenly comes alive, is revitalized, and moves up and on to a success previously undreamed of by anyone, including himself.

Actually, enthusiasm is one of the most effective activation agents. It gets people and results going—really going—and in ways that are often spectacular. As in the case of a young Toronto taxi driver.

I had a friend some years ago in Toronto. He was a chemist by profession, though on Sundays he was the teacher of the largest Bible class in Canada. Dr. Albert E. Cliffe was a highly motivated man and crowds flocked to hear him talk, for he was an outstanding conveyor of enthusiasm for what people could be.

One March morning, when a stormy gale was sweeping the city, Al Cliffe hailed a taxi in Toronto. To the glum and somewhat surly young driver he said a cheery good morning. "Wonderful day, isn't it?" And it was just that, for any day was wonderful to Al. "You should have your head examined," snarled the driver. "What do you mean a wonderful day with this lousy weather!" Then he added, "This country is on the way out. No opportunity here anymore; nothing any good."

Cliffe let the young man empty himself of his gripes and complaints, then he asked kindly, "What's the matter, son?"

This really set the young fellow off. It was soon after the war. The boy said, "I'm a war veteran, gave three years to my country, but what's the country doing for me? I can't get a job in my line. I'm a graduate engineer. I walked the streets of my own city finally taking this job, a taxi driver. I'm disgusted, fed up, completely turned off."

Cliffe said, "My friend, do you want to know what will get you off this negative dead center and start you going?"

"I'd sure like to know that," the driver snorted.

"Now don't discount what I'm going to say. It's enthusiasm that will turn things around for you—real enthusiasm—the genuine article."

At this the driver turned around suddenly to stare at his passenger, nearly running up on the curb. "Enthusiasm," he expostulated. "Aw, come off it, mister. What is there to be enthusiastic about anyway?"

"Life," answered Cliffe. "It's wonderful to be alive and young as you are. Add up your assets. Your future is out there ahead of you, and don't write Canada off either. It's a great land and you and I live in one of the finest cities in the world."

The young driver listened. "Where did you get all this enthusiasm, sir?"

Cliffe's reply was brief, in only two words: "Jesus Christ."

"I was a believer once, too," the driver said.

"Become one again, son. Think enthusiasm, act out enthusiasm, talk enthusiasm, and you will become enthusiastic. Then you will go places and life will become exciting."

About two years later this young taxi driver went to see Dr. Cliffe. "You really got to me that morning," he said. "It wasn't altogether what you said, although that made sense. It was also what you are. And that struck me. Well," he continued, "I gave it a lot of thought and I did as you said. I deliberately tried to make myself enthusiastic. As I did that, I realized I was getting more fun out of driving a taxi."

Then he went on, "One day I picked up a fare at the Royal York Hotel. This man wanted to go to the airport. Believe it or not, it was another rainy day, but I told this man that every day is a good day and spoke with enthusiasm about the country and engineering, in which I was trained, and to which I was going to return one day.

"And do you know what this man said? It went something like this: 'With the cheerful outlook you have and your outgoing personality, you shouldn't be driving a taxi. You say you are trained in engineering? Where did you go to school?' So I told him and he invited me to come to see him at his office to talk about a possible job in his organization. 'I like enthusiastic people working for me,' he said, 'when they are organized and have enough know-how. So come along and we'll check out your education and if all is okay, we will get you started.'

"Well," concluded the former taxi driver, "I guess I'm doing okay. I've had two promotions. And I love it."

When he told me this story, Al Cliffe, who as stated earlier was himself a scientist, commented, "There's a lot more in most people than shows. Sometimes enthusiasm will bring it out, as in this case."

To the important Plus Factor add enthusiasm, intellectual competency, as well as sound spiritual thinking, and you've got an unbeatable combination. You have the makings of somebody special.

America was made by the greatest assembly of enthusiasts the world has ever seen. All of those thousands who trekked west to settle new lands beyond the horizon were enthusiastic or they wouldn't have had the motivation to subject themselves to hardship and danger to have their dreams come true.

The United States despite its problems offers more opportunity for a person who wants to go places and do things than any other country on the globe. This is not an unsupported claim, for I have been on speaking trips from South America to Australia, from Singapore to Tokyo and, believe me, ours is still the land of opportunity.

I personally grew up among motivated, inspired, and enthusiastic people. And we had not yet become cynical. No one had taught us to regard enthusiasm as corny. I believe this cynical attitude came to be called sophistication, which seems an improper use of the word, for *sophistication* according to the dictionary means "to know your way around in the world." And it is certainly not worldly wise to play yourself and opportunity down to the extent that it bypasses you. Even today the real achievers are excited, enthusiastic participants and leaders in creativity. In fact, to be with it in America today, increasingly one has to be an enthusiastic believer in incredible possibilities.

I really think the forefathers would be proud of us. They would see the old spirit of opportunity still at work in the nation they founded. As long as young men and women still are motivated, still follow their dreams, continue to believe in the future, the country is all right, very much all right. I've seen them in a hundred cities at huge motivational meetings—dreamers, thinkers, achievers—all wanting to go places and do things just as their forefathers did before them. And they have the same faith in God, the same faith in their country and themselves. For them enthusiasm makes the difference, a great big difference in their happiness and achievement.

They would appreciate the story I'm about to relate. Though it happened fifty or more years ago, it is still pertinent, for the process is continuously modern.

Harry Moore lived with his widowed mother in Jersey City in three rooms in a run-down neighborhood. They were very poor people but clean, decent, and churchgoing. One day after school Harry came disconsolately into the kitchen, which doubled as a living room, sailed his cap onto a hat rack in the corner (all boys wore caps in those days), and sprawled into a chair. His mother was stirring something that was cooking on the stove.

"Mama," he said, "I sometimes have strange feelings. They're funny. I get 'em every once in a while."

"What kind of feelings, son?"

"Oh, I dunno, but it's like something inside of me keeps saying I'm somebody or can be something. I just don't know what it all means."

"I do, Harry. I know exactly what it means. God is preparing you to be a great man sometime." This simple woman had never heard of the Plus Factor in people, but she had enough sensitivity to know when it was stirring in a boy's mind.

"But, Mama, I can never amount to anything. We are poor and we have no pull or anything. Only the rich and famous can get to the top."

Mama stopped stirring and pointed the dripping ladle at him, drops falling unheeded to the floor. "Listen to me, son. Don't ever let me hear you talk like that again. All you need is just two things—God and gumption."

Gumption is an old-fashioned word meaning common sense and the guts to go out and do something with yourself with enthusiasm and character. Gumption was the stuff of which sturdy, persistent, enthusiastic people were made. It's still a mighty good expression.

Years later when Harry was serving one of his three terms as governor, he was making a speech about America and its opportunity. He was a terrific speaker, with know-how and enthusiasm. Afterward a young fellow came up and said, "Guv, I don't buy that stuff you were handing out. You know as well as I do that unless you've got money and pull and connections you can't get anywhere in this capitalist society. That's why I've about decided to join the communists. They've got a program for us poor people."

"Guess you don't know who you're talking to," answered the governor. "I talked just that way to my mother when I was a kid, all except that communist bit. I never was that dumb, poor as we were." He told about the God and gumption advice. "Okay, son, what is your goal?"

The boy had one. "I want to be the best surgeon in this state."

"Great," said Governor Moore. "What you can conceive you can achieve. Go with God and gumption."

A few years later Governor A. Harry Moore gave the commencement talk at a large university on his usual theme, "You Can Be What You Want to Be." After the ceremony a graduate wearing the green hood of a new doctor of medicine came up and said, "Hello, Guv. Remember me? Thanks to you I made it. That God and gumption bit did it."

Telling me this story a long while after it happened, the governor commented, "Get a person to have enthusiasm and all the other necessary qualities for success are activated—things like a goal, persistence, ability to work hard, determination to study.

"Then," he said, "you know something? God the Creator put an extra something into all of us. Some people let that something atrophy. But when enthusiasm gets to working, that extra quality develops and grows." How right he was! He didn't name that extra quality to which he referred, but what he was talking about was clearly the Plus Factor as we term it.

The most unlikely person may have a huge Plus Factor inside of him. You don't know what a big Plus Factor may be right there within yourself. If you believe it is in you (and that is the first thing to do about it), you will then be ready for the second thing and that, of course, is to develop it and to grow it big—by being enthusiastic about your own potential.

I once knew a man who was considered the most knowledgeable man in the world about radio. And this same man had perhaps the most to do with creating the television industry. At about this time my home radio wasn't working well; so I called in a neighborhood repairman who spent a long time tinkering with it and finally got it going. "I suppose you know all about radio," I said admiringly. "Sure I do," he cockily asserted. "It's simple. Nothing to it."

A short time later I was with the friend who was considered the greatest authority on radio. "It's still a mystery to me," he explained modestly, "that we can actually transmit the human voice through what we call air waves. It's a miracle." His face glowed with an expression of wonder. "I've had enthusiasm since I was a small boy and that enthusiasm has grown to enormous proportion as I have worked with radio and television."

The man to whom I'm referring is the late David Sarnoff, longtime head of the Radio Corporation of America and founder of the National Broadcasting Company. He had a built-in Plus Factor that was activated by enthusiasm, and it was a spectacular Plus Factor. You wouldn't think would you that a young Jewish boy born in Russia, son of poverty-stricken immigrants, growing up in the old Hell's Kitchen in New York City would actually have the Radio Corporation of America and the National Broadcasting Company tucked away inside of him as a Plus Factor? But such is the romantic possibility of human beings. When I think of David Sarnoff, a statement of the German philosopher Nietzsche sometimes comes to mind: "Nothing ever succeeds which exuberant spirits have not helped to produce." David Sarnoff possessed enthusiasm in abundance, and exciting things happen when a person has a burning and unextinguishable enthusiasm.

The Plus Factor requires enthusiasm, for it is that which keeps the individual carrying on in pursuit of a goal. Enthusiasm is what insures the dogged, never-give-up, hang-in-there attitude. As long as enthusiasm is strongly sustained, the extra something within a person that we call the Plus Factor may be counted on to function, and if necessary over great odds. Harvey J. Berman in his magnificent description of the courageous swimming by Florence Chadwick of the English channel from England to France declares that it was the most remarkable attempt ever made on the difficult channel. She came close to death. Agonizing cramps gripped first her legs then her stomach. She became lost as night descended over the sea. But nothing deterred her, she explained: "There was nothing else to do but go on, so I did."

Sixteen hours after she entered the channel on the English side she stumbled onto the beach in France to be labeled "the greatest female swimming star of all time." How did she accomplish this astounding feat? Her explanation, "With God's patient help." And she had a motto that also helped. "Winners never quit; quitters never win."

Beyond all these great assets Florence Chadwick had within her a Plus Factor, which she developed into an extraordinary source of power. And a burning enthusiasm for swimming fired that Plus Factor, keeping the heat on at all times. So she was able to carry on, and to keep carrying on to the victorious end. And that, incidentally, is what each of us must do: Just keep it going, always going until we cross the goal line. And it is a fact that enthusiasm is the power that keeps us in the swim or race or struggle all the way to the end. If you keep your enthusiasm up, you will never even contemplate giving up.

After reading the foregoing human demonstrations of the power of the Plus Factor motivated by enthusiasm, you may very well raise the question, "Just how may I increase my enthusiasm?" In anticipation of that question I made a list of a few ways that enthusiasm may be developed and increased.

1. As stated earlier, employ the "as if" principle; act as if you had enthusiasm and it will tend to develop in your mind. I repeat this for the simple reason that it is so effective.

2. Practice being enthusiastic about simple things. For example, "Look at those fleecy clouds against a blue sky. Isn't that beautiful?" or "Honey, I never tasted a more delicious dinner. You surely are a terrific cook!" You might also admire the nicely cut green lawn or the purring sound of your car motor as you pull out into the roadway. Enthusiasm for the simple things will add up to a general attitude of enthusiasm.

3. Tell yourself every morning as you go to work that you love your job. Think of it as interesting, even fascinating. By so doing you will ultimately get enthusiastic about your work—and you will undoubtedly do a better job.

4. Daily, as you board a bus, train, or subway, tell yourself that you really like people. Do this even when they push and shove you. Look for the interesting and likeable qualities in people. Act toward them as if you were enthusiastic about them. In due course, they will become enthusiastic about you.

5. Every morning say aloud a Scripture verse such as "This is the day which the Lord hath made; we will rejoice and be glad in it" (Psalms 118:24). Another good one is: "Surely goodness and mercy shall follow me all the days of my life" (Psalms 23:6). You'll get to loving God and when you love God, you love life—you become an enthusiast. That is the way it works.

6. See how many "wonderful things" you can identify daily: a spectacular sunset; the face of an old man rugged as a granite cliff; a dogwood tree in full bloom; snow drifted high against an old stone wall. As you emphasize the wonder of life, you will develop that wonder of the attitude called enthusiasm. And you, too, will become more wonderful.

As you do these exercises, and other enthusiasm-developing acts that you yourself will think of, that extraspecial something in your nature that we call the Plus Factor will grow and you will grow along with it.

People today are health conscious. They want their bodies to be stronger, healthier. And so they diet, exercise, walk, jog, run—and this is all to the good. To perhaps a lesser degree, people work with their minds to make them stronger, more knowledgeable, more efficient. They read mind-developing material. Education embraces the old as well as the young and adult education flourishes.

But it is development in the area of the spirit where we are perhaps the weakest. If the spiritual nature is to grow and develop, spirit no less than body and mind needs exercise and thoughtful nurture. The quality of enthusiasm is basically of the spirit, although it is easier to be enthusiastic when the body is healthy and the mind is fine tuned. Thus it is that the holistic principle of body, mind, and spirit is today regarded as increasingly important. It greatly contributes to a general upgrading of one's life, giving to it deeper meaning, enjoyment, and excitement, and is a powerful releasing agent of the Plus Factor.

But there is a method for developing enthusiasm and thereby releasing your Plus Factor, a method superior in my judgment to any other that may be employed. This method is bypassed by some people for what is really an irrational reason. They are mentally and emotionally set against it, because some person they don't like used it; or they had an unhappy experience with someone who taught it; or they encountered unattractive forms of it; or they just don't understand it. What I'm referring to is what I call the Christian-experience method. This, in brief, is the establishment of a definite personal relationship with Jesus Christ as your Lord, your Savior, your friend. A relationship so close and real that He is with you every day helping you in everything.

It creates a new life-style—as if you had been born all over again, this time as a new person. A biblical description of what happens to a person is this, "If any man be in Christ, he is a new creation; old things have passed away; behold, all things have become new" (*see* 2 Corinthians 5:17). People who have this tremendous experience are the outstanding enthusiasts of this world. For them everyday life is more and more wonderful. Things that once threw them, defeated them, and made them disgusted and surly can now be overcome. They rise above problems, or throw them out of the way, or know how to live with them successfully. The Christian experience is method Number One for becoming a genuinely enthusiastic person and for releasing the power of that Plus Factor.

"But," you may ask, "just how do you find this wonderful new life?" There are many ways, but one I recommend is to read the four Gospels—Matthew, Mark, Luke, and John. Read them at one sitting if you can, or at least read large sections at a time. By so doing, you will encounter the most fascinating personality of all time, One who is alive and helping people today, not merely a figure of the dull past. You will find what His teachings really are and how they make much sense. You will become aware that He outlines a way of life that really works and that leads to joy and victory.

You may be quite astonished as you read, astonished that anyone could so succinctly and with such amazing clarity articulate the basic truth about life. Some may even exclaim, "Is this Christianity? I thought it was theological arguments, conflicts between groups, each of which presumes they alone have the truth. I thought it was anything but this plain, simple though moving statement of the way life is at its best."

As you get to know the center of it all, which is Jesus, a strange and marvelous transformation will come over you. He will remove your inner conflicts, heal your hurts, do away with your resentments, strengthen you against your weaknesses, and fill your mind with peace such as you have never known. A new and amazing sense of power will surge through you and you will find yourself able to do things as never before. As the Plus Factor in you is released, an enthusiasm such as you have never experienced will signal the astounding change in you.

Just how can I know this can happen to you? Because it happened to me and I've seen it occur with amazing results in many persons across the years. Because I believe this tremendous experience should not be denied to others who are still stumbling along, being defeated at the same old roadblocks when they do not need to, I am writing this book called *Power of the Plus Factor*.

One night I was speaking at a motivational sales rally in a city in western Canada. Several thousand people were present, most of them in sales. I judged that the average age of the large audience was no more than thirty. All seemed imbued with the desire to get ahead in their respective businesses. That everyone present had a definite desire for self-improvement was indicated by their serious but enthusiastic attitude. I spoke on the subject of "Enthusiasm Makes the Difference" and pointed out that an enthusiastic attitude is an important ingredient in success.

After the speech I returned to my hotel and walking to the elevator, I was accosted by a nice-looking young man who told me he had followed me from the hall because he wanted to discuss something of a personal nature. His problem, he said, was desultoriness. He just couldn't care less about anything, including his work. He knew his attitude was very wrong and wouldn't lead to success, but he had not been able to do anything about it. As a matter of fact, he said he hadn't cared enough to make an effort to correct himself.

But he told me that my message that night on enthusiasm had really reached him and disturbed him. For the first time he realized that he had no future unless he changed from his desultory attitude and became an excited, enthusiastic person. This change would require a miracle he asserted, and he doubted very much that it would happen. "But," he concluded, "for the first time in my life I want to change."

I told him that the desire to change was the first step. "Intensity of desire is the beginning of the process of becoming different," I declared and offered the opinion that he was ready for something great to happen to him.

"I know I've got to become outgoing, enthusiastic, even excited if I am to go further toward real success, but how can this happen to an apathetic, uninterested guy like me? That's the sixty-four-dollar question," he concluded dejectedly.

"What's your name, my friend?"

"Oh, just call me Freddie," he replied.

This conversation lasted perhaps ten minutes, and during it we stood in a rather busy hotel lobby. "Well, Freddie, I will level with you. It's not easy to effect change in a personality where disinterest has long been prevalent. Something dramatically acute is necessary to cause definite change. You may have to spend a long time unlearning defeatist mental habits. But," I said, "there is one way in which a healing therapy can take place almost instantly. It requires that intensity of desire I spoke of, plus an admission you can do nothing for yourself, and finally a complete commitment to Jesus Christ. If it is His will to release you immediately, He can do it. But He may instead put you through the long process of unlearning and relearning new mental habits. The only thing to do is just to ask Him, that's all."

"I understand," he said and he thanked me. We shook hands and said good night. I never saw this man thereafter, but a year or so later at a convention a man said, "I've a message for you. Freddie said to tell you it worked. And also to tell you he will always love you for pointing the way. I might add," he concluded, "that Freddie is one of our top producers. He is a ball of fire, with enthusiasm."

Freddie's Plus Factor was released and enthusiasm became a renewing force in his life and business experience. And the same can happen to anyone who will employ the unfailing method which I gave that night to Freddie. He was smart enough to accept it and go with it.

15.

The PLUS FACTOR Makes Achievers

Just what is an achiever? What image comes to mind when the word *achiever* is mentioned?

Probably to most people the term means a person who accumulates big money, or rises to a high executive status in industry or to stardom in televison or the movies or politics. Such a person is indeed an achiever. But like other words in the English language, the word *achiever* has been somewhat distorted from its original and basic meaning.

Here is its definition in my dictionary: to achieve is "to accomplish something: attain an objective." Achievement is defined as "something accomplished, especially by valor, skill, or exertion; a feat; exploit; the act of achieving."

By these definitions it would seem that simple, unheralded people who never have any publicity, the plain workers of the world who accomplish something worthwhile, are also achievers. In fact, taken together these achievers can well be acclaimed the builders and preservers of our country just as much as the celebrities whose names and pictures are constantly before the public.

The Plus Factor is just as available to these unsung achievers as it is to the more publicized ones. I doubt if my Uncle Will ever got his name in the paper, unless it was printed in the Lynchburg, Ohio, weekly paper as one of the graduates of Lynchburg High School. But he had the Plus Factor and the Plus Factor had him. You see, William Fulton Peale was a poor boy, and anything he attained he had to work for. He was a born salesman. He could sell anything to anyone. That was because he always sold good products, he was thoroughly honest, and had an outgoing friendly way about him.

After high school he got a job selling house to house in the rural districts of Tennessee, and as he sold he left behind him a trail of friends. He worked his way through the University of Tennessee, graduating with honors. "Pa never had to put down a cent to get me through college," he used to say proudly.

Later he taught school in Tennessee and in this work he was equally successful. "Teaching is selling," he declared, "getting young people to buy constructive knowledge to enable them to do great things with their lives."

Young people loved him. "He inspired and motivated me as no other teacher ever did," a prominent businessman told me years later. "Before I met him I had no belief in myself," he added. "He made me believe I had something extra inside of me." Seems that Uncle Will was activating Plus Factors in his students. I know that this must have been true for he had the same effect upon me and I never sat in his classes.

He was always reaching out to do more with his own life. Talents were constantly spilling out of his personality. And he had the important ability to organize and constructively employ his talents. Thus it was that some people who had land in a growing area of Iowa heard of him. They approached him with the idea of selling this land to householders for home sites. Uncle Will would go into a community and announce a week of lot sales by auction. A plot would be laid out with graded streets and staked-off lots. Uncle Will always insisted that mature trees be saved to insure a parklike neighborhood.

He took me along during summer vacations to measure the lots, drive the stakes, and paint them. He gave prizes to attract buyers. He would always have a grand prize, a car, and he gave gold pieces as minor prizes (they were in common circulation then). And he passed out hundreds of one-pound boxes of candy. He drew enormous crowds. Prizes were by drawing and the fortunate person had to be present to receive his prize. Names went back into the box for the grand-prize drawing on the last day of the sale. The crowds stayed with him all through the heat of the Iowa summer.

I have heard some of the greatest orators of America from William Jennings Bryan to the present, but as a speaker I will put Uncle Will right up there with the best of them. I can see and hear him over the mist of years standing before those vast crowds telling those wonderful Iowa farmers what a home means. He drew a picture of the American homestead that brought tears to the eye. He pictured little children playing around the door and on the lawn, then in the golden years a man and wife walking hand in hand under the venerable trees. And he meant every word of it.

His great voice with no benefit of loudspeaker rang over the big crowd. They knew he was one of them, out of a common background of straitened circumstances, a motivated man who loved every one of his hearers and was persuading them to have a piece of America's soil in which to put down roots. And they bought those parcels by the hundreds. It has been sixty years since those exciting days, but whenever the word *achiever* is spoken I think of one of the greatest achievers I ever knew, my creative, innovative, indomitable, lovable Uncle Will.

What were the principles by which he became an achiever? Here they are:

1. He believed that America is the land of opportunity.
2. He wanted to make something of himself. He did not want to stay poor.
3. Money was never his god. He had no god but the Lord Almighty to whom he was ever faithful.
4. He knew one has to think to be an achiever and he did think. He also knew one has to work and he did work. He loved to work.
5. He liked people and they liked him.
6. He had boundless enthusiasm.
7. He had the ability to dream and turn many of his dreams into reality.
8. To him life was romantic and wonderful.
9. Above all, he never stopped trying. He never gave up.

Robert W. Service in "The Quitter" sums up the spirit of persistence:

> It's easy to cry that you're beaten and die;
> It's easy to crawfish and crawl;
> But to fight and to fight
> When hope's out of sight
> Why, that's the best game of all.

And though you come out of each grueling bout
All broken and beaten and scarred—
Just have one more try. It's dead easy to die;
It's the keeping on living that's hard.

I might add that to keep going as the poet so well describes is to have the Plus Factor aiding you in every trouble and every failure and disaster. If you do that, you will be able ultimately to turn every failure and indeed every disaster into an asset and achieve success.

An achiever is also a person who deals in quality. Actually he is himself of quality. He brings something good to other people. There is no phony element in the true and lasting achiever.

Whenever I think about the importance of quality in achievement, my old friend Joe Edison comes to mind. When I was young and single living in Syracuse, New York, where I was a pastor, one evening I found a little restaurant on a side street. It looked clean and attractive and since I was ready for dinner, I entered and climbed up on a stool at the counter. A man obviously of Middle Eastern extraction appeared out of the kitchen and when he saw me, a big smile came over his face. "Welcome, Reverend Peale, welcome," he said.

"You know me?" I asked in some surprise.

"Oh, yes," he replied. "I worship at your church. You see, I'm a Christian and go to church every Sunday."

"What's your name?"

"Well, I'll give you my American name. My Lebanese name might be difficult for you. It's Joe Edison. Call me Joe for short. Now I'll fix you a beautiful steak."

So saying he disappeared behind the swinging doors. Presently he emerged with the same big smile wreathing his face, and set a steak before me as though he was giving me a rare treasure. And it was a treasure indeed, the most delicious steak I had ever tasted. He stood watching me, fully expecting the admiration I was soon expressing. "It's the best," he said as one stating a fact, "the best in central New York, maybe the best in the whole state. I buy only the best western beef. My motto is quality, only top quality, always the best."

I got to know Joe very well as I dined at his restaurant at least twice a week. "What is your goal, Joe?" I asked one night.

His eyes sparkled. "It's to have the best quality restaurant anywhere. I love to cook. I don't want a chain, for I want to do the cooking myself." Joe came out of poverty in Lebanon, arriving in this country with close to nothing. Now he was moving up on the leverage of quality.

Came the day when Joe moved to the West Coast, where in time he achieved his ideal restaurant. His dream came true. Often over the years when I found myself in his area, I would go to his place. No longer was it a counter with stools. It was not large, but it was a place of beauty. Joe would embrace me. "My, but it's good to see you. Now you just sit here and Joe will fix you a nice steak." And it would be of the same delicious quality. It was cooking that never got better, for it was the best from the start. Joe would hover over me lovingly as I ate. He raised a fine family and became a substantially successful man, rising to the top of his profession on the wings of quality and loving-kindness. Joe was one of the achievers I've known in whose career the Plus Factor was uppermost. He is gone now, but there is still one grateful old customer who lovingly remembers him and salutes him as a top achiever, one who accomplished his goal.

On a recent trip to Europe *The International Herald Tribune* newspaper was delivered to my hotel room. A bold headline across the three columns read, "The Fading American Dream." "Never," I said. "Never is the American dream going to fade, not as long as we have men and women like those mentioned in this chapter and thousands more too numerous to mention here. These are achievers, the American way."

The Plus Factor, that extra power source built into each of us, is of superimportance, for achievers often have to pass through dark days and harsh experiences. What is necessary then is the courage and strength to hang in there and keep on believing, keep on dreaming; in short to just keep on keeping on.

I've often studied crowds on city streets thinking, "What are they all striving for? Have they definite goals for which they are working and will those goals bring them happiness and satisfaction?" It is all very well to be an achiever if what you have achieved brings you happiness and a sense of having done something of value. But is the individual who finds only unhappiness at the end of all his efforts really an achiever? For example, was the notable actress I once met who had achieved fame and lots of money really a valid achiever?

At a party in Hollywood I met this famous star and had a short but unforgettable conversation with her. She was very beautiful and sophisticated and naturally she was accepted as a superachiever. A sparkling group of lesser stars hovered around her. She was laughing, sprightly, and witty.

Finally, she came over to me and said she was glad to see me. I said I was glad to see her too and added, "You act happy." She replied, "You're right, it is an act. I'm not happy. Actually, I've never had a dozen happy days in my life. And I would like to be happy, but I guess it's just not for me."

"Well," I said, "at least you've got it over Napoleon."

"What's Napoleon got to do with it?" she asked in surprise.

"You say you've never had a dozen happy days in your life. When Napoleon was on Saint Helena he said that he had had no more than six happy days in his life. You're way ahead of him.

"So," I asked, "your great achievements have not brought you happiness?"

"No, but I know how to be happy without your reminding me. I was brought up in the same faith as you were. I know the way to happiness but in trying to be top dog I've neglected it." And to my surprise she said, "Thanks for reminding me. I'll try to start doing the things I know so well." As we separated, I thought of the statement in the Bible, "These things have I spoken unto you, that my joy might remain in you, and that your joy might be full" (John 15:11).

A famous psychiatrist said that the chief duty of a human being is to endure life. I think the chief duty of a human being is to overcome life, to master it, and thereby find happiness. But how many people really are happy?

I read in a newspaper about a Kiwanis Club whose members tried to give away one hundred one-dollar bills. On the streets of the city where crowds were the thickest they gave every person who looked genuinely happy a one-dollar bill. How many bills do you think they handed out? Twenty-two! Can it be that only twenty-two people out of the great throng were happy?

People of an artless nature seem to find happiness. By artless I mean people who are childlike in their mental attitudes, who are great enough to think childlike thoughts. A child has a sense of wonder and perceptiveness that brings happiness.

I was staying one night with an old friend whose home is amidst the pine woods of southern Georgia. I awakened in the morning and was sitting quietly when all of a sudden the song of a mockingbird burst in on me. The bird was right outside my window in a tree, singing at the top of its voice. It was beautiful. Soaring, cascading, lilting notes ascended from this bird to the God who made it.

I sat listening to the mockingbird, thinking, "It hasn't anything to worry about, doesn't have to pay taxes. It doesn't have to worry about what goes on in Washington or city hall. It's just happy." Then I heard another voice, the voice of an old man, singing an old gospel hymn, "O Happy Day." I caught the words, "O happy day that fixed my choice . . . when Jesus washed my sins away." I called out the window to the old man, "You're happy, aren't you?"

He said, "Yes, sir. I come out here every morning to do the yard work and I sing along with the birds."

"Is that bird here every morning?" I asked.

"Every morning," he said, "and every morning I sing too."

I asked, "Is the mockingbird singing 'O Happy Day' too?"

"Yes, sir, in its own language that's exactly what it's singing. You see we're both God's creatures. The bird sits on a bough and has feathers, and I stand on the ground with gray hair on my head, but we're both singing the same song of happiness!"

I remember what the Bible says about happiness. ". . . in thy presence is fulness of joy . . ." (Psalms 16:11). "Rejoice in the Lord always: and again I say, Rejoice" (Philippians 4:4).

As we have been saying, those persons who do the most creative things in their work, whatever it is, are the exciting top performers of this world, and excellence marks their achievements.

One day, in mid-morning, my brother Leonard and I were driving to the Tampa airport. As we approached a village, Leonard said, "There is a restaurant here that is always crowded. You see, it's famous for its pies. They're absolutely super. The lady who bakes them is top-performer number one in the pie business in my book."

I glanced at my watch. "It's only ten-fifteen and we had a pretty hefty breakfast. It's too early for lunch." Then I weakened. "Tell you what. In the interests of research for the book I'm writing, even if it is only ten-fifteen, let's stop and get a piece of that pie." I was impressed by the alacrity with which Leonard agreed.

We both ordered cherry pie in the rather plain restaurant, which was already well filled. The pie came. It was delicious; big red cherries, the juice deliciously oozing out and the crust crisply melting in your mouth.

"You know something," I said, "this has to be the best pie in the world, but to be sure this one piece is truly representative, don't you think we should sample another one?"

Leonard, always cooperative, agreed and we ordered apple pie this time; and if possible, it was even better than the cherry. After consuming this one I said enthusiastically, "I've just got to meet the lady who makes these pies and shake her by the hand." I made this request to the waitress. "Sure," she said. "She's right out there in the kitchen. Go ahead."

In the kitchen I found several women. All were dressed in blue smocks save a middle-aged woman who had on an immaculate white outfit. "Ma'am, did you bake those pies we just ate?"

She must have been a transplanted Yankee, for she was really closemouthed. "Who else?" she replied.

"Well, ma'am, I want to tell you that I have eaten pies all over the world. And I grew up in Ohio where they have the best cooks and bakers in the world, but I've got to admit that I never really had pie that is pie until now. Yours is by all odds the best pie I ever did eat."

To which she only said, "That's what they all say."

"And may I ask how many pies do you make every day?"

"I make forty-seven."

"And do you enjoy making pies?"

"What do you think? I wouldn't do it if I didn't." And she added, "It's the way I serve."

Having finished this, for her, long speech she clammed up. As Leonard and I resumed our journey, I said, "Do you know something? I've just met one of the most top performers I've ever encountered."

"How do you rate this woman to be that?" asked Leonard.

"Well, she loves what she is doing. She doesn't tire of getting up early six days a week to bake forty-seven pies. She has the highest standards of quality and workmanship. She isn't boastful, just takes praise in stride. Obviously she loves God, goes to her church on Sunday, and bakes pies not to rake in money, but to serve. So in my opinion she has in her nature that extra something that makes her a top performer, maybe number one in her specialty. In her own way she is just as surely a top performer as the most publicized big-time operators, for she is a person of excellence in what she does."

So I philosophized as we drove along. Leonard concurred, "Anyone who does her work with the skill this woman shows certainly has the extra something God puts into human nature, and she has it pretty fully."

And he added, "Another sure thing—we're not going to need any lunch today."

How does one become a top performer? A predominant factor I have observed in top performers is simply that they try and keep on trying. They try to do their best. They do not try to be rich or famous or impress anyone. And they consciously compete with only one person—themselves. They are not out to get ahead of anyone else. But they are always trying to get ahead of themselves by perfecting their skills so as to do better and even better.

The famous artist Eric Sloane was my friend. He lived just up the road a few miles from my farm in Dutchess

County, New York. He was a rare genius of a man who made much of his life from humble beginnings because he took the talent given him and stepped it up by always working and trying to exceed his previous efforts.

He painted rural scenes like old red barns in New York State and Vermont; a haystack in a field, a churn by a milk house. He painted a picture for me, which I cherish and which hangs in my library. It's of a white-steepled church in a small village in autumn. In the foreground is a rambling stone wall. Early in life his paintings sold for very little; later they became collector's items—costly too.

He was one of our greatest painters of the sky above, which Emerson called the daily bread of the soul. He made a life-long study of the sky, its coloring, changing aspects, its cloud formations. His sky pictures were masterpieces, not only of beauty, but of profound thoughtfulness as well.

So he added to the total of American art. Then came the day when he laid down his palette and brushes and quietly went home to God leaving behind the beauty he created.

I conducted his funeral in a little Connecticut town one spring afternoon. His ashes were placed under a gigantic boulder in the garden of the museum honoring him. In the huge rock is carved his name, Eric Sloane, and a statement he often made: "God knows I tried." If God knows that you and I try, He will come to our aid with additional support.

While working on this chapter I was seated in the Admirals Club of American Airlines at La Guardia Airport waiting for my plane. Looking around, it seemed that the proportion of glum faces was greater than usual. This atmosphere of gloom served as a contrasting background for a man who hobbled in on crutches. His neck was also encased in bandages. But he was laughing and exchanging wisecracks with associates. On the way out he spoke to me and I commented, "Your cheerfulness helps make my day."

A shadow of pain crossed his face. "I'm trying," he responded, "and believe me, trying helps. God bless you." And he went through the exit, leaving an upbeat spirit in his wake. In a land of top performers it is a pretty well-known fact that faith in God is an important factor in achievement, for faith keeps people trying and ultimately reaching their goals.

There is an organization known as the Horatio Alger Association of Distinguished Americans. The members are men and women who started in humble circumstances and through consistent effort became outstanding leaders in industry and other areas. I have attended some of the dinners of this organization at which the award winners said a few words. It was noticeable that the awardees always credited their success to the fact that they tried and kept trying and to their faith in God, who helped them along the way, especially in those times when the going got really hard.

The success potential, another name for the ability to do what you are doing with skill and excellence, is, I believe, inherent in every normally intelligent person. If this is true, why then do some persons become top performers and others do not? Motivation or the lack of it seems the most accurate answer to that question. Motivation makes a person believe that he can do things. It causes him to know he can meet and overcome all adversities in the process. And it keeps him going, working, striving, thinking, believing, and forever trying all the way in all the vicissitudes of his career.

I was talking along this line one noonday at the weekly luncheon meeting of the Central Rotary Club in Hong Kong. Afterward a Chinese man, a member of the club, said, "You are so right in what you said in your speech today." He then related his own personal story. It seems that years before, as a young man, he and his wife and two young children lived in Shanghai. The Communists took over the government, and confiscation of property left this formerly fairly prosperous family practically destitute. "Some inner urge," he continued, "caused us to leave our home with only the clothes on our backs and a few extra things we could carry. I remember that I looked around our home and could take only my Bible which I put under my shirt. Then we started walking. We slept at night in open country. We walked to Hong Kong and slipped across the border.

"There we found thousands of displaced, freedom-loving Chinese like ourselves. Like them we found old boxes and pieces of tin and put up a rude shelter. We were fed at soup kitchens provided by the Hong Kong government, standing in long lines at meal times to get our rations.

"To keep up my spirit I constantly read my Bible and prayed to God. He gave me the feeling that I could take better care of my family, that we could rise above this existence, that in fact I could actually be somebody sometime. So I never lost faith. We held on month after month. God seemed to tell me to encourage our neighbors, so we talked to them about faith and belief.

"Then one day reading the blessed Scriptures I came to Philippians 4:13, 'I can do all things through Christ which strengtheneth me.' Now sir," he said with a look of wonder, "I had read that a thousand times but this time it came to me that action was now demanded. So I studied and pondered and then a formula came to me. I put it together this way. I believe in Christ + with Christ I can do it + with Christ I shall do it = I will do it. Then I began to think, really think, and God opened up little opportunities. Wonderful little things happened. Result! Over the years I became a businessman in this city. God has prospered me and always I have worked upon that formula God gave me."

I count that brief meeting with that Chinese man as one of the motivational events of my life. For he gave me in that conversation a priceless formula. I've lived by it ever since. I earnestly commend it to you. It will work for anyone who believes it and works with it. Don't brush it off, for this formula is a pearl of great price.

Prosperity and succcess did not come easily to our Chinese friend. He had to try and try and keep on trying. The going was tough and rugged all the way, but he stuck it out. He never lost heart. He never quit. He continued to believe, to study, to work, to try and try again. He was a positive thinker who never let negatives take hold. He was a man of faith forever. And finally he became a winner. Indeed he became a top performer of excellence.

And what are these stories of achievers meant to do for you and for me? Simply to remind us that with the Plus Factor working and the Lord helping us, we too can achieve our goals.

16.

The PLUS FACTOR and Good Health

The American people today are health-conscious as never before. Newspapers, magazines, radio, and TV feature the subject prominently. Our office receives thousands of communications in the course of a year, as people write to us about their problems. And the number-one problem in the majority of these letters is health, either that of the writer or the health of a loved one.

How does a nonmedical writer go about giving suggestions for having and keeping good health? Obviously, if the writer himself has good health he can share personal information as to the measures he takes toward achieving it. Inasmuch as my wife, Ruth, and I have always worked together as a team, I'm going to share a double secret and outline how we both have maintained well-being and energy.

Our life-style is that of a working couple. For example, we are the executives of two rather large magazine publishing organizations. Ruth edits my books and is also an author in her own right. She travels with me to my many speaking engagements. On such trips we work together on manuscripts and a large volume of mail. Our schedule requires that we be healthy, for energy is needed and only out of health can energy be derived and maintained.

Ruth has had good health all of her life. And so have I. We have been married for over fifty years, and I have learned to regard her as a repository of wisdom and insight. I asked her, "Why have we always been blessed with good health? I am writing this book to help people, so let's give our joint formula for being healthy."

The following are some principles of good health as we have found them in our own experience.

First of all we have found that one way to be healthy and also happy is to have interesting work to do. We are healthy, vigorous, energetic, and yet we work hard every day and have followed this busy routine for years. We have breakfast before 7 A.M. and work at home on papers and manuscripts until 8:30 or 9:00, then go to the office. There we follow a busy schedule of meetings, conferences, interviews, dictation of mail, and telephone calls. Lunch consists of half a sandwich and half an apple at our desks and uses up about fifteen minutes.

When we are not at *Guideposts* or the Foundation for Christian Living, we have a heavy travel schedule of speaking engagements before national business conventions throughout the United States and Canada and occasionally also in countries as far away as New Zealand and Australia. We like this life so much that we take very few vacation periods. And this busy schedule is followed month after month and year after year. Despite it all, or perhaps because of our intense interest in these activities, we are healthy people.

Actually we seldom think of our taken-for-granted well-being except when it comes to writing a chapter of this sort. Then we stop to ask each other why and how in such busy lives we have been able to preserve strength and energy over so many intensely active years. We are not geniuses, just plain everyday people; and the fact that we can continue to be extremely active, going from one business to another, traveling 150,000 miles a year on speaking engagements and still be in the best of health means that others can do the same. If you will think right, pray, and keep relaxed, you will go a long way toward well-being.

Let's discuss eating, which I feel is basic to health. We eat simply. A bowl of cereal with a banana and a piece of toast or English muffin for breakfast, a meager lunch at our desk at noon as previously described, and an early dinner consisting of fish or chicken with vegetables and a salad. If we have meat, it is probably veal. We don't count calories, but we are sparing of sweets, never have a saltshaker or sugar bowl on the table, and keep the total food intake under control. We never take snacks between meals.

We go to bed early when we have no engagements that keep us out late. Before going to bed or before dinner, or both times when we are at the farm, we walk one or two miles and sometimes also swim.

In New York City we walk a mile on Fifth, Madison, or Park Avenue daily. We have a couple of favorite restaurants, one Chinese, the other German, each a mile away, and we walk there and back. Top priority is given to walking, which we believe does much to maintain top condition.

As previously stated, we do not believe work hurts, but rather helps, for if you are deeply and intensely interested in work, it frees you from many ills. We haven't time to be unhealthy. The Lord knows that and generously cooperates by keeping both of us fit to do the work to which He has called us. Our Plus Factors are thus kept in good working order, constantly producing the energy to keep going and handle our considerable responsibilities.

But when at the start of writing this chapter I put the question to Ruth, "Why are we in good health at my age and yours?" she replied, "Well, for one thing we are not people who worry or have fears and we don't hate anyone. And we love God and the Lord Jesus and people and we truly try to do the Lord's will. And that's about it," she concluded.

"Think Positive, Stay Healthy" was the headline over an article in the *Sunday Times* of London on July 27, 1986. The article declares that "depression and anxiety undermine the body's ability to fend off diseases."

> The popular belief that illness is more likely to follow anxiety and depression has recently been substantiated by scientific studies. Immunologists are discovering more about the link between mind and body.
>
> For instance, we know that during stressful periods the body produces large amounts of a steroid called cortisol. This inhibits the work of macrophage cells which are a key part of our immune system. This means the body can no longer respond normally to infection.
>
> Researchers, having evidence that stress depresses the immune system, now will try to find out what sort of events enhance the immune system. . . .
>
> Dr. [Stephen] Greer of the Royal Marsden Hospital has shown how these worries can also affect the patient's physical condition. He looked at the mental attitudes of women who had a breast removed as part of cancer treatment and found that those who had a positive attitude were twice as likely to survive for 10 years as those who were depressed.

> "We will be teaching patients cognitive strategies—that is to say, mental tricks to challenge their negative thinking," he explains.

These and other significant findings being widely reported today substantiate the presence of good health assets in the mind and in our attitudes. This extra supportive power that we call the Plus Factor is a spiritual faculty given to each of us by the Creator to keep us in shape mentally and physically. It only makes sense that God wants those marvelous instruments which He made, mind and body, to work as well as He designed them to.

Having worked closely with people and their problems over many years, I have no hesitance whatsoever in asserting that in my opinion and experience one secret of good health is to have soul or spirit health. To live by the teachings and spirit of Jesus Christ is to be healthy mentally, and mental health leads to wholeness of the total personality. I do not mean that religious people don't get sick, for, of course, they do. But it is a demonstrated fact that religious faith generally speaking has a positive effect on health, and departure from morality, a negative effect.

It is perhaps strange how inner confusion, even deterioration, is often caused by guilt feelings. We are living in a time when some people actually pretend to believe it's okay to engage in wrongful acts as long as it's their own business or doesn't hurt anyone. Well, the trouble is it does hurt someone—you! Wrongdoing eats at your well-being. It can actually affect the body and mind adversely and often causes ill health.

An outstanding ear physician tells me that trouble with the ear—such as roaring in the ear, muffled hearing, imbalance, dizziness—doesn't always result from a physical problem. It can be caused by guilt feelings.

Recently this distinguished doctor, said by other physicians to be the leading man in his specialty in the state, told of a patient, a woman, who complained of pain in her left ear. He examined her carefully and could find nothing wrong. She came back several times and said, "Doctor, there's got to be something wrong with my ear."

The doctor said, "Look, I've been over your ear completely and find nothing amiss."

He studied her intently. She was obese, very heavy for her age and height. He thought she would have been handsome had she not been so heavy. Obviously she was a compulsive eater. There are compulsive drinkers and there are compulsive eaters, and both are driven by inherent emotional conflict. When you see a person drinking or eating heavily, excessively so, you can pretty well figure that he or she is troubled mentally or emotionally. People who overeat are often trying to eat away something that is eating at them.

The doctor asked the patient why she allowed herself to become so heavy. "I guess it's because I'm so unhappy," she lamented. "I was married and was unfaithful to my husband. We got a divorce. Now I've been having an affair with a married man. But what does that have to do with my ear or my eating?"

"It could have everything to do with your ear, and your eating too," said the doctor.

"Okay!" she exclaimed, "what can I do? I admit that I'm really quite miserable and I know what I'm doing is wrong, but how can I help myself?"

The doctor replied, "First, we've got to get rid of your guilt feelings. It's doubtful that you will ever be really happy or physically well until you deal with your inner conflicts and get them resolved. So we'd better drain your mind of those guilt feelings." As a Christian layman he felt competent to handle this matter spiritually.

When she finally came to grips with her guilt feelings, she stopped seeing the married man. Gradually her weight was reduced by thirty pounds. She became a healthy, happy woman and had real peace of mind. Then her ear trouble cleared up.

Guilt feelings can cause trouble mentally and even physically in many ways. Sometimes people are troubled by anxiety and fear due to long-held guilt. Indeed, guilt and fear are so inextricably interlocked that when these two enemies of human well-being gang up they can make life quite miserable. Anyone who suffers from fear or anxiety needs to face honestly the possibility that guilt may be involved. Its elimination is a necessity for healing.

A man I knew became a victim of anxiety in a dramatic reversal of personality, a personality which formerly was free of abnormal fear. It came out that he had developed an enormous sense of guilt based on violation of his moral code. Sadly he discovered that these basic and deeply ingrained convictions could not so easily be set aside without disastrous disintegration of personality.

I recommended several steps designed to bring peace and renewal. First, to stop what he was doing. Second, a complete mental catharsis under the guidance of a competent spiritual counselor. By that I meant he was to empty out all the evil he had thought and done, holding nothing back. A good washing out of the mind can do wonders for anyone. Third, he was to ask and receive divine forgiveness. Forgiveness is quickly and generously given the sincere person. Fourth, he was to forgive himself, which is even more difficult. And no longer was he to condemn himself. The ego instinctively believes it must continually punish and repunish itself. Self-forgiveness is vital, for it turns off abnormal self-punishment. Fifth, he was to rebuild his personality on a moral basis harmonious with his deepest convictions.

We are dealing here with the prevention of ill health rather than the curing of disease. I think it is an indisputable fact that the person who develops and maintains a wholesome, healthy-minded spiritual life pattern will be most likely to preserve strength and energy and a state of wellness. That person will be free of what we may call the "virus" of resentment. "Sick" thoughts will not be able to undermine health.

However, that there can be a healing level where spiritual forces also operate with curative effect seems indicated by the experiences of many perfectly reliable persons. A friend sent me a clipping from *The Daily Review* of Towanda, Pennsylvania, dated August 13, 1985. It carries the story of the healing of Sally Schultz, a mother and highly respected nurse in that community. I do not know Sally Schultz, or have any information about her case beyond the news story by Wes Skillings. But I do find this story of healing strangely moving and also indicative of the operation of the Plus Factor.

> There's an ageless quality about Sally Schultz. She's one of those rare people who seems to have reversed the cycle that steadily robs us of youth and vitality. Her rust-hued hair and delicate porcelain skin, highlighted by roseate cheeks that would put the finest rouge to shame, make one forget that this woman is the mother of three children in their twenties.
>
> It wasn't always that way. She was suffering from a disease that had turned sunshine into an enemy. When she was outside, even in summer, she was wrapped in a cocoon of long sleeves, pants, gloves, hats, and scarfs.
>
> The bottom line was the sun would kill her.
>
> This was a disease called lupus. After an automobile accident 20 years ago, it suddenly came into her life. The accident broke her jaw and cracked and jammed bones and tendons in her neck. She became afflicted

with a battery of problems that caused her body to deteriorate. Pain became her closest companion. Among the most brutal invaders was arthritis that made the simplest movements agony and kept her from sleeping for several nights at a time. She was allergic to everything, particularly aspirin—and it seemed as if all the advances in modern medicine were useless in her case.

Sally started searching for answers. The more she read, the more she became convinced that the power to conquer her afflictions was within her. Though she was not brought up in a religious household, she found tremendous relief in the power of prayer and meditation. In her readings she kept finding one key—the answer is in your head, in some corner of the brain or waiting to be tapped in the subconscious. If that were true, and she knew innately that it was, she wondered if the illnesses themselves, all feeding upon each other, had grown from the seeds sprouted by negative forces somewhere within her consciousness.

"If it's in my head, tell me and I'll accept it," she told the doctors. But, of course, all the physical evidence was there—in the tests and her growing medical records. The more she read, the more she became convinced that there was power within her that could defeat these invaders. Most important, like all believers in prayer, she believed in miracles.

A miracle came for Sally Schultz in the early morning hours. She had been unable to sleep. She dozed off briefly, awakening with a tremendous urge to get out of bed. There was no pain. She got up and walked. No pain. Sat down. Stood up. All the movements that had been so unbearable were now effortless, painless.

It never came back. She was cured somehow. To her the years that have passed since have been years of constant healing. "I've actually gone to a higher plane of healing," she says.

"It's mind, body, and soul," she says quietly. A strong proponent of natural foods, vitamins, and herbs, she is probably best known locally as the proprietor of a local health food store.

"But you need spiritual food too," she says. "None of it can happen unless the ego goes out the door."

She is certain that there is a constant battle between positive and negative energies, on another plane.

"I believe there is an open channel to the Creator," she continues. "He is our past, present, and future." It's a channel into which we can all tap in, she says. "You have to lose you to find Him," is her simple assessment.

As a person who believes in visions and directives from a higher realm, she often feels called to a certain passage in the Bible and has frequently awakened in the middle of the night, suddenly aware of someone else's need for prayer or support. She says these directives have yet to be wrong.

Although lupus is a disease known for its unpredictability, with flare ups and remissions appearing at any time, there is reason to believe that the victim's mental outlook plays a role in its course.

In this case Mrs. Schultz became convinced that a power within her was working to restore health. It would seem that we can identify the power to which she referred as the Plus Factor, that extra something that the Creator placed within us for our benefit.

My brother Dr. Robert Clifford Peale was a physician and surgeon, a graduate of Harvard Medical School. I always thought that he was truly a natural-born doctor. He was generously endowed with a loving attitude and his patients were devoted to him. He told me once, "Norman, you will live a long time even though you drive yourself with work." Asked why he thought so, he replied, "You have learned the priceless secret of having inner peace amidst outward turmoil. And," he added, "Ruth has the same gift, more so than you."

If Bob was right in his diagnosis it is because Ruth and I have been fortunate to find one of the greatest blessings in this world, which the Scriptures refer to as "the peace of God which passes all understanding." You can have it also.

As I write these lines, I am working in my room in Switzerland looking out on a blue lake surrounded by snowcapped mountains. The blue sky overhead is dotted by a few fleecy white clouds. This fabulous spot contains the peace of the world in full measure.

Just a moment ago nature put on one of its most spectacular demonstrations. The widest rainbow I have ever seen stretched from the lake over a high snow-clad mountain to touch down in a deep valley in the Alps. There was about this gigantic rainbow a deep benediction of peace and hope. But as ineffable as nature is in the effect of natural beauty on the mind, it cannot match the peace of God in its healing effect on the human mind. Jesus refers to this comparison, "Peace I give unto you: not as the world giveth, give I unto you" (John 14:27). It cannot be stated too strongly that God-inspired inner peace produces harmony and well-being mentally and physically and is thereby the greatest boon to health.

According to a report in the International Journal of Cardiology (January 1986), religious belief may be protective against heart disease. This was the conclusion of Israeli researchers who found lower heart-attack rates among devout, Orthodox Jews than among nonpracticing Jews. In this study of 500 men and women the researchers cited psychological and social factors as playing possible roles, but said: "The strong belief in a supreme being and the role of prayer may in themselves be protective."

My friend and physician Dr. John C. Carson of La Jolla, California, is always kind enough to give me a physical examination when he spends a month each summer as the doctor at Lake Mohonk, which is situated in several thousand acres of ancient forestation in New York State. John runs daily amidst this quietness and has transmitted to me the sense of peace he has obviously derived from this environment. In a lesser circumference on our farm not far distant, in walking among the trees and meadows, I have found an inner peace that has been reflected in normal blood pressure readings and in good heart action.

While I was writing this chapter amidst the Swiss Alps, a Dutch lady, speaking in perfect English, telephoned and said, "The one thing I want more than all else is an inner feeling of the peace of God." I responded by saying that as she lived closer and ever closer to God in her mind, such peace would be granted to her. As that happens, I am sure this lady will have good health in corresponding measure, for the peace of God and health of mind and body go together. The Plus Factor is released in the form of vitalized energy.

That thinking can affect health both for good or ill has often been demonstrated. The late James A. Farley, one-time postmaster general, was a friend of mine. One day when I encountered him on the street and stopped to chat, I noticed once again his vigorous health. I knew that he was over eighty at the time and admiringly said, "Jim, you actually look the same as you did twenty-five years ago. How come you look so healthy and show no signs of getting old?" He smiled and said, "I never think any old thoughts."

What are old thoughts? Perhaps they are threadbare, worn-out, tired thoughts about life, its cares and troubles as faced by us all. Old thoughts sometimes take the form of resentment, even hatred. If sustained over time, such thinking can produce ill effects physically. Explosive anger has well-known reactions. When anger is perhaps less than heated but seethes constantly, insidious harmful effects can result and in time become acute.

Some people on the other hand constantly infuse their thought processes with the zest, the opportunity, and even the wonder of living. They do not sag and lose their mental and spiritual verve. The Plus Factor is constantly going for them keeping them alive, vital, interested.

It is important to expect good health, for that which is imaged and expected tends to become fact. A few times in my own life I have experienced a crisis in health that caused some concern. But even in such emergency I always expected that the end result would be good. And, in every instance I have emerged in excellent condition. Positive imaging and expectation of good health, I believe, do much to activate a positive response in mind and body. The Plus Factor constantly tries to produce the health status that is imaged positively. Spiritual power gives impetus to the Plus Factor. It is the operation of faith, the kind referred to in Scripture: "According to your faith be it unto you" (Matthew 9:29) or "If ye have faith . . . nothing shall be impossible unto you" (Matthew 17:20).

This spiritual power, which, I believe, transcends physical force, will not work, nor could it be expected to do so, when it is accompanied by practices that run counter to health. Positive thinking, positive imaging, and positive expectation with all their creativity can be frustrated by a life-style that flouts the laws of well-being. But when one lives sensibly, thinks positively, and believes in the best outcomes, good health, while not guaranteed, is more likely to be achieved and maintained. (Of course, professional medical help is needed, and you should let your doctor help you maintain good health.)

To sum up, here are the simple good-health rules that Ruth and I practice.

1. Have interesting work to do. Keep active at something worthwhile.

2. Eat simply. Keep your food intake under control.
3. Go to bed early and get up early.
4. Give top priority to walking every day. Swimming is also helpful.
5. Love God, don't hate anyone, and don't be afraid.
6. Never let a sense of guilt fester in you. Get it cleansed out.
7. Develop spirit and soul health.
8. Cultivate the "peace of God that passes understanding."
9. Expect and image good health.
10. Through spiritual cultivation keep your Plus Factor robust.

17.

Turn Setbacks Into Comebacks With the PLUS FACTOR

Jim Decker's name kept coming to mind. And this was a bit strange, for I hadn't seen him lately. But I have learned that when a person continues to come up in my thoughts, it may mean that I'd better do something about it. And I'm usually glad I did.

I went to see Jim and found him slumped in his office chair the picture of gloom and despair. "What's wrong, Jim?" I asked. "Usually you're right up there on top, happy and positive. Why the gloom? You could cut it with a knife."

"Norman, I've had the biggest setback of my business career," he said dolefully. "I've lost my best account, a third of my business. Now I know you'll give me some of that positive-thinking stuff of yours. But I'm afraid it won't work this time. This one's knocked me for a loop. It's a terrible setback."

"Do you want to tell me about it?" I asked, adding, "I'm no wise man, but sometimes it helps just to talk to someone, especially a friend who thinks you are a great guy, who loves you, who believes in you."

"Yeah," he said, "and it's mighty good of you to come. It's just like you. You're so right. I've been thinking and thinking until I'm getting more and more confused. Maybe it will help to talk it out. How much talk can you take? How much are you good for?"

"When I have to go, Jim, I'll let you know. Start talking." And he did. He laid it all out, condemning himself for "dumb" actions, stupid mistakes, but gradually his talk turned from what he should have done to what he might do, to what he could do. He began to explore solutions. Mentally turning from the past he started facing the future. And that was just the beginning.

When a big setback hits you, the first step on the road to recovery is to start turning from the past and look toward the future. This didn't happen all at once with Jim, however. I entered that office at 3 P.M. and finally left at 5:45 P.M. I listened to over two hours of talk.

And I am glad I did, for by talking it out to a caring friend Jim Decker worked his way past that setback and ultimately wove it into his experience creatively.

Here's how he got the solution for that recovery. Along about two hours after he started talking I interrupted: "Excuse me, Jim, do you ever read *Guideposts*?"

"*Guideposts*? Sure I read it. I think it's a terrific magazine. What do you mean do I read *Guideposts*? You know I do."

"Okay," I said. "Then you know the page we call 'Words to Grow On.'"

He nodded, "Good stuff on that page." He gestured to a pile of *Guideposts* magazines on a table.

I hunted through them until I found the September 1986 issue. Then I said, "Rest your voice and let me read what Grant Teaff, coach of the Baylor University football team, has to say."

> I'm always looking for the right words to encourage my football team. At Baylor University, where I've been head coach for 14 years, I've used everything from praise to provocation to get the best out of my players. But once, the right encouraging words came from a team member.
>
> In 1980 we had a very strong team and had won the first seven games of the season. We were riding high and running a little scared, I think, as the pressure to win increased. Our eighth game was against San Jose State, a team supposedly not up to our caliber.
>
> In a shocking upset San Jose beat us, 30–22. Suddenly our confidence waned. After our loss I kept hearing people say what might have been, shaking their heads over what we could have done. The team seemed to absorb this negative thinking. In the workouts leading up to our next game against the University of Arkansas we couldn't seem to rid ourselves of a lingering defeatist attitude.
>
> Then Kyle Woods came to our dressing room. A year before, Kyle had been injured in a workout that left him paralyzed. He was only a sophomore, a defensive back on the second team, when it happened. Now he would be a cripple for life. This was his first visit to a game in Baylor Stadium since the injury.
>
> Kyle was in the dressing room before the game, in a wheelchair. After our team prayer, I said a few words and then asked Kyle if he had anything to add.
>
> "I sure do," he said.
>
> I walked over to his wheelchair and pushed him into the center of the room. Kyle paused for a moment and

seemed to look every player in the eye. He said, "Here it is: *You take a setback and you turn it into a comeback.*"

Then Kyle dropped his hands to his side. He had no dexterity in them, but he managed to lock his thumbs around the wheelchair's arms. He pushed downward on the chair with his hands, lifting his body up. With one giant lunge, he stood up.

There he stood in the dressing room, to emphasize the point he'd just made, that "you can take a setback and turn it into a comeback." I've never heard a greater message nor seen it so dramatically punctuated.

Then we went out and defeated the University of Arkansas, 42–15, and we went on to become the 1980 Southwest Conference champions.

The Bible says, "God hath not given us the spirit of fear; but of power, and of love, and of a sound mind" (2 Timothy 1:7). The Lord wants us to achieve. Out of every setback we can find the comeback He has in mind for us."*

Jim sat nodding his head. Then he got up, walked around the desk, and put a big hand on my shoulder. "You know something, Norman! God sent you down here today. That's what I needed to hear. Out of every setback we can find the comeback God has in mind for us." He went and looked out the window for several minutes. "Okay, I can make it back now. I know I can. Pray for me and stick with me."

Fortunately, this was an intelligent and spiritually minded man. He knew the source of power, the way to mount a comeback. He drew on the Plus Factor in his nature. Ultimately, he compensated for this loss of one big account by adding a number of small accounts, and so by his own admission was better off in the long run.

*Adapted from *Winning: It's How You Play the Game* by Grant Teaff, Word Books, 1985.

Everyone has setbacks. This is a normal fact of life. And when you have more than one in a row, as sometimes happens, it can be very discouraging. If you allow it to be so, it can take the life out of you. But you should always remember that even so, you still have a lot of rebound left. And when you deliberately start calling on your Plus Factor, you can begin the process that turns setbacks into comebacks.

That is what Jim Decker did. How did he do it? Well, I would say he did it because he is a big man, not physically, because he is only average in size. But he is big mentally, big in outlook, big in faith.

Everyone, every man and woman, has something big in him or her, an extraspecial power put there by the Creator Himself. God knew you would have tough times—when things would go wrong, when everything would seem to be against you. The Creator was aware that setbacks would come and you would be discouraged and feel defeated or that crises would suddenly develop and you wouldn't think you could handle them. He knew that sometime, somewhere along the line, maybe more than once in life, you would be in sore need of extra strength. So He provided a mechanism to produce this power and built it into your mind and body—and it works miraculously. It's one of the wonders that you possess. It is the Plus Factor.

All through the New Testament are passages telling about the gift of power from God the Father to the believer. "I can do all things through Christ which strengtheneth me" (Philippians 4:13). "But as many as received him, to them gave he power . . ." (John 1:12). "Ye shall receive power, after that the Holy Ghost is come upon you . . ." (Acts 1:8). "For I am not ashamed of the gospel of Christ: for it is the power of God . . ." (Romans 1:16).

As a matter of fact, God Almighty made you much bigger than you have ever thought you are. Perhaps you write yourself off, put yourself down as just an average person not able to take much trouble or bear up under the vicissitudes of life. "It's all more than I can take," we say despondently. But when we start growing big spiritually, then we grow big mentally and big, too, in faith—faith in God and also faith in ourselves.

A man once told me he read in one of my books about praying big, believing big, thinking big. He admitted he had thought himself small. So he started to pray big, believe big, and think big. After a while he began to grow big. He developed a bigger faith, bigger thought power, a bigger personality. "I adopted the Twelve Big Plan," he told me. Twelve ways to grow bigger within yourself. Here is the plan he gave me: "Pray big, think big, believe big, act big, dream big, work big, give big, forgive big, laugh big, image big, love big, live big." Carry that list with you daily, look at it often and you will take on an inner bigness such as you've never had.

You and I, and indeed everyone, have lodged within an indomitable, superstrong quality. It can be summoned to our assistance in times of emergency. Physically it is often called "a shot of adrenaline." It results in a sudden access of strength that dramatically supplements normal energy. This may be regarded as a demonstration of the basic Plus Factor.

A man five feet nine inches in height and weighing only 148 pounds was driving behind a huge tractor-trailer. Suddenly the truck swerved, jackknifed, and crashed into a ditch where it turned over. Gasoline spilling out ignited and fire was already spreading over the truck when the driver of the car jammed on his brakes, jumped out, and ran to the cab. He found the driver slumped over the wheel in shock and pinned by the warped doors. He tried the door, but it had been badly jammed in the accident. He tried again mustering what seemed all his strength, but the door would not budge.

The fire now roaring through the length of the vehicle made him terrifyingly aware of the immediate possibility of explosion. He had to get the driver out of there and fast. "Oh, God, help me. Give me strength," he cried. He grabbed the cab door once again and, summoning additional strength, jerked the door open, grabbed the stunned driver, and pulled him out just in time. Where did this extra strength come from? Where else but from the inner Plus Factor called into action by a life or death crisis. What he did not have the strength to do under normal circumstances, he found he did have when desperate circumstances required it.

When a setback hits you, immediately get up, look in a mirror, and tell yourself, "I am bigger than I think I am. I have the great God helping me." Then draw on that big something within called the Plus Factor. You will be strong enough to turn that setback into a comeback.

My friend Smith Johnson is a remarkable man, an ingenious engineer, builder of a successful rubber company, an artist, and a man of positive action. He stood up to fear in his childhood and as a result became bigger than fear. And that is being big, for fear can be very big indeed. Mr. Johnson says, "I am reminded of an incident which happened in my youth when I was about ten years old. I had always been frightened of thunder and lightning to the extent that sometimes I crawled under the bed during heavy storms. It was on such a night about ten o'clock that I made a momentous decision. I would go outdoors and face the elements, whatever the consequences. I left my room, where I had gone to bed, and dressed with overshoes and raincoat, crept downstairs and outside without rousing my parents. Our house was out in the country a mile or so from town. Back of our house was a ten-acre lot and then another ten acres of woods. I made my way across the lot with the lightning blazing and the thunder cracking in my ears. Across the lot I went and into the woods where the only light I had to make my way was the lightning which flashed almost continually. Stumbling over logs and through the thick underbrush I finally reached the back fence which was a half-mile from our house. The storm, if possible, had become worse, and I sat on the top rail of the fence. The rain pelted me and a strong wind tried to take my coat off, but I had a wonderful inside feeling of accomplishment. I had braved the storm and was still alive. Then I retraced my steps back home and it didn't seem half so far. I crept up to my room without waking my parents. I slept the sleep of the happy, even going to sleep before the storm stopped.

"The next test to which I put myself was overcoming the fear of a building on my way through a park to school. This was called the pavilion because many years before they had held dances in it. It was boarded up and generally shunned by the townspeople because it was said to be haunted. I was so terrified by it that I usually ran past as far from it as possible. But one evening with my newfound courage I took this shortcut home instead of going by the road, which was farther. I went boldly around the building looking for a way to get into it. By good fortune I found a loose board, which I removed. Through this opening I forced my skinny body. It was indeed spooky as I walked across the creaky floor from one end to the other. I even explored the long unused kitchen, which was particularly dark and to my wrought-up imagination very hazardous. Again I felt that sweet feeling of accomplishment as I stood my ground in the deserted building.

"I feel that these two experiences had a great and profound effect on my life which is drawing to a close at eighty-eight years. Was it God who gave me the strength to do these two simple things, but most important to me? I don't know. But my faith in God and myself, I believe, have helped me during a life when there were many narrow escapes from disaster or death. And I am most thankful for it."

The fact is that we *can* handle and rise above things much better than we think. Yet, sometimes mere common everyday difficulties that we all have can add up and eventually defeat us if we allow them to do so. A lady wrote me from Florida. "About sixty years ago I had trouble getting to sleep. My mother told our minister about it because she figured a twelve-year-old should not have that trouble.

"The pastor took me aside and said he heard I had a problem with insomnia. He then took a piece of paper and printed eight words: quietly, restfully, easily, patiently, peacefully, trustfully, serenely, joyously. He handed it to me and said, 'Repeat these words slowly and think of the meaning of each one. By the time you reach the end, I am sure you will have dozed off.'

"I still have it in my Bible and when a restless night comes I repeat the words and think of that kind, understanding minister."

As a twelve-year-old girl this woman found a technique that worked on the problem of sleeplessness and years later when she had become elderly, it was still working. I've believed and taught in books and speeches that there is a workable formula for every trouble. It's like finding a cure for a disease: Discovery goes on constantly. There is a way to attack every setback and it is often some simple, tried and true method.

My mother often said, "Whenever a door shuts, it means that God has an open door for you down the way." She believed this, for it operated again and again in the life of my parents. So she taught it to her children, my brothers and myself; and the three of us believed it, having seen it work for Mother and Father. Our firm belief in it proved effective for us as well. We were not much upset with setbacks for we believed that a comeback was just waiting down the road a piece. And do you know that is exactly the way it worked out for Bob and Leonard and for me and for many to whom we have suggested this principle.

Often a so-called setback is actually a blessing in disguise. Many times setbacks not only lead to comebacks but to even better circumstances than before. "To every disadvantage there is a corresponding advantage" is a statement often made by W. Clement Stone who has had enough disadvantages to know something about them and what can come of them. By a strong positive attitude and intelligent effort he was able to turn the majority of his setbacks into comebacks. And he says he learned something from each experience. One thing he learned was to look intently into a setback situation for what know-how it might contain, for usually there are some direction signs to that comeback down the road.

A case in which I had some involvement concerned the chief financial officer of a fair-sized investment counseling company. His goal was to succeed to the presidency of the company upon the retirement of the president and chief executive officer. He was sure he would. And why not? He was widely considered to be one of the most knowledgeable men in the investment-counseling business.

Yet when the vacancy occurred, he was not selected. Instead a man from a branch office was brought in as president. The bypassed official was, of course, deeply disappointed and angry. He felt that he was unfairly treated and humiliated by this rejection. He loudly declared that the new president "knows nothing about investment counseling; he is just an ordinary salesman."

The new president, whom I happened to know quite well, a kindly, thoughtful, Christian man, telephoned me and said he would like to come and talk over a problem with me. The problem was the one I am relating. He told me that it was indeed a fact that the treasurer was the best man in the business—without any question—and he added, "He has forgotten more about the business than I ever knew. I feel sorry for him, for this is a terrible setback to his career."

"Why then did your board bypass him and select you?" I asked.

Floyd replied, "It's because he cannot get along with people. He is a genius in finance, but at the same time he's an unapproachable man who just turns people off. The board wanted an administrator who could make decisions and who also liked people and was outgoing and could therefore lead." He grinned, "Since he didn't need much ability, they picked on me. But," he continued, "I want to help Frank. I won't be in this job all that long at my age, and I'd like to help him recover from this setback and later make a real comeback and succeed me as president."

"Call on him in his office," I suggested, "or better still, go to his home some evening. Let him know how you respect him and his ability and try to help him to change his attitudes toward people. Tell him you're going to have to depend upon him. To change a personality requires delicacy and patience, but you've got both qualities. Later at an appropriate time, if you are sure your board would select him if he changes, you could level with him and the reason he was not promoted."

Subsequently these two men became good co-workers. The treasurer was completely loyal to his president. Gradually some of the chief executive's affability and caring rubbed off on the other man. At any rate, five years later when Floyd retired, he recommended Frank for the position. Frank was elected by the board and became, so I have been informed, an excellent well-liked administrator. His setback had within it the makeup of his comeback. Fortunately, he was cast in a big mold and did not persist in anger and hostility. He cooperated, he learned about himself, he corrected his weaknesses of personality, and therefore he qualified for a comeback.

I've often thought that Floyd was able to handle this delicate situation so well because for years he had been growing spiritually. His Plus Factor it seemed was working very well indeed.

This is a case where the rebound from a setback to a comeback was engineered by another person. All of which highlights the importance of having friends who know our good points and emphasize them creatively. The more such friends we accumulate, the more we guarantee successful recovery in times of setback. We can build up comeback resources by becoming involved in our communities, always being sensitive to the needs of the other fellow. Not that we do these good deeds to assure a payoff in the form of help for ourselves, but just because it's the right way to live. It is a fact, however, as the Good Book says, if you "cast your bread upon the water, you will find it after many days" (*see* Ecclesiastes 11:1).

When his setback came, Jules Matsoff found that his many friends were the source of his comeback.

When he walked into his clothing store one day in March, he felt about as low as a man can feel. His failing business, Esther's of Hartford, Wisconsin, with aisle after aisle of women's fashions, had been a local institution since 1920. Jules and Roz, his wife of 44 years, had purchased the store from Esther in 1958 and kept the business growing—until now. Now business was shrinking and the outlook was bleak—not the customary outlook for Jules Matsoff.

A talkative, energetic, people-loving, risk-taking businessman, Jules had done an amazing thing for his little town of 7,000 souls. He had made it a magnet for shoppers from the big city. His sales technique was advertising his store heavily on radio and TV stations and in newspapers in Milwaukee, the major metropolitan area 27 miles southeast of Hartford. He even rented the Hartford City Hall every summer and had such a whale of a sale that it drew customers from six counties. A goodly number of retailers in town admit that it was Jules' advertising that brought customers to *their* stores as well.

In 1980 Jules and Roz decided to expand. The Downtown Development Authority was willing to lend them a million dollars at 10 percent interest to build a mini-mall. Two years later Esther's moved into a modern, red-brick complex with room for nine other stores. Business buzzed. But not for long. No matter how hard he tried, Jules couldn't rent four of the nine stores in the mall. The empty space ate up his profits and he couldn't afford to continue advertising in the Milwaukee media—which sharply curtailed the business generated by city shoppers.

By 1984 newspapers and news stations had noticed that the little mall seemed to have permanent "For Rent" signs in many windows. Suddenly, "Financially Troubled" became Esther's first name. Rumors flew that Esther's was on its way out of business. Panicky brides-to-be started calling. "Mr. Matsoff, I'm getting married in a month! What's going to happen to my wedding gown and bridesmaid dresses?"

Jules assured the young women that their gowns would be delivered on time. But some weren't convinced and canceled their orders. Two top salespeople quit to work in Milwaukee because they believed the business was going under.

In 1985 the Redevelopment Authority had to file a lawsuit demanding the $50,000 the Matsoffs were behind in loan payments. Foreclosure loomed.

Jules' fund of optimism was finally depleted. "Maybe it's time to call it quits," he told Roz.

"We can't give up now," Roz insisted. "Remember, Esther's even got through the Depression."

A few months later, Jules found a buyer for the mall. Though his enthusiasm for retailing was at low ebb, Roz persuaded him to look for a new location for Esther's. Halfheartedly, he decided to rent the old closed-up movie theater across the street. Then the Matsoffs did just enough redecorating to make it usable.

Jules continued to worry. "Roz, we're going to lose too much money when we close the store to make the move. It'll take a week. I've hired five men, but they'll need hundreds of trips to carry everything by hand, out the door, down the sidewalk and across the street!"

Roz stayed calm. "It'll all work out. What happened to your faith?"

Jules shook his head. "Maybe God wants us to retire."

On that March morning of the move, Jules dragged himself downtown, unlocked the door of his beautiful mall store for the last time and heaved a heavy sigh. Just as he flipped on the light switch he noticed a local bakery truck pulling up in front of the store. Two men got out with two huge trays filled with doughnuts and pastries and plopped them down on the jewelry counter.

"Hey, wait a minute. I didn't order that. You must have made a mistake."

"No mistake, Mr. Matsoff, it's all paid for."

Before he could call the bakery, another truck from a local restaurant arrived with two 100-cup coffee makers.

Jules did a 180-degree turn. That's when he saw all the people, over a hundred of them, streaming toward the store. His attorney was wearing jeans and a sweatshirt, as were many of the other professional people and business owners. Even Mayor Witt was there in his natty three-piece business suit. Soon they were all chatting, laughing, wolfing down doughnuts and coffee.

"We're here to make the move, Jules. You just tell us what to take first and how to carry it."

"Hey, ol' buddy," grinned Dick Furman, manager of the local J.C. Penney store, Esther's biggest competitor, "We figure you won't have to close the store for a minute. If somebody wants to buy something we're ready to move, we'll just send 'em right up to the cash register!"

Mike LaCrosse, the six-foot-two, 240-pound owner of the Jock Shop, the local sporting-goods store, hollered, "Hey, Jules, wanna give us a crash course on how to carry these long fancy dresses?"

Jules phoned Roz in the theater store, "Roz, I don't know what's going on, but there are some crazy people here and they're moving the whole store right now."

And that's exactly what they did that crisp, sunny March morning in downtown Hartford. Even the police helped direct traffic while Esther's army marched 14,000 items—lock, stock and mannequins—across the street.

They finished the job in just over two hours. Then the movers, en masse, marched back inside the empty store and surrounded Jules like players surrounding a coach after the season's most exciting victory. "Lift him up, guys!" shouted Jim Sarafiny, Jules' attorney.

Before Jules knew what was happening he was hoisted shoulder high and carried out the door, down the sidewalk, across the street and right into the old theater.

"Hey, Roz, here's the last piece of merchandise. Where do you want us to put it?"

Roz giggled. "Oh, that's a mark-down. You can toss it in the corner."

And so it all ended on a happy note. For a certain discouraged small-town retailer had seen a wholesale demonstration of God's Golden Rule.*

Using the principles listed here will help you turn your setbacks into comebacks.

1. Always believe that with God's help you can ultimately turn any setback into a comeback.
2. Picture yourself as having a lot of rebound left in you. Your Plus Factor is still unimpaired.
3. Think positively, especially when you feel the lowest. Remember, in that setback may be the answer to your comeback.
4. Remind yourself that you are bigger than anything that can happen to you.
5. Never be afraid. Stand up to your fear with God. He will give you faith and faith is always bigger and stronger than fear.
6. Pray big, believe big, think big.
7. Always be helpful to others and you will have friends who will help you turn setbacks into comebacks.

Remember always that you can turn setbacks into comebacks with your Plus Factor.

*From "Hartford Shows Its Heart" by Patricia Lorenz. Excerpted with permission from *Guideposts* magazine. Copyright © 1986 by Guideposts Associates, Inc., Carmel, New York 10512.

18.

THE PLUS Factor and the Skill of Growing Older

Actress Marie Dressler once said, "It's not how old you are that matters; it's how you are old." What a lot of wisdom packed into just thirteen words! We've all known elderly people who seem to pull down the shades and retire from life. They think of themselves as worn out, nonproductive, unattractive, full of health problems. They feel sorry for themselves and expect us to feel sorry for them.

On the other hand, there are older people who sparkle with vitality and the joy of living. They admit cheerfully that they're no longer young, but that doesn't bother them. They think of themselves as wise, experienced emotionally mature, creative, intellectually alert . . . and usually they are. Some mysterious, unseen force keeps them going, sometimes far beyond the allotted biblical span of seventy years.

What is that mysterious unseen force? I think it's yet another manifestation of the Plus Factor.

I am past that biblical span myself, and I think there's a lot to be said for these terrific extra years. The culture we live in tends to put a premium on youth. Our television commercials endlessly extol products supposed to make us look or feel young. The models in our magazine advertisements look as if they had just escaped from the cradle. But aside from an abundance of raw energy, youth is often likely to be lacking in the qualities that make for real happiness: judgment, balance, wisdom, self-control, experience . . . all the values that come as you move along the pathway of life.

It has been my observation that older people are likely to be less self-centered than younger people. They have had time to learn more about loving . . . and living. They are more philosophical about disappointments or setbacks. They are less impatient. They have learned the value of waiting. They are more serene.

In other word, reaching the high plateau of your later years can be a satisfying—even exhilarating—experience, if . . .

If you bring the right attitudes along with you.

One of the key attitudes, certainly, is a strong religious faith. Not long ago a major life insurance company carried out a survey of its policyholders who had lived to be 100 years old . . . or more. One of the question was: What is the most important thing you've learned in your long life? The most frequent answer: Love thy neighbor as thyself.

People who live according to that great commandment are almost certain to live longer than people who don't, because they have freed themselves from deadly negative influences like anger, hatred, suspicion, jealousy, guilt, and anxiety that upset body rhythms and can actually cause organic illness. Such people have more vitality, more resistance to disease, more curiosity, more eagerness, more energy. As the Book of Isaiah puts it: "They that wait upon the Lord shall renew their strength; they shall mount up with wings as eagles; they shall run, and not be weary; and they shall walk, and not faint" (40:31).

Another thing that keeps many spiritually minded people going long beyond the average life expectancy is their feeling that God has a reason for their continued existence, even though often they are not quite sure what that reason is.

In the village of Carmel, New York, there was a remarkable man named Mort Cheshire. He lived for over 103 years, and he never lost his enthusiasm. Mort was a professional expert in the use of a musical device that has almost become extinct—he played the bones. They were a great favorite in the old-time minstrel shows that I remember as a boy. Mort was famous in old-time vaudeville.

One of the last times I saw Mort, he had reached the ultraripe old age of 102. We were at a Christmas party of the employees of *Guideposts* magazine, which is published in Carmel, New York. Mort was called upon to play the bones. He stood up and played with such enthusiasm and gusto that everyone clapped and cheered and there were even people wiping away tears. Why tears? Because the crowd knew that this proud and remarkable old man still had a firm grip on things. He hadn't quit. He hadn't given in. He had accepted the gift of life and he was still giving something back. Making his cheerful, lively music, he transmitted something wonderful to the crowd of onlookers. We all felt it.

I remember saying to Mort, "You're terrific! Now tell me, why are you a hundred and two years old and still so vital?"

He said, quite simply, "Because that's what Jesus wants me to be. He must still have some purpose for me here on earth. That's why I'm here."

He died at 103½, still strong in the faith. How did he do it? He did it because God gave him the gift of the Plus Factor, that's how.

I hear of people like Mort Cheshire frequently. In 1908, for example, Martine Tompkins of Owensboro, Kentucky, became an instant celebrity when she drove down the main street in a Stevens-Duryea touring car. Today, nearly eight decades later, she's still a legend in Owensboro for her perfect driving record, no violations ever. Someone asked her when she might give up driving. "When I'm old!" said Martine Tompkins tartly. When she said that, she was only ninety-four.

One thing is certain: The Plus Factor will never fail you just because you're getting old. Let me tell you about another ninety-four-year-old, Effie Ford, who lived all alone in a suburb of Richmond, Virginia. Late one afternoon she decided to walk down to the end of her driveway and take the newspaper, *The News Leader*, out of her mailbox. It was at the end of October; the weatherman had predicted freezing temperatures before morning. Effie wore a thin housedress and a sweater that she had wrapped around her shoulders for the quick trip.

But it wasn't a quick trip. Near the end of the driveway Effie's heel caught in the gravel, and she fell. When she tried to get up, she found that her knees, weakened by arthritis, would not support her. Painfully, the rough concrete scraping her knees and elbows, she managed to drag herself to her own back door. But then she was too weak to get up the steps.

It was about five o'clock; the short autumn afternoon was dying. She called for help. Nobody heard her. Temperatures were dropping rapidly. She tried to cover herself with the doormat at the foot of the steps, but it did little good. Headlights flashed as cars passed by her driveway.

But no cars turned in. She felt the warmth of her body draining away into the cold ground.

The hours passed, each one darker and colder and lonelier than the one before. Ninety-four-year-old Effie Ford felt the stealthy languor creeping over her that is the prelude to death from hypothermia. It would have been easy just to accept this, to relax, to go to sleep forever. But something in Effie Ford—that power we call the Plus Factor—would not allow her to give in. She began to twist her body and kick her legs, trying to keep warm. She would count aloud as she kicked, five times with the right leg, five times with the left. She wondered if it were God's will that she should die like this, alone and almost helpless. She decided it was not. She decided God wanted her to fight as long as there was a spark of life in her.

So this daughter of a coal miner, who had raised seven children and endured hardship all her life, refused to give in. All night long, sometimes only half-conscious, she kept fighting. At seven the next morning, a neighbor was horrified to look out his window and see the old lady lying on the ground. He rushed to her side, brought blankets, called an ambulance. And Effie Ford survived.

An incredulous doctor said to her, "Mrs. Ford, I'll never understand how you survived that freezing night all alone."

Effie Ford smiled. "I wasn't alone," she said. She meant that God was with her . . . and God's gift to people facing almost hopeless odds—the Plus Factor.

I'm sure that this hidden reservoir of power that saved Effie Ford exists in all of us. A well-known doctor said: "If tension and conflict can be removed from the mind by enlightened self-analysis, and if muscle tension can be removed by a conscious effort to relax the body, then the psychic energy latent in all of us is unchained, and the results are increased creativity, a sense of physical well-being, and general enthusiasm for living."

The psychic energy latent in all of us . . . what is that but the Plus Factor? You can't see or touch it. You can't measure or analyze it. But it's definitely there, waiting to be summoned forth in a crisis, as was the case with Effie Ford.

Older people can accomplish astonishing things, and so can you as the years begin to mount up. I'm sure the good Lord put exactly the same amount of latent Plus Factor into each one of us. Some people are better at activating it than others, that's all.

Here are a handful of suggestions that I've drawn out of my own experience that may help in this business of growing older.

1. *Stop looking over your shoulder.* Some older people seem always to be reaching back into the past. It's good to have pleasant memories and okay to go back to them in memory occasionally, but don't stay there. It's much better to face forward, to focus on the future and all the exciting opportunities that it holds. Remember the advice of the great black baseball player Satchel Paige, who remained a star athlete for longer than the average player. "Don't look back," Satchel Paige used to say, "'Somethin' may be gainin' on you." He didn't say what that somethin' was, but he might have meant the regrets and mistakes that are better left behind and forgotten. Live in the now with zest.

2. *Keep elasticity in your attitudes.* Don't let them harden like cement. The world changes. Customs change. Ideas change. You need to retain enough flexibility to change with them. This doesn't mean you have to abandon your basic principles. It just means that you need to let fresh ideas into your mind. Listen to different points of view. Expose yourself to opinions with which you don't necessarily agree. Read books that will push back the boundaries of your mind.

Recently I heard a businessman described like this: "He has a steel-trap mind, all right, but it snapped shut years ago." Try not to be like that! Hold on to your tried and true values. If they are of the truth, they are ageless.

3. *Expect health, not helplessness.* As one grows older, it becomes very easy to say, "Oh, I can't do this; it's too late." Or, "I can't try that because I'm too old." I am sure of one thing: If you expect poor health, if you think poor health, if you proclaim poor health, that is what you are going to have. If on the other hand you see yourself as vigorous and energetic regardless of age, that is the way you are very likely to be. As Oliver Wendell Holmes said, to be seventy years young is sometimes far more cheeful and hopeful than to be forty years old. He was absolutely right. Affirm health, affirm well-being.

4. *Dont' say yes to loneliness.* A lot of people do that as they grow older. Their friends die off or drift away and they make no attempt to replace them with new friends. They never volunteer for activities that would bring them into contact with people. They seem to grow more isolated and solitary as the years go by. And more unhappy as they do.

But you don't have to be like that! Loneliness is primarily a state of mind, and the curious, eager, interested mind seldom has time for boredom or room for self-pity. One of the surest antidotes for loneliness is to look around for someone who has troubles and try to help them.

5. *Don't take leave of your senses.* I'm not writing about mental faculties so much as the five basic senses that the good God gave to all of us. How long is it since you brought a fresh-cut rose close to your nostrils and smelled that incredible fragrance? How long is it since you went out at night and looked—really looked—at the stars? How long since you listened to the music and magic of poetry read aloud, or to the murmur of the surf on a lonely beach? How long since you tasted hot homemade bread fresh from the

oven? How long since you scuffed your way, ankle deep, through the gold and crimson leaves of autumn? Or smelled the scent of wood smoke? Or heard the wild calling of Canada geese passing across the face of the harvest moon? Too long, probably.

It may be true that some senses like eyesight or hearing grow less keen with the passing years, but usually you can rectify that. Get a magnifying glass and study the composition of a piece of quartz or the texture of a flower. Turn the volume up a little on your favorite recording; if the neighbors complain, invite them in to listen. Get up early some morning and watch the sun come up; you don't need reading glasses to watch the miracle of sunrise.

Don't take leave of your senses just because you're older. And don't let your senses take leave of you.

6. *Live your life forgetting age.* An eighty-six-year-old friend was the owner and manager of a big hotel in Chicago. With admiration I watched him supervising a dinner of 1,500 people where I was the speaker. "Frank," I asked, "how old are you anyway?" "What's the matter? Isn't your room okay, the service here satisfactory?" "Well, I know how old you are for you went to school with my mother."

"Listen, son," he said—and that "son" went over big with me. "Live your life and forget your age." Then he told me that when he looked into a mirror, he didn't see Frank Bering, an old man. He saw Frank Bering—period.

7. *Don't ever retire from living.* I warn you that the Plus Factor will begin to desert you if you do. Keep your capacity for wonder alive. Keep in touch with the amazing and astounding world around you. Keep trying new things. You're never too old to be creative. We're told that Titian painted *The Battle of Lepanto* when he was 98, and Verdi composed the soaring music of *Aida* when he was in his 80s. Goethe and Tolstoy did some of their best work in their later years. Most of us can never be such towering geni-

uses. But it's possible to remain creative as long as you live. Remember this great fact: If you don't give up on life, life won't give up on you.

8. *Enjoy being yourself.* Dr. Hans Selye, the great expert on stress, said that most emotional stress is caused by trying to be something you're not. Older people can usually stop worrying about what the Joneses think. They can express opinions freely. They don't have to conform so much. They don't have to be so aggressive, so striving, so materialistic in their outlook on life. They have more time, and sometimes more inclination, to help other people. Your later years can be a very pleasant and productive time—if you can find the serenity that comes from just being yourself.

9. *Live a day at a time.* View each day as precious. Live it to the full. Skip any idea that "you're running out of time." Take every day and its abundance of opportunity and make the most of it. You'll be surprised at what you can do.

I spoke to a big dinner of over 2,500 people along with General Jimmy Doolittle. General Doolittle, one of our greatest American heroes, won the Congressional Medal of Honor for leading sixteen bombers in 1942 on America's first bombing raid against Japan. It was one of the most heroic exploits in American history.

The general, now at ninety years of age, thrilled the vast crowd at that dinner with his speech. Asked how he handled age, he replied, "I do just what I've always done. I live one day at a time." And I might add, his Plus Factor seems to be working as well as it always has.

19.

How to Keep the PLUS FACTOR Going

To keep the Plus Factor going I suggest doing this:

Incorporate into your thought pattern and life-style the ten golden attitudes: They are:

Faith
Positive Thinking
Persistence
Confidence
Positive Imaging
Prayer
Affirmation
Belief
Love
Work

They do not necessarily need to be in the order listed above. But if all ten, or even a majority of these attitudes, are employed regularly, the result will be that the special quality called the Plus Factor will be kept going in you always. And your life will thereby be filled with joy and satisfaction and achievement.

I have been teaching and advocating this way of life for quite some years. And I have received many messages from persons in nearly every section of the world telling that they have applied these principles and that they have worked successfully. Many of these communications have borne enthusiastic testimony that the incorporation of the ten golden attitudes have turned lives around and led people to a quality of success and happiness they never dreamed of attaining.

So in this final chapter I want to explore just how these attitudes which I have chosen to call "golden" have worked successfully in the experience of so many individuals.

The first person I wish to tell you about exemplifies the positive effect of creative discontent. He was a New York City taxi driver who drove me to Kennedy Airport. His cab was spotlessly clean—immaculate—as was the driver himself. This man had a streak of genius, for not only was he contented—he was also discontented. But he told me right off that he was a confirmed positive thinker.

While driving along, the radio news gave a brief rundown on a speech made the night before by the governor. It was an impassioned declaration that he, the governor, was committed to driving all rats out of New York City.

The driver flipped off the radio saying, "I don't know whether the governor knows how to get rid of rats. But I do. In fact, I used to live in a ghetto section of Manhattan. But," he declared, "there were never any rats in my house."

"How come?" I asked.

"Because our house was clean, spotlessly clean. And I mean clean. My wife is a terrific housekeeper. She hates dirt and so there just wasn't any dirt in our place. It doesn't make any difference how poor a neighborhood may be, there is no excuse for your own house not being clean. And there is another way to outsmart rats," he told me. "I just filled any kind of opening with shattered glass. That makes it so tough for a rat that it gets discouraged and bypasses your place.

"Even in a so-called ghetto neighborhood I was a contented man," he smiled broadly, "and why not: lovely wife, good kids, and a nice home? What more could you ask? I was a contented man and a positive thinker . . .

"But . . ." and then came good old creative discontent. "I wanted something better: a house out of town with grass and trees and flowers. So I worked hard and saved my money and one of my passengers, an investment man, gave me an idea on how to invest the little I had and what do you know?"

"Okay, what?" I asked, fascinated by this story of good old American self-reliance. Well, he got his house—on Long Island. It had a few scraggly trees and a beat-up lawn and no flowers. The man knew nothing about how to make a lawn or grow flowers. But he got some pamphlets on flower and grass culture. And a Sunday newspaper supplement gave him tips on gardening. Eventually he had a lawn and a garden that was the talk of the neighborhood. So much so that all the envious housewives on the street pressured their husbands to get to work gardening. An entire neighborhood was transformed into a place of beauty.

"Wonderful," I said, "positively wonderful! Isn't it something—what a human being can do when really motivated by contentment powered by discontent? Someone who doesn't wait for a government housing program but who gets along on his own.

"So now you're really contented, I'm sure."

"Sure am," he replied proudly. "I'm a contented man. Lovely wife, good kids, beautiful home and garden . . . but . . ."

He started telling me what was on his drawing board for the future, and it sounded mighty like driving discontent for something better.

That this New York City cab driver has his Plus Factor in top working order was obvious. The next time I have the good fortune to ride in his taxi he may have some harsh experiences to tell me about, but that he will also be able to tell of his victories over them I have no doubt. For he is the sort of man who rolls with the punches and comes out a winner. And the creative discontent that prods him always to something better is one of the reasons.

Now let me tell you of one of my inspiring friends, Pete McCulley, quarterback coach of the Kansas City Chiefs of the National Football League. He had been, successively, receiver coach with the Baltimore Colts and Washington Redskins. Then he attained his dream and goal by becoming head coach of the San Francisco 49ers in the eighteenth year of his highly successful professional coaching career. Then the devastating blow came. He was let go from this athletically exalted position.

But despite this shock and adversity, Pete McCulley's Plus Factor was working magnificently. Ed Jacoubowsky, sportswriter for the *Palo Alto Times* said of him, "But McCulley exits with dignity. 'I'm not going to blame anyone but me,' he says. 'You're either successful or you can't stay around in this business. You can't go through life blaming others.

"'You hope when you get a chance in the NFL—that's the ultimate in coaching—you just hope things work out better than this.

"'But it's history,' he concludes, 'It's done with, it's over.'

"Maybe for some people, but not for Pete McCulley. Whatever he does, he'll be successful. He's a winner."

As one of the most qualified coaches in professional football, he soon landed a top coaching job with the New York Jets. It was then that he wrote me the following letter. It is the letter of a real champion with a big Plus Factor going for him. And as you will see from this communication, he knows how to keep it going. He practices the ten golden attitudes. Well, here is the letter:

Dear Dr. Peale:

Two years ago when we moved to Long Island to accept a coaching position with the New York Jets, I felt as if I left my heart in San Francisco. I had been released as head coach of the San Francisco 49ers after attaining my career dream of being a head coach of a National Football League team. It was like swallowing a square pill and my morale was so low that I felt like I would have to dig up to get to the bottom. However, the New York move was a blessing because it located me in an area where one of God's own could provide positive aid for a wounded spirit.

As a coach, I have experienced numerous victories over every kind of defeat and difficulty. In fact, ordinarily when I fall in a mud hole, I check my hip pocket to see if I've caught a fish. However, in this case I needed a good dose of your practical approach to Christianity for a full recovery and peace of mind.

Recently I have been toughening up my physical and spiritual muscles in my foxhole. My foxhole is located in our basement where I have weight-lifting equipment, an indoor bicycle and a tape recorder. In addition, I have at least thirty of your sermons on tape. Each morning at 6:00 A.M. when I work out, I listen to two of your tapes in my effort to hone my physical and spiritual muscles at the same time. In athletics, it is said, fatigue makes cowards of all that compete for a high goal. I believe this applies to the spiritual as well and I certainly don't want to get fatigued and fall short of the goal.

Thanks for providing the fuel to flame the hungry kind of feelings that burn inside of me to find God's will in a meaningful life. It is indeed as promised, the victory that "overcometh the world." God bless you every day.

Sincerely,
Pete McCulley

Currently Pete has an assistant coaching job at Kansas City. Through his strong faith and mature understanding of the ups and downs in football as in life itself Pete McCulley has become a great positive thinker. He kows that positive thinking works when the going is good and that it also works when the going gets rough. And that to meet life situations masterfully is what the ten golden attitudes help us to do.

In fact, a major ability we must cultivate is how to react when the rough times come. These golden attitudes are not designed to make life a bed of roses, but rather to toughen us up to meet and handle trouble and difficulty like strong men and women. The constant and sincere use of those ten principles stated on the opening page of the chapter will make life better, even great, and will lead to real success. But they will also give strong sustaining power when the hard knocks come. They will, in fact, pull you through anything and get you going again even when everything seems hopeless. So say the many persons who have communicated with me.

Scheduled to speak to a public meeting of sales people in Pittsburgh one night, I entered by the stage door and sat backstage waiting for the program to begin. A rather stocky athletic-looking man came back and introduced himself as the master of ceremonies for the meeting. He was an animated person, full of vigor and enthusiasm. His positive attitude came through impressively.

He told me he had been a helicopter pilot in the war in Southeast Asia. Shot down, he was so seriously wounded that his life was despaired of. Because of suspected brain damage, doctors came to a tentative diagnosis that if he did live it would "be as a vegetable." He underwent a brain operation that left a small plate in the top of his head. Moved to a military hospital in the United States, he was paralyzed in both legs and both arms. His speech, however, was not affected nor was his mental ability.

One day he said to his wife, "Bring a book I once read about positive thinking and read it to me." Day after day his wife read about the powerful creative and recreative principles of positive thinking until this desperately wounded man developed an extraordinary positive attitude.

Then came the conviction that he, too, could be healed despite the disheartening prognosis.

He told his wife that he was going to reprogram his mind to take charge of his broken body. He entered upon an intensive and persistent routine of positive thinking and spiritual affirmation, infusing his mind with a powerful directive force. His eventual healing did not come in a miraculous way, nor did it come all that easily; but that it did come was evidenced by the physically strong and mentally alert man who told me this story of what a motivated human being can do with himself when his faith is strong enough in content and force. He knew how to keep his Plus Factor going.

Later as I watched this remarkable man emcee the meeting with humor and spirit that set a positive and enthusiastic tone, I once again reaffirmed my own certain belief that an in-depth positive attitude wins over all difficulties. So keep it going—always keep it going. Miracles are built into persons who program their mind to in-depth belief.

Even deteriorating marriages based on the golden attitudes program reverse themselves and do well, as the following letter illustrates. It is from a lady in Australia, where I have spoken on several occasions.

Dear Dr. Peale:

I managed to get two tickets in the last row for your meeting and talked my husband into taking me, because I wanted him to hear your positive ideas.

My husband has been a very negative and anxiety prone person, coming from a large family without any love or affection. We have been married nearly thirty years and have five children and up until now my husband was not a very good husband or father, nor was he a success financially. He had a heart attack three years ago but thank God he recovered.

I picked up a copy of your book *The Power of Positive Thinking* and decided to put into practice some of the principles in your book and a miracle has happened in our marriage. We are closer now than we have been for nearly twenty years. My husband has become the person he should have been all these years.

Thank you for helping me to look at my God in a more positive way. I am a Catholic but the idea of taking HIM into partnership with me had never occurred to me, and I know we could not have repaired our lives without His help.

We enjoyed your lecture so much. The hall seemed to be filled with your presence. I hope you are spared for many years to do God's work in this present time. I am,

Yours sincerely,

Several references in her letter indicate that this lady is a practitioner of the ten golden principles or attitudes. In times of difficulty she has moved through to victory. The Plus Factor within, coupled with faith and prayer and positive thinking, has been her secret all the way.

One should never face a difficult problem negatively. Never assume that nothing can be done about it. The first thing to do is to think. Practically every problem is solvable if we think coolly, objectively, and intellectually. Never give in to emotionalizing. Instead, think and pray and affirm that the power, the insight, the wisdom is given you to handle this troublesome situation. Affirm by saying, "I have a Plus Factor in me. It is now coming to my aid in power so that I am well able to handle this problem."

Then summon your faith to aid you. Remember always that great promise, "If you have faith as a mustard seed, you will say to this mountain [this difficulty], 'Move from here to there,' and it will move and nothing will be impossible for you" (*see* Matthew 17:20).

In this superlative manner the Plus Factor that was built into us by the Creator and the ten golden attitudes given to us by Jesus Christ work together. Thus the problems of life are solved, overcome, or lived with victoriously. By consistent affirmation you are firmly fixing the success image in consciousness; you are in effect praying the powerful prayer of faith. And this quality of high-level prayer overcomes because it is indicative of faith. Remember the promise "According to your faith be it done unto you."

In addition to the activation of the inherent Plus Factor and the development of the power to keep it going, those ten golden attitudes are of prime importance. Look carefully at them again:

Faith
Positive Thinking
Persistence
Confidence

Positive Imaging
Prayer
Affirmation
Belief
Love
Work

In my opinion, which is based on thousands of personal cases over many years, the best way by far to get out of trouble and to have a creative and happy life is to live by the ten golden attitudes. I mean this not only sincerely, but also enthusiastically. This way of life will release your own native personal abilities as nothing else can. Your plus power will produce ideas one after the other which will contribute to your ability to handle things more successfully. I've seen it work in the experience of too many people of all types and backgrounds to have the slightest vestige of doubt about the truth of what I am writing here.

The experiences which have been related in this chapter bear out the fact that teachings of Jesus Christ produce the best values in life and endow the believer with the ability to meet and overcome even the most difficult problems. I am not saying that they will produce riches and give a person everything he wants, for what he may want cannot be assumed to be what God wants for him. But I am saying that his needs will be fulfilled and God in His great generosity will provide him with His good in full measure. Remember this promise:

> . . . for your heavenly Father knoweth that ye have need of all these things. But seek ye first the kingdom of God, and his righteousness; and all these things shall be added unto you.
>
> Matthew 6:32, 33

I have always noted that those people who do not only follow the teachings of Jesus but who also possess His spirit of love, compassion, and esteem for others have their own Plus Factors always going with extra force.

And old friend, Ben Sweetland, a well-known writer, was respected and loved by many. He was a positive personality who loved to help individuals. And he often performed such help in innovative ways. How he activated the Plus Factor in a house painter is a story he told me over dinner one evening in San Francisco.

Ben was having some painting done in his home by a man named John Doyce, who one day said, "You're so lucky. How I would love to have my own home!" Knowing that the painter was about forty-five years old and married, Ben asked him why he didn't. John then proceeded to recite a long list of the expenses involved in raising two children in a time of an ever-increasing cost of living. He just about came out even.

Ben left John to his painting, but later in the day came back with a box in his hand. It was a simple candy box that Ben had transformed into a makeshift bank. He asked for a coin. Puzzled, the painter pulled a dime out of his pocket, which Ben took and dropped into the slot in the "bank." He then handed over the box saying, "John, you're on your way to owning your own home."

John looked surprised, but Ben explained that he needed to establish the habit of saving. Every time he earned any money, he was to take some part of it, no matter how small, and put it in the box. Ultimately, the dribs and drabs would amount to something. The painter took the "bank" with him, but Ben could see he was dubious about the whole thing.

A few years later, though, Ben received in the mail an invitation to a housewarming—from John and his wife. The home was not simply adequate, but charming and imaginative.

John told Ben that it wasn't the saving of the money that was the most important factor in the building of the house—and in other areas of his life as well. It was learning to change his attitude—replacing "I can't" with "I can." Once he saw his savings overflow the candy box into a bank account, he took on extra jobs and put the whole amount earned from them into the "building fund." Persuading John to take that all-important first step, Ben Sweetland helped to activate his Plus Factor. A change in attitude kept it going.

To help anyone to realize that "he can" instead of "he can't" is actually an act of love. For by so doing you are activating and releasing that extra talent, that greater something that the Creator placed in that person. To care enough for people to assist them to be what they can be is a high form of Christian practice. And further to do something that will aid another person in keeping his Plus Factor going and developing is to add to his success and happiness and to your own also.

As I come to the closing pages of this book, I find myself remembering a little church in Switzerland and some words I heard spoken there.

One Sunday in Zermatt my wife, Ruth, and I went to the little English church that stands in the heart of the village. Conducting services that morning was a bishop of the Church of England, tall, stately, white-haired, with long, expressive, blue-veined hands. He read from the prayer book in his correct British intonation, each syllable as clear and distinct as a fresh-minted coin. Finally he closed the book, came down from the pulpit, stood in the aisle, and said he would just like to talk to us informally for a few minutes. And what he had to say was memorable indeed.

He told us about the little cemetery in the center of the village where some of the climbers are buried who lost their battle with the great Matterhorn. On some of the graves, he said, you can see the ice-axes that belonged to these brave men. Then he asked some questions. "Why are you here today? Why am I here? We may have lesser reasons, but our true reason for being here, whether we're aware of it or not, is to have fellowship with the mountains." He quoted the majestic words from Psalm 121: "'I will lift up mine eyes unto the hills, from whence cometh my help.'" A hush fell over the congregation as he spoke. One could feel the quiet strength of the great mountains enfolding us, stealing into our hearts, bringing peace and tranquility and a deep awareness of the mighty Power that had called those mountains into existence.

The bishop pointed to the church wall. "Do you see that plaque over there? To me it's not merely a plaque; it's a boy who lies in the graveyard. An English boy. I knew him well. I knew his parents. The boy came here when he was only twenty-one. He was climbing the Matterhorn eagerly, confidently, when a rope broke and he fell . . ."

The bishop stopped speaking. All around us the hush seemed to deepen.

Finally the bishop spoke again. "But was that the end for this young lad so full of life and promise? Those who knew him don't think so. His parents don't think so. I don't think so. In that graveyard where he lies with the others there is a sentence carved in stone that says, 'In the sight of the unwise, they seem to die.' Death is the illusion; the shortsighted view. Those with more wisdom know that this boy died climbing. He was moving up. And in the life beyond this life he is still moving up, he is climbing still. . ."

Again the bishop paused. There was not a sound in the little church. Finally he went on, "And so I say to you, when you go forth from this place, find a mountain to climb. Find a difficulty and overcome it. Find an obstacle and master it. All around you are the great life-giving, life-sustaining forces of the universe. Give yourself to them. Trust them. Lift up your eyes to the hills. Keep them fixed on the highest peaks . . . and you will always find the strength you need."

Ruth and I left that church inspired and uplifted. Wherever you are, whoever you are, have faith in God. Experience the life-changing power of Jesus Christ. Develop your God-given Plus Factor. Do these things and you can live magnificently and handle creatively anything life brings to you.